ALSO BY RONIN RO

*Tales to Astonish: Jack Kirby, Stan Lee, and
the American Comic Book Revolution*

*Bad Boy: The Influence of Sean "Puffy" Combs
on the Music Industry*

Street Sweeper

*Have Gun Will Travel: The Spectacular Rise
and Violent Fall of Death Row Records*

Gangsta: Merchandizing the Rhymes of Violence

RAISING HELL

RONIN RO

RAISING HELL

The **Reign, Ruin, and Redemption** of **Run-D.M.C.** and **Jam Master Jay**

Amistad

An Imprint of HarperCollins*Publishers*

HarperCollins books may be purchased for educational, business, or sales promotional use. For information, please write: Special Markets Department, HarperCollins Publishers, 10 East 53rd Street, New York, NY 10022.

FIRST EDITION

Designed by Jeffrey Pennington

Printed on acid-free paper

Library of Congress Cataloging-in-Publication Data

Ro, Ronin.
    Raising hell : the reign, ruin, and redemption of Run-D.M.C. and
Jam Master Jay / Ronin Ro.—1st ed.
        p. cm.
    Includes index.
        Contents: Grandmaster get high—Son of Kurt—Disco sucks—Party
time—The broken arm—Jason Mizell—Krush Groove 1—Disco fever—
Rock box—Taking the throne—Russell and Rick—Kings of rock—The
silver screen—The kid with the hat—Proud to be black—The
Mainstreaming of hip-hop—War and peace—The Long Beach episode—
It's the new style—Def pictures—Rhyming and stealing—Suing Profile—
It's called survival—Leaving hell—Ohio—You talk too much—Run ruins
everything—Endgame—The party's over—Loss and remembrance.
        ISBN-10: 0-06-078195-5
        ISBN-13: 978-0-06-078195-8
        1. DMC (Musician). 2. Jam Master Jay, 1965–2002. 3. Rap musicians—
United States—Biography. I. Title.

ML400.R65 2005
782.421649'092'2—dc22
    [B]   2005041075

05 06 07 08 09 BVG/RRD 10 9 8 7 6 5 4 3 2 1

For the Ramones: Joey, Johnny, and Dee Dee
"I Remember You"

And my daughter,
Rachel, because
"She's the One"

(((ACKNOWLEDGMENTS)))

To Robert Guinsler: Thanks for being an excellent agent and an even better friend. You believed in this project, and created an opportunity for me to tell a story six years in the making. I appreciate everything you've done. Editor Stacy Barney: You were patient and supportive, gave me extra time, and never stopped believing in this book. Thanks. Run: Thank you for being so generous with your time. D.M.C.: Thank you for your honesty and unfailing support of this work. It was an honor and a pleasure to speak with you. Bill Adler: Thanks for the copy of *Tougher Than Leather* and more. (I owe you a copy of *TTA*.) Russell Simmons and Rick Rubin: You guys worked hard, and in the mid- to late 1980s created some of the greatest hip-hop of all time (together or apart). Both of you turned this music into an industry that provided opportunities for people like me, and for that I'm grateful. I'd also like to thank King Ad Rock (and the other Beastie Boys), Chuck D, Bill Stephney, Hank

ACKNOWLEDGMENTS

Shocklee, Doctor Dre (creator of the 808 Bass sound), Kool Moe Dee, T La Rock, Spinmaster Finesse, Runny Ray, Hurricane, Glen Friedman, Tracy Miller, Cory Robbins, Larry Smith, Adam Dubin, Grandmaster Flash, Whodini, the Fat Boys, Kool Lady Blue, Ryan "DJ Doc" Thompson, Spyder D, Mark Skillz, and the many people who spoke off the record, providing insights into the greatest rap group of all time, the greatest manager, and two of the greatest record labels (Profile and Def Jam). The following works also proved helpful and come recommended to anyone interested in learning more about the evolution of rap music: *Rap Attack* by David Toop, Y*es Yes Y'All* by Jim Fricke and Charlie Ahearn, *The New Beats* by S. H. Fernando, *Moguls and Madmen* by Jory Farr, *The Hip-hop Years* by Alex Ogg and David Upshal, *King of Rock* by D.M.C. and Bruce Haring, *It's Like That* by Reverend Run and Curtis L. Taylor, and *Life and Def* by Russell Simmons and Nelson George. I'd also like to thank Jon Shecter, David Mays, Edward Young, Reginald C. Dennis, James Bernard, Rob Tewlow, Jeremy Miller, Darryl James, Bonz Malone, Sheena Lester, Adam Dolgins, Rob Kenner, Cheo Coker, Allan S. Gordon, Michael Gonzalez, Havelock Nelson, Frank Owen, Jody Hotchkiss, Nelson George, Glennfoye Stewart, Enrique Melendez, Mike Kirkland, Danae DiNicola, and the late George Jackson (rest in peace). Finally, for helping me through a difficult period, David Patrick Crowley, Matthew Clifton (for spotting me in the gym, the beats, and the support), Kathy Carney, Carlos Flores, and Rachel Flores. And the readers, for all the support over the years.

Ronin Ro
March 2005

(((contents)))

Contents

*F*riends: How many of us have them?

—WHODINI

RAISING HELL

(((PROLOGUE)))

*O*n October 30, 2002, Jam Master Jay (JMJ) was in Jamaica, Queens, back from touring with Run-D.M.C. Behind the wheel of his black sport-utility vehicle, he rolled through rain-slick streets, heading to the recording studio he owned and operated with his old friend Randy Allen. Jay (born Jason Mizell in 1965) was a father of three, a husband, a legend in the rap music genre, and reportedly strapped for cash. Jay's old friend Wendell "Hurricane" Fite, who had joined Run-D.M.C. on many a tour as a bodyguard and then as part of co-headlining acts, would later claim Jay was also worried over stolen funds from a studio account. "Jay and I asked Randy about missing money and he denied it. They were definitely on the outs by the end."

Allegedly, Jay also worried about a business deal gone bad with Curtis Scoon. Six feet four inches tall and 250 pounds, and having spent time in jail, Scoon had reportedly been calling Jay's studio to demand repayment of $15,000. According to a report in *Playboy* Jay had responded to career woes and rising tax debts (the thirty-seven-year-old performer owed the IRS over $400,000) by arranging drug deals, and in one, Jay's friends later claimed, he had asked Scoon to put up $15,000. Jay had put up the same amount. Supposedly they used the combined $30,000 to buy cocaine in California, then had the drugs shipped to another dealer in Baltimore, who was then to sell the drugs, giving the duo a return on their outlay; but the guy in Baltimore ran off with the drugs. Allegedly Scoon blamed Jay for the robbery, but he has denied any involvement in any drug deal, and has never been charged or convicted of any wrongdoing in this matter.

With tax debts rising, a business associate rumored to be embezzling funds, his wife taking a job at the Banana Republic clothing store (to pitch in), and a bandmate in Run-D.M.C. leaving the group, effectively ending it, Jay hoped to leave music behind and transition into producing films. "Now we can start fucking with these movies," he had told his friend Shake. "I'm through with the rap shit."

Despite tensions between Jay and Randy Allen, Jay had continued to work alongside him on an album for Rusty Waters, a southern-style rap duo that included Randy, and Jay's teenage nephew Boe. The group rapped about "Cornbread" and hoped to release a debut album on major label Virgin Records. However, friends recall that after finishing the Rusty Waters album, Jay planned to close the studio. "I'm glad that Rusty Waters is signed to Virgin," Jay reportedly told Shake during this period. "I'm happy that Randy is finally out of my pocket."

Night was falling when Jay parked his SUV in front of the two-story building that housed his studio offices. In addition to finishing the Rusty Waters album, Jay had to perform a show with

Run-D.M.C. the next day. Though Run—the outspoken lead rap-per—had recently told Jay and rapper D.M.C. that he no longer wanted to stay with the group, he had decided to join them in Wash-ington, D.C., for a halftime show at a Washington Wizards basket-ball game. Jay figured he'd help Randy finish the Rusty Waters album and then head home to his wife to pack for the next day's trip to the nation's capital.

After entering the building's front door and walking up a flight of stairs, past a video camera, Jay reached the locked door to his studio. Someone opened the door and let him in. He entered, and saw the two couches in the lounge, walls that were bare save for one or two picture frames holding Run-D.M.C.'s gold and platinum records, the wide-screen TV complete with an Xbox game system hooked up to it, and Lydia High acting as friendly as ever. Then Jay faced the huge window that overlooked the recording room. The curtains were open, so he saw Randy standing over the controls of the huge mixing board, working on the song "Cornbread." Randy nodded a greeting. Jay returned it. Jay then walked to one of the two couches. Randy's friends Mike B—reportedly homeless and sleeping on a couch in the studio each night—and Pretty Tone slid over so Jay could sit, and before Jay knew it he was playing video games with them.

In the past, Jay would have hung out with people like Hurricane, or Run-D.M.C.'s road crew employee Runny Ray, or Jay's good friend Darnell Smith. But over the years, members of his circle of friends had started families, moved to other states, or found ways outside of Run-D.M.C. to earn income and support their families. Jay would have hung with Run and D.M.C.—his partners in the group—but since the problems associated with the making of their last album, 2001's *Crown Royal*, they hardly spoke to each other anymore. "All of those people toward the end that ran with Jay were all Randy's people," one JMJ confidant explained. "None of them were people Jay grew up with. Everybody was from Randy."

Instead of heading into the recording room, Jay settled into playing video games and kept his eyes glued to the TV. He figured Randy, also a producer, was more than capable of completing work on the Rusty Waters' song.

A young woman entered the studio lounge then, claiming she wanted to play Jay a demo. It was strange because someone had to have opened the door to the studio, if not the building, to let her in; friends knew that Jay, though an avid talent scout, preferred that aspiring artists leave demo tapes with employees. Jay and Randy were on a tight deadline to get the completed Rusty Waters album to Virgin Records, but Randy emerged from the recording room to tell the unexpected visitor he would take the time to listen to her tape, and returned to the recording room with the young woman in tow.

Around Jay, Randy's friends began to light marijuana cigarettes. Jay relaxed and smoked a little himself. Someone had shut the curtains in the window overlooking the recording room. Jay, mellowed by the marijuana, sat unaware on the couch with a video game handset in both hands. Lydia headed toward the front door, and opened it. Then the guy was there, the people in the studio claimed, and yelling, "Look at the ground!" The guy supposedly knocked Lydia to the floor, out of harm's way, and approached Jay with the .40-caliber pistol in hand.

Jay, sitting near Randy's friend Pretty Tone, reportedly yelled: "Oh, shit. Grab the gun!"

Then the visitor yelled, "What about this? What about this?"

And raised the gun up to Jay's face and . . .

CHAPTER 1

Grandmaster Get High

During the spring of 1978, thirteen-year-old Darryl McDaniels was finishing eighth grade at St. Pascal-Baylon Elementary, a Catholic school that required students to wear blue and yellow uniforms each day. The short, stocky black kid with the close-cut Afro and earnest expression was also taking care to avoid being robbed by larger, poorer bullies waiting outside the school each day to run up on kids, tap pockets, steal hats, loot, and shoes, chase them in packs, or send them home naked on the bus.

Hollis was working class, but these ruffians acted as if the neighborhoods south of the Grand Central Parkway, west of Francis Lewis Boulevard, north of Hollis Avenue, and east of 184th Street were the drug- and crime-infested South Bronx. So he'd literally cross streets to avoid someone coming his way while he was in uniform. Only after rushing past the group standing by the store on his block, getting home, and changing into streetwise jeans and sneakers would he go back out to buy whatever he needed.

He'd lived here since at least age five, among aluminum-sided one- and two-family houses, tiny patches of lawn, concrete driveways, and teens trying to live down the fact that their parents—many from down south—owned real estate and provided middle-class comfort. And because other boroughs were battling to determine which was toughest, and didn't consider Queens anything but a good place to come rob a wealthy soft kid, D's young neighbors and friends were acting even worse.

Unlike other neighborhoods, Hollis was filled with private houses, not apartment buildings, with black working-class neighbors, and bustling main streets with stores and movie theaters. It had a small-town feel, with everyone inevitably running into everyone else. If D and his friends weren't hanging out in an alley behind the only high-rise building in Hollis, a place they referred to as "the building," they were playing basketball in 205th Street Park near where the Hollis Crew, a group of somewhat older, tougher teenage neighborhood residents, spent their days and nights. Or D and his young neighbors passed each other while crossing the street at the corner near the park, where local dealers ran their drug supermarket. It was a small, remote enclave for the black working class and the children these hardworking adult parents hoped would have easier lives.

A typical weekday for Darryl involved going to school, then drifting over to "the building" after dinner to get high with his friends Butter, Ray, and Cool T; during weekends, he went to one of three local parks to shoot basketball, get a little high after the game, and escape his parents' strict rules. He didn't really fit in with the neighborhood tough guys, the drug dealers, the stickup kids, the older college students, the athletes, or the neighborhood DJs.

One afternoon in the spring of 1978, he reached his modest home and saw his brother Alford—three years older, bookish, into

sci-fi and comics—playing new tapes he'd bought on the street. Alford liked this new street music kids in other boroughs created with
turntables and microphones in city parks, house parties, or rented
halls and community centers. Darryl had heard it before, in concrete school yards in the neighborhood and on portable radios in
Hollis, but had never paid much attention to it. But Al's new tape by
Grandmaster Flash and the Furious Five was different.

Amid the usual calls for zodiac signs, a teen named Melle Mel
(Melvin Glover) rapped about a high school dropout turned stickup
kid who gets locked up and raped in Rikers Island. Darryl wanted to
hear Mel's unsettling story-rap again.

The verse was cinematic, cautionary, and reflective of D's private fears about his own lifestyle of the past two years. Until 1976,
D had been a quiet, meek, acquiescent A student, the sort neighborhood toughs would point at and call brainiac. Leaving St. Pascal's back then, he'd come straight home and stay in the house. His
father usually left at four to work as a station agent for the Metro-
politan Transit Authority. His mother arrived from her job as a
nursing coordinator at a nearby hospital at about five. After cook-
ing dinner she usually went to bed by seven so as to be up early
enough the next day to cook everyone breakfast before heading to
work again.

After a certain hour, D found himself alone and unsupervised.
For a while he'd been content to sit in his mother's neat living room
with some of the thousand comic books he and Al owned, or at a
table in front of a window, spending hours drawing pin-ups and
comics. And if that got boring, he'd pull out his collection of G.I.
Joe dolls or little green plastic army men and engage them in epic
battles. But this too got boring, so at age twelve he gravitated to
football, and spent a year lifting weights, feeling good about his
broadening shoulders and the attention he received from girls, and
seeing his reputation in the neighborhood change. With eighth-
grade graduation coming up, he learned his parents planned to send
him to a high school in Harlem that didn't have a football field. He

then gave football up and fell into the habit of sneaking out of the house after dinner. With his mom sleeping, he'd walk to "the building" and join his friends to share joints, crack jokes, and drink quart bottles of Olde English 800 malt liquor.

The Flash tape ended. Darryl felt this new music offered a new, safer way to escape his boredom. He carried his mom's turntable down into the wood-paneled basement and tried to scratch a record. In the background, Alford stood, offering moral support and encouragement.

Days later, Darryl arrived from school with plans to spend the afternoon playing basketball at the new hoop their father had installed in the backyard. But Al led him into the basement instead. Darryl's eyes widened with silent amazement. He saw that Al had purchased a second turntable and a $50 mixer, and had set DJ equipment up on a table. "I didn't really have to struggle," Darryl recalled. "It was all set up, prepared for me." The equipment became a major part of his daily routine. He kept smoking weed and drinking quarts when his parents were at work or asleep, but spent more time at home, where he couldn't get into serious trouble. Quickly dubbing himself Grandmaster Get High, he also collected beats he heard on tapes, wore headphones while cutting and mixing records, and fantasized about competing with Grandmaster Flash. Behind his turntables, Darryl played two copies of James Brown's "Funky Drummer." He would let one copy of the record play until its short percussion break was ending. He would then use a mixer to switch over to a second turntable playing the beginning of the drum solo. In this manner, he was able to keep his favorite part of the record going for an eternity.

Shortly after D became Grandmaster Get High, his best friend, Doug Hayes, who called himself Butter, introduced him to a thin cat named Joseph Simmons. They were about to play ball in the school gym. D recognized Joe from the neighborhood. He had been seeing this skinny, long-haired kid in school since first grade, in the same blue-and-yellow uniform that he wore, but since they were always in different classes, they never hung out.

Joe looked repressed, angry, and a bit pampered. He was shorter, with smaller shoulders, lighter skin, and an arsenal of frowns and smirks. Joe also had a reputation in Hollis. He was supposedly a shrill and sarcastic mama's boy. During basketball games in 205th Street Park with Butter and members of Butter's Hollis Crew, Darryl saw opponents stop the game because Joe was scurrying past, usually heading to the store for a loaf of bread. The players hurled insults: "Yo, DJ Bum! Your brother's a homo!" Within minutes, Joe would emerge from the store and rush back toward his two-story house (with a driveway so narrow his dad's secondhand green Mercedes couldn't get into the garage). Joe ignored the insults, headed into his house, and shut his door. "Hollis was too hard for him," one later member of Run-D.M.C. recalled. "On his block he got picked on."

Darryl also knew that the Hollis Crew's disdain extended to Joe's older brother Russell. Seven years older than Joe, Russell had once run with a local street gang, used drugs, and sold marijuana. He'd then reinvented himself as a party promoter. In many ways, Russell was a success story. He'd changed his life for the better— but all some of these kids in the Hollis Crew remembered was that Russell had allegedly worn leg warmers one day. They put that together with the fact that he sometimes spoke with a lisp, and spread unsubstantiated rumors about Russell.

But in the gym, Butter said Joe would join the game. Darryl had no objection. Joe had never done or said anything to offend him, and Darryl had no reason to think anything negative about Joe or Russell. In fact, Darryl enjoyed Joe's jokes and comments during the game so much that he didn't object when he saw Joe with Butter in his backyard later that day.

For Darryl, Joseph Simmons was cool, ambitious, and quick-witted. And as the school year continued, when he left St. Pascal at 2:20 p.m. every afternoon, Joe was usually by his side, chattering away on bustling Hollis Avenue. They'd shoot hoops in Darryl's backyard until about 4:30 or 5:00, then smoke weed and drink Olde English in Darryl's basement. Darryl then started taking Joe to his hangout, "the building," where he and friends Butter, Ray White, and Cool T got high. They also hung out in school, in the school gym, on the basketball court in a church basement that hosted Police Athletic League sports programs, in Darryl's backyard, and in the park during weekend afternoons and evenings.

Darryl didn't really like anyone coming into his house, but months after they met, he invited Joe in and led him to his set of equipment in the basement.

"Oh, shit!" Joe said. "You got turntables and records?"

"Yeah, I'm Grandmaster Get High."

"That's cool. I got turntables too. I perform as 'the son of Kurtis Blow,' DJ Run."

DJ Run was a little-known performer—not in the big leagues at all—but D remembered seeing Run's name on one or two flyers. "Really?"

"Yeah, I get onstage with Kurtis and play the record while he raps. And I call him out. I'll bring a tape for you."

"That's cool."

Darryl turned his equipment on and started mixing two copies of Captain Sky's "Super Sperm." As Joe watched with amazement, Darryl made the Sky record go from singing "soup-a-sperm" to chanting "soup-soup-soup-soup." Between sips on his quart of beer, D pulled out other break-beat albums: the opening beat on the Monkees' eleven-year-old "Mary Mary," the fiery horn blast on John Davis and the Monster Orchestra's disco song "I Can't Stop," the Incredible Bongo Band's salsa-styled "Apache," and Bob James's jazzy, dreamlike remake of a Paul Simon song, "Take Me to the Mardi Gras." Soon Joe started asking questions, so Darryl taught him how to quick-mix, backspin, and cue the record up.

CHAPTER 2

Son of Kurt

Joe went home excited about what D had taught him. He could apply these lessons to his own career with his older brother Russell's friend Kurtis Blow. Until now, his home life had been wonderful, filled with love, gifts, and middle-class comfort. If he wanted something, he had only to ask his parents. He never went without, and never had money problems.

Born in November 1964, Joe first got into music at around the age of ten after hearing WBLS on the radio. "I got interested in where is the best radio station." said Joe. "How do I do it? Give me a radio." At home, an adult taught him to turn the radio on, "put it on FM, and turn the dial a little bit and get to BLS. There it was. It was extremely easy." Since then, he'd tried to express himself through music, dubbing himself "DJ Joe," taping songs from the radio, attending block parties where residents played guitars and drums, and banging away on a drum set his father bought and installed in the attic (with an older next-door neighbor named Spuddy giving him lessons).

His father, Daniel, supported Joe's dream. An attendance supervisor for New York City's Public School District 29, and professor of black history at Pace University by night, his father had spent the second half of the 1960s as part of the civil rights movement. Now in the late 1970s Joe saw his father reading aloud from *Hamlet,* espousing the value of a college degree and traditional nine-to-five establishment jobs, and reciting his own politically charged poetry. Joe's mother, Evelyn, also supported Joe's new hobby of playing drums and writing song lyrics. A slim, light-skinned artist with degrees in sociology and psychology from Howard University (where she had met Joe's father), Evelyn worked as a recreation director for the city's Parks Department. She was easygoing and sophisticated, and had always been willing to listen to Joe's nonstop chatter. But in 1978, her marriage to Daniel was disintegrating. "That messed little Joey up 'cause he was close to his mother," said one of Joe's close friends, who spoke on condition of anonymity (since this matter has never really been discussed in the media). So Joe retreated to his room at night to cradle his radio in the dark, and to tell himself, "I'm in control."

Once he heard this new park jam music at a block party, and saw Russell immerse himself in this exciting new scene, Joe wanted to be part of it too.

Russell (born 1957) shared Joe's bedroom on the second floor of their Queens home. Russell had attended an integrated elementary school instead of the all-black one and a mostly white junior high, and had played baseball at August Martin High. But he surprised everyone by joining the fearsome Seven Immortals street gang, partly so he could earn money to buy flashy clothes by selling marijuana. And though he left the gang at age sixteen, after their nemeses, the Seven Crowns, killed one member and left his colors on a lamppost in the park, Russell kept selling weed on the corner of 205th and Hollis Avenue, near a park where children played basketball.

Their father tried to get Russell a job at a hot dog store in Manhattan's West Village, but Russell quit this job and instead chopped up coca-leaf incense, claiming it was foil-wrapped blow. Russell was not above lying to make some money. In his lizard-skin shoes, sharkskin pants, and Stetson hats, Russell both sold and used drugs. He kept twenty nickel bags in bushes in front of the house, spent nights in fancy nightclubs, ignored his parents' rules, and didn't seem to care about anyone's feelings but his own.

By his senior year in high school, spring of 1975, Russell was taking LSD every Friday, running down Jamaica Avenue, and on one occasion had shoved into people and said Mickey Mouse was after him. He started attending City College of New York in Harlem in the fall of 1975. He was supposed to be studying to become a sociology teacher, but was more interested in smoking angel dust, wasting days in the student lounge and going to Harlem's hottest clubs each night.

Then during the autumn of 1977, everything changed. Russell came home excited about a party he had attended in the Harlem nightclub Charles' Gallery. He'd seen a DJ mix two copies of P-Funk's single "Flashlight," and a young guy named Eddie Cheeba, holding a microphone, tell a crowd of blacks and Puerto Ricans, "Somebody, anybody, everybody scream!" He smelled money in this new music. He stopped selling weed, and enlisted schoolmates Rudy Toppin and Curtis Walker (already rapping as Kool DJ Kurt Walker) to help him throw parties. He barked orders, printed thousands of flyers and stickers, rented halls and charged admission, and changed Curt's stage name to the Eddie Cheeba–like Kurtis Blow (which Walker, an affable communications major, didn't initially like). Soon Russell's flyers claimed the Harlem-bred Walker was really "Queens' #1 rapper."

Russell came home one night to complain that no one had come to one of his events and he had lost all his money. Their dad urged him to treat this as a lesson and return his focus to school, but their mom handed Russell $2,000 in $100 bills she kept in her "personal savings" and encouraged Russell to continue. Russell kept throwing parties and littering the city with thousands of flyers headlined "Rush Productions in Association with Rudy Toppin and Kurtis Blow." Once his minor success in Manhattan threatened to eat into other promoters' profits, however, his competitors started telling people, "Hey, Russell's gay!" Said Russell's friend Dave Sims: "The partying community was very tight and a rumor like that could hurt a person." Sims added: "Suddenly it was, 'Is there something else about this guy?' But no matter how hard they tried, Russell shot past them. Russell had that drive."

In late 1977, only two or three months into his new career as a party promoter, Russell started concentrating on Queens. The uncorroborated rumor had made its way to Hollis, but he stood in front of crowds at a block party, holding a microphone, welcoming his guests, and inspiring Joe to want to become part of Russell's events. Joe was also able to see more of Russell's main draw, Kurtis Blow, who had done a few things in the street but also encouraged Joe to stay in school. Other rappers who performed with Kurtis said Kurtis mimicked rappers from the Bronx (even if they were right onstage with him), but Joe didn't care. At local parties, Joe watched Kurt come onstage with his neat Afro, fly clothes, and jewelry. Kurt played MFSB's string-heavy *Love Is the Message* on his turntables, and rapped into a microphone: "When Kurtis Blow is on the go, he's gonna make you hate your radio," he'd say. "When Kurtis Blow is ready to rock, he's gonna make you tick just like a clock." He'd rhyme until the MFSB record was ending, then play it from the beginning on a second turntable, and speak some more. In Kurtis, Joe saw a mentor, and a gateway into this new music and Russell's circle of performers.

Joe had decided to pattern his own embryonic lyrics after Kurt's. And when Kurt slept over in their second-floor bedroom after a show, Joe would let Kurt hear his newest rhymes. Kurt listened, and offered tips and suggestions, but couldn't induct him into the act. Only Russell could do that.

And Russell was busy trying to get audiences to view Kurtis with the same respect they accorded groups from the Bronx. Russell tried to pair Kurt with Grandmaster Flash, approaching the Bronx-based DJ (born Joseph Saddler) after a show to ask if he'd play Queens.

Flash had asked, "Queens? Who'd want to hear me in Queens?"

Russell said he had a club out there. "I want you to play with my boy."

For this party, which Russell hired Flash to perform at, Flash arrived at the nearby club Fantasia one evening in a flashy Lincoln Continental (really, a cab).

Inside, the rail-thin DJ stood near the turntables he'd be using to play for Russell's audience, and watched a Queens-based disc jockey—the opening act that night—perform a few Flash-like turntable maneuvers. After the show, Flash became a fixture at Russell's events and let Kurt join some of his famed Furious Five MCs onstage. Joe wanted to be part of the act but couldn't persuade Russell to let him perform. He kept auditioning new rhymes for Kurt and volunteering to spend weekends putting stickers and flyers on walls, but Russell wouldn't give him a chance.

But then Russell changed his mind. Kurt was doing two shows a night, and Russell wanted to change his image, make him more like popular DJ Hollywood. Kurt approached Joe one day and asked, "Joey, do you want to come spin?" Joe knew he would be a novelty act, but didn't care. " 'Cause there was a son of Hollywood, DJ Smalls. I'm young, I'm thinking, 'This is the coolest thing ever.' "

Before his first show in early 1978, Joe was in his backyard with his dad. Joe heard Russell and his promoting partner, Rudy, in the kitchen in his home, discussing how to bill Joe on the flyer. Joe heard Rudy say, "DJ Run."

Joe ran to the kitchen. "Where'd you get that from? That name! Where that come from?" For Joe, it was as dramatic as Flash.

Rudy said someone already had the name.

"That's got to be a lie, that can't be true, anyway it doesn't matter, I got more juice, I'm with Kurtis. . . . I got it, that's my name."

Alone in his room that night, Joe sat in bed with his radio playing and thought, "DJ Run. I get to have that?" He thought people would bug when they heard it. They'd say, "From this DJ Run it sounds like you're very fast on the turntables or something."

In early 1978, Joe accompanied Russell and Kurt to a rented hall in the Hotel Diplomat in Times Square. He saw crowds waiting to see Kurt, Flash, and "Kurtis Blow's Disco Son—DJ Run." Inside, Flash said he would handle the mixing. Kurt performed a few rhymes, then passed Joe the mike. With Russell watching, Joe yelled, "I'm DJ Run, son of a gun, always play music and has big fun. Not that old but that's all right. Make other emcees bite all night."

As winter turned to spring in 1978, Russell kept including Joe's stage name, "DJ Run, Son of Kurtis Blow," on flyers. And Joe felt he'd arrived. He was only in eighth grade but had people from every borough coming to see him perform. And he was making money, $35 a show. "So I was big-time as a kid. I was a huge star in my mind." In Hollis, before he meet Darryl, Joe felt other kids were acting jealous. They hurled insults when they saw Joe on Hollis Avenue. When Joe dribbled his basketball in 205th Street Park—the center of social life in the neighborhood—kids ran up and kicked his ball down the street. He couldn't even walk the eight blocks to Darryl's yard, friends recalled, without people taunting him. "He was a thin little kid with long hair looking like a girl," one witness felt. "They used to say, 'Yo, your brother's a homo.'" But Joe ignored them. He took the side streets to reach Darryl's section of Hollis, and told himself that one day he'd show them all.

CHAPTER 3

Disco Sucks

During the summer of 1978, D (still calling himself Grandmaster Get High) would leave his home at about 10:30 every morning to join basketball games in Jamaica Park, in the concrete courtyard behind Junior High School 192, or in the park on 205th. Run usually joined him out there for games until 8:00 p.m. At that point, Darryl would head home for a shower and change of clothes, then quickly return to the park because people usually brought their turntables and records outside to throw a jam.

Usually Darryl watched Solo Sounds, a Hollis crew led by young, light-skinned DJ and guitarist Davy DMX (David Reeves). "He had just as many records as Bambaataa did," said Darryl. "'Cause he was rolling with the Bronx and Manhattan. He was up to date." But Davy couldn't cut loose and play the break beats he loved. "Queens wasn't really into hard-core hip-hop like up in the Bronx," said DJ Finesse, an associate of the Hollis Crew who attended Davy DMX's parties in the park. "Queens was bourgeois, on that R&B tip." Hollis residents wanted to hear the songs popular radio DJ Frankie Crocker played on WBLS, but Davy and his friends eventually reached for break-beat albums and handed microphones to aspiring neighborhood MCs. Some nights Darryl would see his friend Butter up near the turntables, saying a few rhymes.

September 1978 arrived, and with it, cooler temperatures, brown leaves on trees, and a new schedule. Darryl had to take two buses and three trains to reach Brother Rice, the only Catholic high school in Harlem. His parents thought it was a haven from a violent public school system, but Darryl arrived with a fresh shave, shined shoes, and formal attire to see older Harlem kids bringing guns to school, discussing drug deals, and griping about the cost of repairs to their BMWs. No one sold drugs in the school, but many students that year used them. Darryl fell in with a group that drank malt liquor and played all the latest jam tapes by Grand Wizard Theodore, Luv Bug Starski, and Afrika Bambaataa. And his exposure to this raw form of park music changed his opinion of the tapes Run brought to his house every Sunday afternoon. Run's tapes (Run and Kurtis Blow in concert) were enjoyable, but struck Darryl as softer than the ones he heard at Rice.

Once Run's latest tape ended, Darryl would turn his equipment on and start mixing break beats that reflected what he felt this music was really about. Not the soft disco sound of Kurt, Russell, and Run.

Run kept sharing stages with Kurtis Blow and playing the nearby nightclub Fantasia. Run—still a little kid—stood by Kurt's turntables onstage, facing two hundred or so people and playing Kurt's beloved disco breaks. He'd hear a gunshot, see the audience scatter, and calmly step to the side of the stage to avoid being shot. But after a show one night, he, Russell, and Kurt left the club and encountered armed robbers. One fired a gun and they ran. Russell slid under one car with the night's receipts while Kurt and Run hid under another. For a few tense moments they held their breath and watched gunmen's sneakers run past. Later that night, Russell said no more shows at Fantasia.

For his fourteenth birthday in November 1978, Run installed his own set of turntables in his attic. He told people he had saved money to buy them, but most people felt they were another gift from his educated, middle-class parents. Whatever the case, "They were called Quantas," said Run. "I picked them out myself." They weren't name brand like Technics or Pioneer, but "they were good," he added.

Darryl agreed, so he carried one of his turntables and his mixer to the pawnshop. He received $15, spent it on weed, and looked forward to practicing in Run's attic. But Run didn't let him get on the turntables. Instead, he'd pass D a microphone and say, "Start rapping. Say a rhyme."

With a heavy sigh, D performed lighthearted raps and listened to Run tell their friends, "Yo, get D a beer. Keep going, keep going."

As time passed, D came to enjoy rapping more than spinning records. As a rapper, he could tell people—not show them—how great he was. He changed his nickname to "Easy D" and started writing rhymes. And in the spring of 1979, after hearing a jam tape by the Funky Four Plus One More—a female member named Sha Rock saying rhymes with an echo chamber—D told himself, "This is what I want to be."

That thunderous echo was on his mind in English class, when the teacher let students spend the last five minutes of each period on creative writing. D started filling his black-and-white composition notebook with lyrics about fistfights, Puma sneakers, British Walker brand shoes, angel dust (something he smoked for three weeks, then gave up), Olde English, Hollis, and rocking the mike.

He wrote an entire song in one sitting, and stopped whatever he was doing to write another if inspiration struck. Soon he had filled seven notebooks. "In school, on the train, on the bus; I was always writing rhymes," he remembered. One day his English teacher read a few and asked, "What is this? Where's this stuff coming from?"

With a shrug, the laid-back student said, "I'm an MC."

CHAPTER 4

Party Time

One afternoon in the summer of 1979, Run was out in Hollis hanging posters for a Rush party. A bespectacled thirtyish black man with an Afro came over to ask about Rush Productions. His name was Robert "Rocky" Ford, and he worked for *Billboard*. He was also writing a story about break beats. Run accepted his business card, handed it to Russell at home, and within days saw Russell hanging with Ford, who lived in nearby St. Albans, Queens.

Russell and Ford were looking to create a rap record, and Ford wanted to record DJ Hollywood, a jolly disco-style DJ who stole the show during intermissions at concerts by major black music acts like the Ohio Players and Kool and the Gang. Since he couldn't get Hollywood, Ford then wanted to record the Hollywood-like Eddie Cheeba. As Russell and Ford went back and forth about whom to record—

Russell pushing for Kurtis Blow—Run kept joining Kurt onstage in local nightclubs. One night D came by his house to hang. Run had no time to stop and talk, since a long limousine was waiting out front. He and Kurt ran past D, leaped into the car, and took off.

Darryl, Joe knew, wanted to attend his concerts but couldn't since his mom was so strict. D tried, though. He'd face the shorter, older woman and say, "Russell's giving a party, and I want to go with Joe and them. Can I go?"

She'd reply, "No, you ain't going over there. It's bad over there! Go watch TV with your brother or go to sleep."

D would barge into his bedroom, slam his door, and actually cry. One night he even told himself, "I hope she die! I hope she get hit by a car!"

Since Run usually made it a point to have someone in the crowd hold a recorder over his head and tape his latest gig, D was able to hear his concerts on late Sunday afternoon. Run would play him the tapes, and let D come to his attic to practice on his turntables. But one day, D surprised him. In his attic, Run saw a black-and-white notebook lying on a table. D always had it with him. Run lifted the book, flipped through a few pages, and saw dozens of rhymes. "Yo, who wrote these?" he asked.

"I did. Why?"

"Yo, they are incredible! When Russell lets me make a record I'm gonna put you down with me."

With Russell working to convince his friend from *Billboard* to record a song with Kurt, Run figured it was just a matter of time before his brother let him make a record too. But when that happened, he didn't want to be alone onstage. His confident, abrasive facade concealed that he was racked with fears and doubts, and in need of moral support.

As the summer of 1979 continued, Run and D spent more time together, and Run continued to tell D he'd someday join him in a group. They had a plan now, to record together, and spent so much time working on rhyme routines that D's other friends became jealous. D would smoke and drink with them at his neighborhood hangout, the alley they called "the building," until about six, leave without saying good-bye, and go to Run's attic to record his latest rhymes. If Run started acting grumpy, D would rejoin his friends at "the building," and notice some were angry. One night, Butter (who had introduced him to Run) went so far as to say, "Yo, why don't you go over to your girl Joe's house?" D understood that they wanted him to hang out more and didn't like Run's confident attitude, but he kept practicing and developing material with Run anyway.

"I didn't give a fuck," D explained. "We were positive and negative. We worked. Everyone else was like, 'D, how could you be around this motherfucker?' I'm like, 'That's my man. We got something in common.' "

Later that summer the duo made their way over to Solo Sounds' jams in Two-Fifth Park (named after 205th Street). Solo Sounds included their friend Cool T, Davy DMX, and Hurricane (who had once hurled insults at Run and kicked Run's ball, one Run confidant claimed). Solo Sounds was also, Hurricane said, "the hottest group in Hollis, Queens."

Run was going to change that. Performing shows with Kurtis, and sharing stages with some of the biggest acts in this burgeoning scene at famous clubs like Disco Fever, increased his confidence. Where he once endured taunts, now Joe was the aggressor, some people explained. Wearing the very latest styles, he told his former tormentors that in other boroughs, their sneakers, pants, or shirts were already considered old-fashioned. They got upset and wanted to fight, one person recalled, and Run either was hit or talked his way out of it.

At a Solo Sounds jam in the park, Run would wait in the crowd of kids, hoping Hurricane or Cool T would let him perform. "He was more into wanting to be 'seen' on the mike and wanting the fame," Hurricane explained, and though Run was cool with Davy now (he had introduced the DJ to Russell), Hurricane would still tell him, "Get out of here, man, you ain't getting on the mike, beat it!"

CHAPTER 5

The Broken Arm

In August 1979, Run saw Russell move closer to achieving his goal of convincing his *Billboard* friend Robert Ford to record with Kurtis Blow and not Eddie Cheeba. Russell invited Ford to Kurt's August 31, 1979, show at the Hotel Diplomat near Times Square. That night, Kurtis rapped while Grandmaster Flash mixed records. Ford decided Kurt had star quality. By mid-September, Run (a freshman at Andrew Jackson High School in Hollis) saw Ford's *Billboard* coworker, ad salesman J. B. Moore, become part of the project. Moore, a former bass player, composed a lyric about Santa in the ghetto. Russell and Ford accepted it, and Moore offered to invest $10,000 he'd saved in studio time at Big Apple Studios and for a group of musicians.

They were midway through recording the story rap song "Christmas Rappin'" when New York radio stations started playing the Sugar Hill Gang's

fifteen-minute single "Rapper's Delight." The Jersey-based trio—
Big Bank Hank (a former bouncer at a Bronx rap club), Wonder
Mike, and Master Gee—were unknowns. But story raps, boasts,
and crowd-pleasing chants over the melody line from Chic's recent
hit "Good Times" made "Rapper's Delight" a pop hit that sold a re-
markable 100,000 copies each week in New York alone. Though
Sylvia and Joe Robinson, the couple who owned Sugar Hill
Records, beat Russell to the punch, at Big Apple, Russ, Ford,
Moore, Kurtis, and a group of session players kept working on
Kurt's record.

"Kurtis had a voice like Melle Mel or Hollywood," said bass
player Larry Smith. "He had star quality. He didn't say a lot or do
a lot of tricks, but he had a voice." Once they had a Chic-like
groove on tape, Kurt recorded a vocal that fused a Christmas rap to
party lyrics he and Run had performed onstage.

Robert Ford then used his *Billboard* connections to contact
twenty-three labels. All of them rejected Kurt's song. Russell decided Polygram, which had Kool & the Gang, the Gap Band, and
Parliament on its roster, would be a good place for Kurt.

With test pressings of Kurt's song in hand, Russell visited every
major club and record store in Manhattan, Queens, Brooklyn, and
the Bronx. He told everyone they could buy the single from Polygram. Stores placed orders with the major label, and Polygram executives wondered why they were receiving orders for a single by
an artist that wasn't signed to the label. The executives then noticed
how many copies various record stores were ordering and wondered whether they should in fact sign Kurtis to a deal.

New Polygram A & R guy John Stains in Los Angeles heard the
song and told his bosses that the R & B promotions department
could easily push lyrics about Santa to radio. "I can get your money
back out of London," he added. "Sign them up." Polygram did, for
$6,000, then released "Christmas Rappin'" on its Mercury imprint,
and watched it quickly sell 100,000 copies.

On Christmas Eve, with the Simmons family gathered around

the tree and presents, Russell ran downstairs to yell that Frankie Crocker was playing the song on WBLS. And in early 1980, Kurt's debut "Christmas Rappin'" sold another 300,000 copies.

At home that winter, Run—who didn't appear on the song—looked forward to DJing for Kurt and helping Kurt perform the hit in concert. Since D had taught him how to cut and mix, Run had been practicing with break beats "Keep Your Distance" and "Frisco Disco" or with Spoonie Gee's new single, "Love Rap," which was set to nothing but a beat. Run's skill so improved that he amazed Russell with how he played Chic's record "Good Times." One day in the attic Russell watched Joe let the song's title play. Then Joe cut to the next turntable and repeated the title: "Good Times." Then he returned to the first: "Good Times." Then the second—"Good"—then back again—"Good"—then back and forth until the two records said, "Good, good, good." Then even faster: "Guh, guh, guh." "He was like Grandmaster Flash," said his friend Ray, who hung with him in "the building." "He practiced every day."

With Kurt's "Christmas Rappin'" a commercial hit, Run designed a stage show. He placed a copy of Kurt's record on a turntable. When Kurt's voice said, "I am the man called Kurtis Blow," Run's hand flew out and moved the disc back and forth: Kurt-Kurt-Kurt-Kurt Kurtis Blow.

During their gigs, Joe performed this on his turntables to rile the crowd. Kurt stood backstage, out of view, waiting for the crowd to become hysterical. When they were yelling for him to take the stage, Kurt came into view, took his time crossing the stage, grabbed the microphone, then asked, "What's my name?"

With Kurt becoming one of the genre's first superstars, Joe felt things were looking up. His father even allowed him to travel with Kurt and Russell to play concerts in North Carolina, South Carolina, Detroit, Cleveland, and Baltimore. And in April 1980, Mercury wanted another single. J. B. Moore helped with the lyrics again, session players created another Chic-like groove, and Kurt rapped about hard times on "The Breaks." Fans quickly bought

500,000 copies, making "The Breaks" the very first certified-gold rap record.

Now Mercury wanted a Kurtis Blow album. And Russell told their father he didn't want to study sociology anymore. Daniel Simmons objected: Russell was in his senior year, with only four or five credits to go, and a black man with no degree or job wouldn't get anywhere in life. Russell felt guilty, as if he'd let his father down, but decided to follow his dream. Kurt's career was taking off—the Commodores wanted Kurt to open during their big tour.

Run was just as excited. He liked being on the road, away from Hollis, and performing for larger crowds. And doing this tour, he felt, would bring him money, let him see more of the country, and hopefully convince Russell to begin working on a DJ Run solo single.

He was all ready for the tour, and the next phase of his career, when disaster struck. He was playing basketball with D and Butter in a church basement one night. Run got the ball and tried to shoot for the basket, but the larger, stocky Butter blocked the shot so roughly that Run fell to the court and shattered a bone in an arm. Everyone was stunned. His doctor put his arm in a cast, but Run told Russell he could still tour with Kurtis. Russell and Kurt talked about having Davy DMX from local crew Solo Sounds replace him. Run went to his attic to teach himself how to DJ with one arm. He didn't want to lose the gig or his place in Kurt's show, and actually managed to play records with one hand, but Russell and Kurt still tapped Davy DMX for the tour. During those weeks in 1980, Run sat at home with his arm in a cast, reflecting on how his exciting eighteen-month adventure as the Son of Kurtis Blow was over.

CHAPTER 6

Jason Mizell

While Run's arm healed, Russell became even more involved with the music industry. As Kurt's manager, he booked shows, accompanied Kurt on the road (even traveling to Amsterdam), networked with other executives and rap artists in clubs in Manhattan, and worked with Robert Ford, J. B. Moore, Kurtis, musicians, and executives from Mercury Records on Kurtis Blow's self-titled debut album, which Mercury wanted to release as soon as possible.

Run and D meanwhile spent the summer of 1980 hanging in Two-Fifth Park, playing basketball until about 6:30. When the games ended, older people would head home, and Jason Mizell would arrive to throw another jam.

Every street kid in Hollis knew Jason, who called himself Jazzy Jase and led a DJ crew called Two-Fifth Down. For the past two years he'd been impossible to ignore. Broad-shouldered, swaggering, Jason was the leader of the Hollis Crew. One night, D's friend Butter, part of Jason's crew, led D into the park and up to tough-looking Mizell. "Yo, this is my boy D," Butter said.

D faced Jason's b-boy gear—sneakers, jeans, jewelry, and black mobster hat—in awe. "I've seen him around," Jason said. "He's the one who look like Hurricane." They would have shaken hands, D recalled, but Jason was holding two large handguns, then started chasing some Five Percenters (an offshoot of the Nation of Islam) out of the neighborhood: "Yo, motherfuckers, take that shit out of here!" But afterward when D came to the park and saw Jason, they'd play ball.

Jason Mizell came to Hollis from Brooklyn in 1975 with his mother, Connie (a teacher), his father, Jesse (a social worker), and his older half sister, Bonita (a high school student). Jason was ten years old, and nervous about gang members in denim jackets victimizing him and his public school classmates. But these thieves took their lunch money once too often. One night in 1975, young Jason told his friends, "Yo, fuck that, man!" He outlined a plan to get the thieves off their backs. The next day Jason and his friends stood in front of their public school, flashing money. The thieves took the bait, but Jay and his pals, as a team, beat the hell out of them. "It was a turning point," Jay explained.

In 1980, Jason attended Andrew Jackson High, and though he was a grade behind Run, Jason continued to lead his crew and command the respect of the entire student body—they had to stay on his good side. Jason and his crew marched through the school hallways like an army, had teachers and security guards asking them to break up fights, took over benches in Hollis Park, and dealt with gang members and kept having it out with Five Percenters.

The Five Percenters harassed Jay and his crew because they supposedly objected to the petty crimes some of Jason's friends committed in the neighborhood. Jason meanwhile felt some of these Five Percenters were committing their own crimes. One day,

Jason saw a few of them intimidating kids in Andrew Jackson High and decided he'd had enough.

Jason told these Five Percenters to leave these kids alone. One slugged him in the face. Word quickly spread through the halls, and before Jason could stop them, his loyal friend Hurricane organized a posse. In school the next day, they confronted these Five Percenters, and a melee ensued in the hallway. Someone, it's unclear who, pulled a gun and fired a shot. Jason saw Hurricane stumble. "Why the fuck am I falling down?" Hurricane remembered thinking. Jay grabbed his friend, who had been shot in the leg. "I got you, 'Cane," he said, leading him away. "You're all right."

Despite his tough crowd, Jason was a bright student. He attended class with the school's most intelligent students and earned high grades. And at home, he refrained from cursing, played drums and guitar, showed an interest in philosophy, and listened to his parents warn that some of his friends were no good. But once he got outside, these friends continued to ensnare him in their troubles. Some—including his pal Randy Allen, also originally from Brooklyn—reportedly liked to burglarize homes in the nearby affluent, predominantly white neighborhood Jamaica Estates. "We'd take everything," another member of this burglary crew told *Playboy*. "Jewelry, guns, money, drugs, stereo equipment, televisions—even food for a meal afterward." The crew knew Jay's father Jesse Mizell was a decent man, and didn't want to get Jay in trouble, so they generally kept Jay out of it. "But Jay held stuff in his basement, where his parents didn't go," this person claimed.

When Jesse asked Jay whether he was committing crimes with these kids (as a social worker, Jesse knew all about peer pressure), Jay told him, "Nah, I ain't messing with nothing. I'm cool. I'm doing everything right, Dad, for real."

One night in 1980, on Hollis Avenue, a friend ran up to Jay and reported that he and some others had robbed a doctor's house in Jamaica Estates. Suddenly a detective ran toward them. His friend bolted, and Jay did the same, but the detective caught and arrested

Jay, despite the fact that witnesses to the burglary described seeing a light-skinned black man with an Afro, attired in blue and black clothing, while Jay was dark, with a Caesar haircut, and wearing green clothing and sneakers. At a nearby police precinct, police officers asked for his telephone number. Ashamed and frightened of what his parents would say, Jay at first claimed he didn't have a phone.

A court sent Jason to Spofford, a juvenile prison in the South Bronx where older inmates supposedly took younger inmates' sneakers, and sodomized them. To prepare for his stay, Jay later explained, "I said to myself, 'I'm going to love it here. I'm going to love someone bothering me. I'm going to love the fights I get into. I'm going to love it all.' " He was eager to use his fists, make an example of someone; instead, he befriended other inmates and had the time of his life. "It looked like school facilities. Pool table, Ping-Pong, and basketball in the backyard."

Four days later, his father picked him up. After a silent drive back to Hollis, his mother, Connie—a God-fearing woman—asked if other inmates had mistreated him. To avoid upsetting her, Jay said, "I had a lot fun, Mom."

In tears, she repeated, "You had a lot of fun?"

Seeing her cry inspired Jason to instantly change his life. He bought a $39 mixer, and invited highly intelligent former classmate Jeff Fluud (rapping in parks as "King Ruler") and a few other DJs to perform with him as Two-Fifth Down.

Though Jason dropped out of school (to avoid more battles with Five Percenters), Run saw the rough-mannered kid attend meetings Russell now held in the Simmons family's basement. During these informal talks, Jason and other local residents discussed local happenings, music, and new developments in their lives. "People would come and have talks," Jay's cousin Doc (born Ryan Thompson) remembered. "They were meetings of the mind where they kicked facts and enlightened each other about life in general."

Jason continued to hang with old friends, but was nonviolent. If

Doc felt someone got out of line during one of his weekend visits to Jay's home, and yelled, "Yo, I'm cracking some heads," Jay quickly said, "Yo, chill. He messed up, but chill. Let's not do that." The focus, he reminded everyone around him, was on music, DJing at parties.

Jason's Two-Fifth Down displaced Davy DMX's Solo Sounds as the best-known DJ crew in Hollis in 1980, and Run wanted Jay to DJ for them. One afternoon in the park, Run and D watched Jay and his friends emerge from his back door, which faced the park. After lugging armloads of equipment across a neighbor's backyard and into the park, Jason and his friends set everything up, plugged a cord into an electrical outlet in the redbrick Parks Department building in the center of the park, and played music that drew a crowd of three hundred. As Jason played break beats that night, most of the three hundred people wanted to get on the microphone. Jason handed out three mikes, and saw three aspiring rap artists try to rap at the same time. Run waited for his turn, seeing some of his detractors conspicuously hand the mike to anyone but him. "It was even hard for Joe to get on at Two-Fifth Park," D recalled, but Jay usually made sure Run did.

D could have performed also. Jay liked him and knew he wrote rhymes as Easy D. Jay also knew D carried his book around and often opened it to read Hollis Crew members his newest rhymes about rum and coke, the Q2 bus that ran down Hollis Avenue, smoking angel dust, his Puma sneakers, gold chains, Olde English 800 malt liquor, and his ode to Hollis: "H is for Hollis, it's for Hollis town, O is for only Homeboys that are down." Someone offered D the mike; "Take the mike, D."

But before he could accept it, Run stepped forward. "Nah. D don't take the mike," he said. Then a few feet away, to D: "Nah, you just rhyme with me." D later felt that perhaps Run told him this because Run did not want to risk losing a potential rhyming partner to another group.

Run and D kept attending Jay's parties even though at about two in the morning someone always pulled a gun and fired shots that sent the crowd stampeding for every available exit. The next day, people gossiped about how someone had started shooting again and had people climbing fences to escape, but when Saturday arrived, everyone reconvened in the park to watch Jay throw another jam.

Feeling Russell would inevitably let him create a record, Run wanted Jason Mizell to be his group's DJ. For him, the bearded, broad-shouldered tough was the perfect candidate. In addition to talent, Run felt, Jason had the fearsome Hollis Crew to protect them at shows and in Hollis. Jason, however, kept telling Run he was busy with Two-Fifth Down, so Run tried to invite Jason's assistant, Nellie D, to spin for them even though D still refused to perform in public.

Once "The Breaks" took off, Russell began coming home with tapes of the album Kurtis Blow was creating for Mercury Records. Russell saw Run and D practicing their own routines in the attic and invited them to hear the new songs and give their opinions. They *wanted* to like them, but felt that Kurt's music was overproduced, and that his lyrics—"Rappin' Blow," "Way Out West," "Throughout Your Years," his ballad "All I Want in This World (Is to Find That Girl)," and an unexpected cover of Bachman Turner Overdrive's rock song "Takin' Care of Business"—were tame compared to other rap singles. They liked what Russell did with "Hard Times" (a song that began with Kurt telling someone who asked if he had money, "Yo, my brother, I ain't really got it like that . . . What we got here is hard times"); but for the most part, they felt *Kurtis Blow* featured too many Chic-like grooves, party raps, and cries of "Everybody say ho." And on his album cover, instead of cool b-boy wear, Kurt posed without a shirt, with a gold chain on his chest, trying to look tough. Despite their rejection of his sound and image—D repeatedly opined that Kurt was corny—Run and D saw 1980's *Kurtis Blow* enter the R & B Top 10 sales chart.

Since Run kept saying they'd be in a group together, D told him they should sound like a tape he heard in between classes at Rice High School in 1981. The tape featured unsigned Bronx rap group the Cold Crush Brothers battling the Fantastic Five at the Super Showdown party in the nightclub Harlem World. Instead of backing tracks that mimicked disco records, the Cold Crush rapped on the beat from Aerosmith's "Walk This Way." Other groups offered crowd-pleasing boasts and call-and-response routines, but the Cold Crush insulted rivals and chanted lyrics to the melody from Harry Chapin's "Cat's in the Cradle." While members of groups rapped separately, one after another, the Cold Crush shared sentences. "Oh my God," D thought when he first heard the now legendary tape. "What's going on here?"

After saving $9, he bought the tape, and seemed to be inspired by Cold Crush member J.D.L. when he changed his nickname from Easy D to DMcD—the way he signed his work in typing class— and then to the less awkward D.M.C. "I can't even describe what happened," D later said of the tape. "It changed my life."

He coaxed Run—who liked rapper Spoonie Gee's smooth single "Love Rap" and "verses by Reggie Reg of the Crash Crew"— into creating routines in which they shared sentences. And whenever they hung out, D kept playing his Cold Crush tape.

They prepared a few routines, and practiced them for friends at their old familiar hangout, "the building." Emboldened by Olde English 800 malt liquor, D yelled lyrics until neighbors opened windows and the super came out to yell, "Y'all got to stop that noise! Take that someplace else!"

D and the others ignored his complaints, so the super would return with a stick to chase them off. Even while running away, though, D would turn and yell: "Don't tell me to be quiet! Don't you try it! You know my rhymes are def! You can't deny it!"

Their sound came together (D's powerful lyrics, inspired by the

Funky Four's echo chamber, Run's smooth Spoonie Gee–style delivery, and a Cold Crush–like tag-team approach), but Russell ignored them. In late 1981, Russell was busy helping Kurt create his second album, *Deuce*, and playing Run and D early versions of his songs. D, who now dressed like a b-boy (baggy hooded sweatshirts and dark jeans), agreed to hear the songs, though his friend Ray from "the building" said, "He wasn't feeling them."

With hood over head, facing Russell's radio, D heard more of the funk grooves, call-and-response routines, and soulless raps that had made Kurt's debut album one of his least favorite rap products. Joe liked Kurt's number "Do the Do," but D felt that it, and Kurt's other new works—"Deuce," "It's Gettin' Hot," "Getaway," "Rockin'," even "Take It to the Bridge," his attempt to create a tape-styled routine—all sounded stilted and bland. Songs played, but D didn't move. When they ended, he told Russell the songs were corny. Indignant, Russell told him this sound made money. D said Kurt needed to sound more like Cold Crush or Funky Four, and recited a few of his own rhymes to show what was cool—but Russell said, "It's too hard. It's too aggressive. It's not commercial."

"You dummy!" Run yelled. "D's the best rapper in the world!"

But Russell wasn't convinced, and in private told Run, "D will never be a rapper. If he nods his head to a beat or a record, it's def." D didn't like Kurt, but Russell still paid attention to D; Russell felt his views might reflect those of a younger audience that wanted far less music on the rap singles they bought, and wanted rap artists to dress in clothing they—the younger audience—could actually afford and wore every day.

Even though D kept saying Kurt was corny, Russell kept playing him new Kurtis Blow songs. He respected D's honesty and wondered if D wasn't right, after all, about this live music sound not being as exciting for teenage listeners as break beats, scratches, and tougher lyrics. In Run's house another night, with Kurt present, Russell played D "Starlite," a song that included tinkling piano, gentle guitar, and women singing the title. D sat motionless as it played, causing Russell and Kurt to face each other, and Russell to think, "Oh, shit! We're not gonna sell any records!"

When it ended, D said calmly, "Uh-uh, y'all are finished."

Run agreed with D's appraisal of Kurtis's music, and decided that when Russell let him make a record, he wouldn't rap over "Good Times" and sound like a sucker. But the more he told his brother "You should let me make a record," the less Russell seemed to listen. If anything, Russell's mind was somewhere else. By now singer Deborah Harry, a white woman who fronted the new wave band Blondie, had included a few raps on her song "Rapture" and seen it become a major pop hit. "Russell was talking about getting a white rap group together very, very early on," said Kurtis Blow songwriter J. B. Moore. "He could smell how big that was going to be and he was actively looking."

Run kept saying they'd make a record, but D told himself, "Yeah, right. I have my life. I'm going to school; I'll be in St. John's."

Run was counting on Russell's help. By 1981, Russell was booking Kurt, who had two gold-selling singles to his credit, on major tours. And with no other company (besides Sugar Hill Records) actively managing rap acts, Russell was working with other artists. Russell was also busy trying to learn how to actually operate as a manager; he didn't know what he was doing, but told himself he'd take meetings, make calls, produce records, join Kurtis on tour, book shows, and somehow get the hang of it. Instead of working on a DJ Run single, Russell teamed with musician Larry Smith and concentrated on recording other musicians, and managing their careers from an office at 1133 Broadway in Manhattan. Then Russell received his first royalty check for his work with Kurtis and moved out of the Simmons home.

Just as Russell left, friends recalled, Run was coping with the fact that his parents were heading for a divorce. "It was crazy in Hollis, and crazy at home," one of Joe's friends said, under condition of anonymity (for fear of angering Joe by discussing this barely reported period of Joe's life).

Even if Russell had been around and wanted to work with him, Run knew his father was opposed to the idea. He wanted Run to focus on improving his grades, which had slipped to the point where Run had to attend night school to make up for lost credits. To keep the peace, Russell agreed to put Run off until Run received his diploma. Run kept saying, "Russell, let me make a record," but Russell kept ignoring him.

Run kept DJing in his attic and expanded his dream to include his friend Ray. Ray, who hung out with Joe in the neighborhood, was usually near the turntables, handing Run whatever record he needed from his crates. And because Ray literally ran to get some of these records, Run nicknamed him "Runny Ray," and wrote a rap for him to perform.

In Ray's living room, on days they all played hooky from high school, after hearing tapes by Grandmaster Flash, Bronx DJ Afrika Bambaataa, rapper Melle Mel, and the Cold Crush Four, Run and D practiced their tag-team routines while Ray made beats by banging on a radiator. Then Ray would say the lyric Run gave him: "Toot the horn, ring the bell / I am the man with the clientele / Ring the bell and toot the horn and then you know that Runny Ray is on." But Ray soon told them he'd rather stick to making beats.

Around his neighborhood, Run saw crews refuse to let him perform at their jams. Then he heard records on the radio by acts on Sugar Hill and thought, "If *I* could be down, I'd be a lot better. Imagine a young rapper making a record, *this* young, with *this* voice." The more people rejected him, pushed him aside, the more determined he became to make it in music. "When he became DJ Run," one of Joe's bandmates later said, "it was for revenge."

Meanwhile, D.M.C. was beginning to lose hope. D was drifting further into street life (stealing forties of beer from Dolly's Deli, suckering a white man out of $5 by claiming he'd buy drugs for the guy, stealing from his mother's purse, going on a three-week angel dust binge, and messing up in school). Run did what he could to keep D focused and feeling confident about himself and his music.

One afternoon, while playing hooky again, both rhymed at the top of their lungs while walking to a porno theater on Jamaica Avenue. D wore his b-boy Kangol hat without fear of stickup kids or hard rocks; Run swaggered a bit. "Something jumped in me around seventeen where I thought I was the baddest little *hood*lum that ever did anything," Run explained. Both carried bottles of Olde English malt liquor.

After sneaking into the theater, they headed for the men's room. It was out of service, so they made a detour into the empty ladies' room. There, D opened his schoolbag for some reason. "He pulled out these glasses and put them on to see something," Run remembered.

Run asked, "What are those?"

D, who had recently failed an eye examination, explained, "My mother bought them yesterday. She told me to wear these glasses." D didn't want people calling him "four eyes" or "goggles," so he'd worn them to one class, then hidden them in his bag. "They look doofy," he added.

Run asked, "What? What do you mean? I would trade my life for those big dumb glasses! You're like Preach from *Cooley High*! What do you mean you look corny? We'll *win* because of these big dumb black glasses! They're not Cazals! They're retarded incredible! Put them on and never take them off!"

D looked like he wanted to cry. "But they look funny," he repeated. "What do you mean?"

"Do you know how cool those glasses are?" Run said. "Your mother did you a good justice. Wear these glasses every day."

After that D not only wore them, he did so with pride. But he still wouldn't perform in public, so Run was alone when he made his way over to a block party Russell's production partner, Larry Smith, threw in nearby St. Albans one summer day in 1981.

A thin, sharp-featured bassist with a mustache, Smith (a former schoolmate of Run's oldest sibling, Danny junior) was a well-traveled veteran of bands that played blues, R & B, funk, and disco, and numbers from *Your Arms Too Short to Box with God* for a production in far-off Canada. Larry liked Run, and felt he showed promise. "But that was Russell's little brother, so Russell always used to push him to the side," Larry felt.

Run grabbed the mike that day in 1981 and "put Kurtis Blow to shame," Larry continued. "He put a lot of rappers to shame. And they wanted to beat him up after the party." Another afternoon, Run showed up midway through a jam in nearby Jamaica Park, cut across the throng of rappers waiting for the mike, and, said Ray, "was busting them on their ass." On another occasion, Run persuaded D finally to stop being shy and rock the mike at a crowded block party. That day, D surprised Run by facing a friendly audience and segueing from amiable call-and-response chants to yelling insults in people's faces.

*B*un soon became known in Hollis for humiliating any opponent trying to battle him at a jam. "His brother, who was a hip-hop promoter, didn't want to give him a chance, so he had to blast everybody out," Larry Smith explained. "He did it everywhere he went." And though he had long since stopped performing with Kurtis, he kept lining up shows in local clubs, on his own, as the "Son of Kurtis Blow." Since he liked how D rocked the mike at the block party, Run decided to use these shows he booked to introduce D.M.C. to his small but loyal core audience.

One Friday afternoon he called D unexpectedly to say he'd be doing a show in a few hours with rapper Sweet G., whose single "Feel the Heartbeat" mimicked Tanya Gardner's recent "Heartbeat" and was a big hit on local radio. "Yo, D, I got a show at the Le Chalet," he said. "You know where that's at, right?"

D said he knew about the venue on Hillside Avenue.

"I want you to come and be down with me," Run said. "I got DJ Kippy-O."

D was surprised by the invitation but accepted: "All right. All right. Cool." He ended the call and sat there for a minute. Then he went to his basement, opened a bottle of Southern Comfort, and drank half the bottle in an effort to steady his nerves. By 6:00 p.m. his mom, Bannah, was asleep, and his pop, Byford, was at work; but instead of meeting Joe, he drank some more. Hours passed quickly, but he finally left his home. It was a ten- to fifteen-minute walk to Joe's block, 205th, and along the way D wondered if he'd remember his rhymes, if he'd say the right ones, if anyone would like them, if the DJ would play break beats that fit his lyrics (each designed for a certain one). He thought up reasons to go home, even telling himself, "Man, I am drunk," and on Run's block he actually stopped in the middle of the street to change direction. But he reconsidered, marched up to Run's house, and knocked on the door.

Run opened it. "You want something to drink?" he asked.

D said, "Cool. Yeah, give me a lot."

By the time they reached the club Le Chalet, D was smashed. He didn't know how he had got there. It was early, so the club was half empty, but before he could fully take in his surroundings, Run started his fifteen-minute set. D stumbled over to the side of the stage and stood behind a speaker while Kippy-O mixed the bass-heavy record "Seven Minutes of Funk" on two turntables. Then Run yelled, "Easy D, my man! Get on the mike with the master plan."

D couldn't make it to center stage. For a millisecond he wondered why he had come. "I was drunk and sat down and rhymed with my back to the crowd," he recalled. The rest of the night was a blur, but bright and early the next morning Run called him on the phone. "You were drunk last night."

D felt embarrassed.

"You don't know what you did?" Run asked.

"What'd I do?" he answered.

"Yo, you were good," Run said. "Your rhyme was dope. But, motherfucker: next time, stand up and look at the crowd. And if you gotta sit down, sit on the front of the stage, have your hood over your head, and rhyme at the crowd!"

CHAPTER 7

Krush Groove 1

un kept asking Russell to let him make a record, and finally, in early 1982, Russell told him, "Okay, Trevor got something."

Trevor was Trevor Gale, drummer for Larry Smith's band, Orange Krush. Together, Russell and Larry had produced a record called "Action" for the group, found them a deal with Mercury Records, and seen Sugar Hill Records use its drum track as the basis for their group the Treacherous Three's single "Action." Gale had recently asked Russell to find a rapper for a new lyric, "Street Kid," and Russ told him, "No problem. I've got just the person for you. Joey will be perfect."

But despite suggesting seventeen-year-old Run for the single, Russell continued to avoid working with him. "I didn't have enough belief in my own brother," Russell wrote in his autobiography, *Life and*

Def. "I knew how good he was, but it just didn't occur to me that he could be a star."

Though he'd told D.M.C. they'd form a group, Run agreed to record as a soloist. But his dream soured when he saw the lyrics Gale had cowritten with his wife. Like "Christmas Rappin'" and "The Breaks," the lyric had a theme—a young b-boy asking old people not to dismiss him as a hoodlum simply because he wears his hat backward and his trousers with one leg rolled up—but Joe thought it was hackneyed.

He complained to D about the verse and tried to personalize it, make it a little tougher by referencing Hollis and his friends from "the building." "I went to Hollis Ave. just to see who's there," Run wrote. "People judge us by how we look and by what we wear. My man Darryl Mack thinks its all a joke. But me, myself: I think it's wack 'cause I'm a cool-out folk." Then someone drove him out to a studio in New Jersey, where Gale played him a track with a heavy keyboard riff, commercial-sounding bass, and a computer voice chanting the title, "Street Kid."

"I kicked the rhymes," Run remembered. "Some were written and I changed some." Run also tried to add "fast rhymes" to make it more street, but Gale and his spouse wanted him to plead for understanding. Facing the mike, Run cried, "Adults out there, we've all got brains. Why don't you treat us like you oughtta?" It was all for naught. Gale pitched the idea to various major labels, but found no takers. "Never released," Run said tersely.

In a way, Run was relieved. Back in his attic, he practiced on his turntables with Jimmy Spicer's record "The Bubble Bunch"—produced by Russell and Larry Smith—and Kurtis Blow's "Do the Do," playing it backward to create an otherworldly sound. Though he sold Larry a few passages from a "Hard Times"–like message rap for $100, Run focused on improving his grades, selecting a college to attend, and dating a schoolmate named Valerie, a serious relationship that would lead to an engagement and then, by 1984, a marriage and the birth of their first child.

)n spring of 1982, Run and D felt the pressures of adulthood. High school was ending. Their parents expected them to go to college. They weren't particularly excited about four more years of school (already both of their grades had slipped because of partying and focusing on music). And they didn't look forward to having bosses at whatever careers they stumbled into. D had had only one job in his life. He and a friend—he never publicly identified who—had signed on to distribute handbills on the street. But D quickly tired of it and threw all the flyers in a trash can.

Run also didn't have any idea about what sort of career to pursue. He loved music, smoking marijuana, getting on the mike and doing shows, and dreaming of someday having a hit record and supporting a family.

In their respective high schools, teachers and guidance counselors asked to what colleges they'd be applying, so to buy time until they could figure out what they would do with their lives, and to keep their parents from complaining, the music-minded duo applied to local universities.

At Rice High School in Harlem, guidance counselors asked D to pick a course to study. Exhausted by the night before—he gave the impression that he had been partying—D checked off business management on a list of possible majors given to him, since it was near the top of the list. And since his friend Butter would also be attending the school, D applied to St. John's University. "I had no idea what the hell I was gonna be," he said.

At Andrew Jackson High School in Hollis, Run was just as confused. He faced a checklist similar to the one given to D, but on an application for La Guardia Community College. The words "mortuary science" caught his eye. He had an uncle who did that. "And Joe said, 'Everybody has to die, so that's what I'm gonna take up,' " said Larry Smith.

He really didn't care. He had to check something. He applied to La Guardia Community College. "But then I went to the community college and there were no classes for it," he said. "It was crazy."

In autumn 1982 Run began attending college and considered applying for work at a nearby Woolworth department store. He decided not to work there. Instead, he attended classes, did his homework, and tried to figure out what he would do with his life. At St. John's, D did the same but immediately started screwing up. "I'd hang out in Hollis, in the game room, 'cause I didn't like what I was going to college for," he said. "I wasn't able to find something to do."

Music, they felt, continued to be an option, and Run continued to invite Two-Fifth Down member Jason Mizell to DJ for his group with D.M.C. Jay, who had by now dropped out of high school, earned his general equivalency diploma, spent most of 1982 caring for his sick father, Jesse, at home (Jesse died in October of that year). When Run issued his latest invitation into the group, Jay surprised him by saying, "Let's do it, baby!"

At Rush Productions, really a desk in someone else's office space at 1133 Broadway, Russell and Larry Smith wondered what to work on next. As a production team, they had created two solid hits, Jimmy Spicer's novelty rap "The Bubble Bunch" and Orange Krush's R & B–rap fusion.

By late 1982, rappers mixed with whites in downtown nightclubs. Graffiti artists like Fab Five Freddy and Phase II released singles like "Change the Beat" and "The Roxy" on Celluloid Records. Afrika Bambaataa's "Planet Rock" sounded like German duo Kraftwerk's radio hit "Trans-Europe Express" and sold a whopping 600,000 12-inch singles. "It was all about dance music at that time," party promoter Kool Lady Blue recalled.

Russell figured they could position Orange Krush as part of the dance-rap scene downtown, and by Christmas of 1982 he'd told

Larry they should include Kool Lady Blue, an Englishwoman who worked in fashion by day and promoted mixed-race events at the Roxy. They could include Blue in the lineup, call the group OK Crew, and have new members rehash the beat from "Action," Russell felt.

And since Run kept asking to record, just as Run was deciding to apply for a job at Woolworth, Russell told him, "Here, let's do this." As Run worked on lyrics and planned to rap over the beat from "Action," Kool Lady Blue recalled, "Russell kept pestering me about joining them." She told Russell her days in a punk band had soured her on being in a group, but Russell kept asking her to sing on the record. "He handed me the demo and would call me at the Chelsea Hotel daily and proceed to sing 'my part' to me over the phone, thinking I'd change my mind," she said. "I thought he was out of his tree. It was funny."

Then, D.M.C. remembered, Run insisted that the group name change to DJ Run and the OK Crew. (Run denies this.)

Ultimately, nothing came of this Run solo project, either. Kool Lady Blue would not join the OK Crew. "No, thanks," she told Russell. Run also backed out of the musical group, telling Russell and Larry, "I want D with me. We're gonna do what we do when we in the attic, in the basement."

That would have been it, but then Run's next-door neighbor Spuddy—who taught him how to play drums when Run was ten, and was also Russell's trusted friend—told Russell, "Man, you better get with these kids. Your brother and Easy D—they're off the hook. These kids are amazing!" Russell called Larry Smith to say he wanted to work with Run again, on something like "The Message" by Grandmaster Flash and the Furious Five, which the *New York Times* had just named most powerful single of 1982.

R un got D on the phone. "D, I'm really gonna make a record this weekend. It's called 'It's Like That.' " He wanted help. "Go home and write about how the world is." Though he already had a few message raps from his high school English class, D sat and filled another fifteen pages with writing. When he saw the new lyrics, Run was excited. "These are great! We're gonna make that record!"

D, however, felt something was lacking. That night, he considered the chorus; Run yelling "It's like that" felt plain. Something like Flash and the Furious Five's "Message" sequel, "Survival," would be better: "Its called survival, survival, survival."

The next morning he called Run to say, "I'm thinking, when you go 'It's like that,' there should be something to answer: 'It's like that/ and that's the way it is.' " Run liked it. So did Russell, who told Run he should record it.

Run didn't want to do this alone. He wanted a partner onstage. "I'm not making a record unless you put D on it," he said.

Russell admired D's fashion sense but felt Run was going too far. "Because he didn't like my voice," said D. "I was like 'Peach to the apple, apple to the core,' " he yelled as an example. " 'I am the man with the rhymes galore, from the Hollis Crew, and I'm doing it too. . . .' And he was so used to 'Clap your hands every-*body*!' "

Another concern was that Run's hyper voice and D's monotone wouldn't mix well, Larry Smith explained. "And you had Spoonie Gee out there. Maybe we figured it would be easier to lock down one person than to have a group. And Russell knew he could control his brother. He didn't know about D.M.C., if his parents would go along with it because they were still in school."

In the end, Russell said all right. They performed for him in Run's living room, and he told them to bring their lyrics over to Larry's house in Jamaica, Queens.

Larry and Russ were already there when they arrived one afternoon in the autumn of 1982. Larry stood near his eight-track reel-to-reel tape recorder, mixing board, microphones, guitars, and

other instruments, and played them what he and Russell had created—their take on "Planet Rock." Run and D loved its stark beat,
intimidating horn blast, and quirky little synthesizer effects. Instead
of the live music and disco grooves on Sugar Hill singles, Larry
recorded a pummeling track.

Russell thumbed through D's rhyme book and allotted lyrics to
Run and D. They entered a recording room and yelled their lyric,
but the music stopped. Russell wanted them to sound more like DJ
Hollywood and Kurtis Blow. They deepened their voices and tried
again.

At home, Run played the studio tape for his father. Ray was also
there, nodding along.

Run's father pointed at Ray. "Watch his head! When he bob that
head that means that record's gonna be a hit!"

Russell had second thoughts, Larry recalled, and in a formal
Pilgrim-like tone, he asked, "What's my little brother saying?" A
record label wouldn't sign a group cursing as much as this. The
group edited their verses. "We had better lyrics," Larry sighed.
"But that was the most commercial of them all. We had some profanity. And Joe, even at a young age, didn't like cursing."

Back in Larry's attic again, they recorded "It's Like That" with
the inflated, Blow-like voices. But D.M.C. yelled, "Nah, let's do it
like 'Planet Rock'! Let's make this shit flow! Let's be loud! Bring
some energy to it!"

Russell wasn't there, but Larry—who usually preferred commercial elements like live music and party lyrics—let them try it.

D faced the mike and Run, who stood across from him. Then he
yelled: "Un-em-*ploy*-ment at ay wreck curd high!" Larry was
stunned. He called Russell on the telephone to say, "Yo, this shit is
def. We got a hit. We need a name." Larry then extended the telephone to Run.

Run grabbed it and listened, then started to look defeated. D
knew this couldn't be good. Run was near tears from stress when he
passed him the phone.

Russell said, "The name of y'all is Runde-MC."

D felt rage billow inside him.

"See?" Russell asked happily. "It sounds so good, Runde-MC."

They wanted something as descriptive as the *Furious* Five, *Fearless* Four, or *Treacherous* Three. Even the "Tough Two," D recalled. "Not fucking 'Runde-MC,' the fakest name in the world."

They literally cried. "Russell, you're ruining us!

"It's stupid . . . it . . .

"Runde-MC?

"Please don't call us that! Please!"

Russell ignored them. "Joe was younger—he was on the street—and Russell looked at it from an old perspective," said Larry. "So Joe had to shut up and learn."

Bussell started acting as their manager and saw every major label reject the song. "They're bourgeois blacks," Russell complained about label executives. They wanted "sophisticated" upscale images like Chic (who performed in suits), or gentle music like Peabo Bryson's ballads. "It's also *too black* for them," he felt. Rejections piled up, but then Russell stopped in at Profile Records.

During the past two years, the two young white guys (Cory Robbins and Steve Plotnicki) who started Profile in 1981 with $34,000 had enjoyed the demos Russell brought, but not enough to actually sign any of his acts.

Instead, they released dance music singles before investing $750 of their final $2,000 on Dr. Jekyll & Mr. Hyde's "Genius Rap," a November 1981 12-inch that was set to the Tom Tom Club's hit "Genius of Love," and sold a remarkable 150,000 copies, keeping Profile in business.

Runde-MC was harder than anyone signed to the label—Dr. Jekyll & Mr. Hyde, the Disco Four, Hurt 'Em Bad, and dance music singers like Sharon Brown ("Specialize in Love")—but Russell handed young label president Cory Robbins, a former DJ from up-state New York, the tape. There was only one song on it, Robbins recalled. "And not only that, Run-D.M.C. was spelled differently: R-u-n-d-e, one word, 'Runde' dash MC."

Robbins asked Russell, "Why is it called that?"

"Oh. 'Cause my brother's Run and the other guy is D.M.C."

"Well, why isn't it 'Run-D.M.C.'?"

"Yeah, okay, we'll do that!"

Robbins listened to "It's Like That" and had to make a decision. "We were very familiar with all the rap records out at that point because there weren't that many," he said. "Sugar Hill was having a lot of hits and everything had a full band and a lot of instruments. And this had bass and drums and was very, very empty sounding, sparse and different." He'd never heard anything like it. That night he drove around town, playing it repeatedly. "And I kept liking it more and more every time I played it." He enjoyed the chorus, "It's like that and that's the way it is," and told himself, "Oh, that's a pretty good line. That's a good hook. And this record is really so different. I don't know if people are gonna like it, 'cause it doesn't really have many instruments, but it's different, it's original, the lyric is really good, the hook is *great*, and it's worth . . . let's give a shot."

Robbins made an offer.

Russell wanted more money.

Robbins said, "No. We'll do it for half that money." Profile was ready to let it go.

Russell thought it over, then accepted Profile's offer of 10 points and a $25,000 advance for an album.

D.M.C. was confused. It wasn't Mercury. "It wasn't a major label."

Profile drew up a contract. "Actually Russell was signed to Profile," D.M.C. explained. "He was signed to bring Profile Run-D.M.C. records. And we signed to Russell." In addition, Robbins said, the group signed a contract directly with Profile. This way, if

Russell and Profile stopped working together or had a falling-out, the group Run-D.M.C. would still be signed to Profile Records. "They had to sign the Profile contract also, but the money got paid to Rush, and Rush paid Run-D.M.C.," Robbins explained. "Rush collected all the money from Profile and then paid it out to the artists."

The contract covered "It's Like That" and gave Profile the option to request more singles and albums.

As Rush Productions and Profile finalized terms in March 1983, Run and D found themselves spending more time in the city. "We had to bring contracts from the label to the lawyer's office," said D. "We had to do the footwork."

*B*ussell and Larry called Greene Street Studios in lower Manhattan and played engineer Roddy Hui the demo for "It's Like That." Hui (pronounced "way") had helped with Kurtis Blow singles when the studio was known as Big Apple. Hui now called studio owner Steve Loeb into the room and put Russell and Larry on speakerphone. Loeb heard the song, and said they could record, and pay him later.

Run and D were excited. "Larry's house was good," Run said. "Greene Street was better."

They recorded "It's Like That," and then Russell began creating something else. On a drum machine, Larry tapped in the beat that drummer Trevor Gale played on Orange Krush's popular single "Action," the same beat Russell had wanted Lady Blue to sing on.

Run was about to record an old routine about riding in a chauffeur-driven Cadillac to buy marijuana uptown when Russell said, "Just be sure to mention Orange Krush and tell them where you go to school."

Run revised his opening lines. Then D let Russell hear his verse about St. John's University, what D called his light skin, living in Queens, and eating chicken and collard greens. "Russell was like, *oh shit*," D recalled.

Russell and Larry let them rap the entire song without stopping, and while mixing it, they took the drums out when D started rapping and had DJ Davy DMX—Kurtis Blow's DJ until he and Kurt had a falling-out for unspecified reasons—scratch behind D's voice. Run and D wanted Jason Mizell in the group, but Larry included Davy instead. " 'Cause he was the DJ for Kurt, he was the DJ for the Orange Krush band," said D.M.C. "They were cool. It was their little clique: Larry, Kurt, Russell, and Davy."

Russell and Larry then alienated Run and D by saying they should add melody at certain points.

Run and D objected.

"Turned out they were right," Russell said later in his autobiography.

Eight hours after they started, Run-D.M.C. left Greene Street Studios with a tape of a song called "Sucker MCs (Krush Groove 1)."

In Hollis the next day Run and D faced Jay and explained why they hadn't attended the going-away party Jay had thrown for their pal Nellie D at neighborhood club Dorian's. By the turntables all night, Jay had dismissed MCs. "I wasn't letting anybody rhyme," he said, even after he sensed they wouldn't show up.

Now Run stood there in his black leather jacket and white Lees, with his Afro and sideburns; D, in his cloth trench coat and glasses, his hair cut in a severe round Caesar style that, combined with his square-framed glasses, made him look odd. They told Jay they'd been in the studio, and then played "It's Like That." By the fade-out, admiration had replaced anger on Jay's face, and he nodded and said, "Okay." Run and D then reported that they were heading over to Hollis Avenue to shoot their publicity photo, and told Jay they wanted him to join them. Jay understood that they really wanted him in the group, that it wasn't just talk. He happily slipped into his black leather bomber jacket, his billed black leather cap, and his chunky brass belt buckle that spelled out "Jay."

They stood in front of a brick wall: Run on the right, in profile with hands tucked in his jeans pockets; D to the left, leaning over, hands stiffly at his side; Jay between them, shorter, holding his belt buckle with both hands. At the last minute some neighborhood toughs in a passing car saw them posing and sneered, "So what, niggas!" Run was crushed, and it showed in his eyes.

Larry felt Davy would be a better DJ but accepted that Run had his reasons for wanting Jay. "He would be like the ghetto pass," Run admitted. "You with Jay, everything's cool. I won't say protection, but Hollis was rough. If you ran with Jay, he had everything under control."

But Jay needed a better stage name, one that people wouldn't confuse with Jazzy Jay, who performed with Afrika Bambaataa's group the Soulsonic Force. "I called him Jam Master Jay," said D.M.C. " 'Cause he's the master of the record and the master of the party."

Two months had passed since they signed the deal with Profile, and Run was impatient. He wanted everyone to hear his record, so one morning he slipped into an ill-fitting plaid jacket, combed his pork-chop Afro out, and led a friend to the Jamaica Bus Terminal, where everyone waited for the Q2 bus. "And homeboy was out there with his giant JVC Biphonic box playing 'Sucker MCs,' " Finesse, a DJ and neighborhood friend of Run's, recalled. The radio belonged to D.M.C., and while Run stood, another of Run's friends—not Finesse—sat and pointed at Run. "Yo, yo, this is my man's shit," this other person, Run's companion, yelled. "Yo, this is my man right here! My man Run!"

Run started mouthing the words to the song. "It was funny," Finesse continued, " 'cause we were standing in a terminal."

People were used to radios playing well-known records. If they didn't hear familiar beats or songs, they paid no mind. "But he was playing 'Sucker MCs' and everybody sitting around the Q2 bus stop was just sitting there, looking at him, like 'okay.' " Like Run had a big ego and craved attention and adulation. "You know?"

Profile released "It's Like That"/"Sucker MCs" in May 1983. "It was out there and it wasn't really reacting right away 'cause it was so different," Cory Robbins said. "Every week it would sell like 500 copies."

Run and D did what they could to let people know about their record, including traveling to Adelphi University on Long Island (fifteen minutes from Hollis) for their first radio interview, on radio station WBAU with Bill Stephney. Run and D.M.C. were familiar with the station's rap shows and energetic rap tapes promoting various programs. They entered the station (Jam Master Jay wasn't with them) and met hosts of other WBAU shows, including members of a Long Island DJ crew called Spectrum City, who threw parties, and were at the station that night to meet Run and D, whose record the DJ crew loved playing.

Butch Cassidy, who rapped alongside Chuck D in Spectrum City and cohosted Chuck's radio show, explained that he had been at the Encore nightclub in Queens and heard a DJ play "It's Like That." Since the Encore's DJ hadn't mentioned the song's title, Cassidy had told people at WBAU, "Yo, the beat was big. It sounded a little bit like 'Action' and it had cats rapping over it." A day later, another WBAU associate, aspiring producer Keith Shocklee, brought a promotional copy of Run-D.M.C.'s record to WBAU and told everyone, "Yo, man. Listen to this."

As "It's Like That" played, Butch Cassidy yelled, "Yo, that's the cut they played last night at Encore." WBAU host Bill Stephney, whose show mixed punk records with rap singles, loved what he heard and immediately made WBAU the first station to play both of Run-D.M.C.'s songs. "Many of Run-D.M.C.'s friends in Hollis and southeast Queens called the station to say Run-D.M.C. wanted to come on the show," said Stephney, a former freelance writer who met Russell Simmons in 1980 while trying to arrange an interview with Kurtis Blow. "Then I found out Run was Russell's little brother and told them, 'Well of course, come on up!' "

At WBAU for their interview, Run and D posed for one or two quick photos before sitting in front of the station mike. Stephney kept praising the stripped-down sound of "Sucker MCs." "This thing is beyond anything," Stephney told them. "This is like a revolution on wax. How do you guys feel?"

Run and D didn't provide many eloquent answers. "They were shy, nervous kids," Spectrum City member and Run-D.M.C. fan Chuck D remembered. "We joked that the record said more than they did: 'Two years ago a friend of mine . . .' " Off the air, however, Run and D joined everyone at WBAU—Bill Stephney, Chuck D, local DJs Hank and Keith Shocklee—for a spirited conversation about the rap genre, what fans liked best, and the direction they felt the music was heading.

Kids on the street loved the beat on "Sucker MCs," but major radio stations ignored the song. Run and Jam Master Jay decided to get involved. "We started calling WBLS," Run admitted.

Jay requested the song and told station employees his name was Jim or Jason Murdock. "Making up a lie like they were gonna know," Run quipped.

Within minutes, the radio DJ said, on the air: "We're getting ready to play 'It's Like That,' Jim."

Run yelled, "Oh my God! They're gonna play our record!" He called D.

It was about 8:00 p.m., and at home, D was listening to the same station. The DJ said, "Here's something brand new." The song began, and he was stunned. "Ma! I'm on the radio! Come listen! Yo, check it out! Yo! Alford!" The family gathered around the radio, and the telephone rang. D answered and heard Run yell, "D! It's, it's . . ."

"I know, I know!" he shouted back. "I'll call you back afterward."

The station played "It's Like That" every three hours. "And it started selling more copies and we got the next station to play it," said Profile president Cory Robbins. "It was bigger. Then we got the third big station to play it. It was even bigger."

But radio continued to ignore the B-side, "Sucker MCs." If WBLS played it, it was as backdrop for a commerical for Kamikaze motorcycles. Run-D.M.C. and Jam Master Jay did their part to draw fans to their first single. They spent weekends riding in producer and road manager Larry Smith's Cadillac, performing five shows a night in just as many cities. After picking them up in Hollis, Larry would drive a hair-raising 90 miles per hour to get them to Boston on time. While the group set up Jay's turntables, Larry would collect their performance fee from the promoter. After this show, they would load everything back into Larry's car and speed toward clubs in Connecticut (Hartford, New Haven, and Greenwich). Once these shows were finished, they rushed to gigs in the Bronx and Westchester, then ended the night onstage at Manhattan's Roxy. Back in his car, Larry would then hand each member a stack of bills, said D.M.C.; "then Larry would get so happy because he was going to the Fever." Jay and D would go with him, while Run rushed home to his pregnant wife, Valerie.

The hectic touring paid off. Listeners started calling radio stations to request "Sucker MCs." "Then one of the stations started playing 'Sucker MCs' and that started getting big," said Cory Robbins. "And KISS used to have the Top 8 at eight and 'It's Like That' was in the Top 8 every night. Then it was number one. Then 'Sucker MCs' was number one." Within six weeks, Robbins said, "it was selling 10,000 copies a week. But it was *not* instant."

At St. John's University, D.M.C. heard schoolmates play "It's

Like That" and "Sucker MCs" on the school's PA system. Then Russell called to say he had booked a show in North Carolina, a state Russell had visited while managing Kurtis Blow. D.M.C. figured it was a good time to tell his parents he wanted to take a leave of absence from college. "I want to make records," he told them.

They weren't happy, but understood that his music career was taking off. "All right," his father, Byford, answered. "Take a leave of absence. But remember you're going to go back. You're going to go back to it." For nineteen-year-old D, the one-day trip to North Carolina was a good way to give his parents time to get used to the idea of him leaving school.

Run-D.M.C. and Jam Master Jay arrived at a mostly black high school to perform at a concert thrown by a local radio station. Run was nervous and hesitant to enter, but Jam Master Jay grabbed his big portable radio, started blasting a tape of a beat he'd cut up on his turntables, and then marched into the venue. Run and D.M.C. followed. The waiting crowd cheered at the sight of them. On an outdoor stage, they ignored the dark skies and wintry chill in the air, rushed headlong into "It's Like That," and saw the black audience go crazy.

The next night, back in New York City, they played a show Russell had booked in the four-story downtown Manhattan club Danceteria, which usually held concerts by artists on Sugar Hill Records. "There were about sixty weird niggas in here and some weird-looking motherfuckers, a whole lot of punk people," Jay said later. They did "It's Like That" and "Sucker MCs" on a small, cramped stage and saw this mostly white crowd react as fervently as the audience down south.

CHAPTER 8

Disco Fever

Russell booked them at the Disco Fever, a small, rowdy club in the South Bronx that was a favorite watering hole for many of the rappers Run and D enjoyed hearing on tapes. Russell had been going there for years to hang with Flash, party, and hand house DJ June Bug test pressings of singles he was promoting.

The Fever was an all-star place: Flash and Love Bug Starski DJed there, and everyone from Melle Mel to Busy Bee to the Treacherous Three to Kurtis rocked the mike. The Fever also attracted a tough crowd: violent drunks, dusted b-boys, drug dealers, and stickup kids who robbed departing patrons at gunpoint. Run and D were glad Jay would join them for the show. Jay knew many drug lords from Queens who partied at the club, so once the drug lords saw Jay was with Run-D.M.C., the drug lords would protect Jay *and* the group.

Before the show, Run and D discussed what to wear. Since b-boys now wore plaid pants, Run suggested plaid blazers. Instead of going to Jamaica Avenue to buy one, D pulled a jacket out of his father's closet. He tried it on and instinctively knew it looked wack, but still asked Run what he thought. Run already had misgivings about the tartan jacket he planned to wear, but on the eve of the show, both decided they looked fine.

Jay looked forward to the show as well. He'd been going to the Fever for years and had looked to the club for inspiration before he and Hollis friend Randy Allen started promoting parties. He couldn't wait to enter their state-of-the-art DJ booth and show the Bronx how Hollis threw down. And since Larry always went on about the club's turntables, Jay was even more excited.

Before the big day, Jay told Larry to pick him up at six. The day of the show, Jay dressed in his best b-boy gear: a black leather suit, a new pair of Adidas, and a black velour hat like something out of *The Godfather*.

That afternoon, D and Run waited for Larry to arrive in his giant light blue 1978 Cadillac Coupe DeVille. Both wore ill-fitting jackets with checked patterns. D's was beige and brown; Run's, white, black, and gray. With his, D wore a beige mock turtleneck sweater and dark jeans. Run had a black shirt and baggy white pants. D's hair had grown out into a short Afro, while Run's own Afro was pretty tall, and long sideburns made him look eccentric.

Larry's ride pulled up at 4:30 p.m. and Run and D saw Spyder D in the car. They liked Spyder's single, "Smerphie's Dance," and knew flyers called him the "King of Queens." They also knew Russell was managing him.

The older rapper said, "What's up?"

Larry said they had to get going.

The first stop was a club called Lola's in New Jersey. The group looked forward to rocking a young crowd but saw older yuppies and secretaries in suits, ties, dresses, and shoes. D shook his head

with contempt. "The first thing we did was like a little press conference," Spyder recalled. "It was one of them after-work clubs
with more of a suit-and-tie crowd, and there were members of the
press there because everybody was waiting to see this group that
the radio kept playing. So Run and D were nervous."

Larry ushered them toward the stage, and they noticed Lola's
had only one microphone. Performing "It's Like That" would be a
nightmare, since they shared sentences and yelled certain words in
tandem. Since Larry hadn't picked Jay up for this show—why
Larry didn't remains unknown—someone, its unclear who, played
Run-D.M.C.'s record, and Run and D did what they could. D stood
right near Run. Russell watched from the audience, looking angrier
about every word. Run finished his part, and D grabbed the mike,
did his part, then shoved it back, hoping they didn't mess up or skip
any words. "It was kind of embarrassing," Spyder said. "D's glasses
fell off. They were kind of standing there and had on these plaid
jackets. D still had his 'very big' glasses on and the lens fell out
and broke."

After the show, Russell griped about how stiff they looked.

Back in Larry's Cadillac, Larry yelled, "Y'all were wack! Yo,
y'all do the Fever like that tonight y'all gonna get shot! New
Edition was in there last week and they were wack and they
started shootin'!"

Spyder tapped Larry on the shoulder. "Yo; yo, Larry, don't tell
them this. We need to be pumping them up."

They traveled to a skating rink in Yonkers for the next show. Jay
wouldn't be at this performance, either, because the shows were
booked back to back, with no time for Larry to drive to Jay's home
and pick him up, or even to stop at a pay phone to call Jay and say
they wouldn't be coming to get him. "I performed 'Smerphie's
Dance,'" Spyder said; then he faced the predominantly black
teenage audience and said, "I appreciate the love but I know y'all
really came to see my homies from Hollis!" For minutes, he stirred

the crowd. "They not coming out until they can hear y'all from all the way back in the dressing room." The longer he spoke, the more this adolescent audience wanted Run-D.M.C. "They came out and when D said 'Un-em-*ploy*-ment!' they went crazy. They lost their minds."

Minutes earlier Run and D had been sulking. Now their confidence was back. After their set, Run asked Spyder, "How did you do that? At least I got D onstage with me. How do you come out performing by yourself?"

Spyder answered, "You wouldn't be human if you didn't get the jitters. But if you're playing a club and your record's hot or all over the radio, you can't be anything *but* good because they already love you."

Larry pulled up to the Fever on Jerome Avenue. Run and D waited while Larry called Jay to tell him they had gone to do a show in Jersey first. Larry then told Jay that he could not drive out to Queens to pick Jay up and bring him to the Fever to join Run-D.M.C. onstage. Even if Jay wanted to come there on his own, he'd arrive after they performed.

Run and D learned Jam Master Jay wouldn't be coming and that Jay had sounded distraught on the phone. He had been pacing in his house and on his porch all day. He was in his new outfit and everything. When he realized he wouldn't actually be playing the Fever, Jay sounded like he was about to cry.

Why Jam Master Jay never attended their earlier concerts is unknown. Larry picked Run and D up at 4:30 p.m. that day, and told Jay he would pick him up at 6:30 p.m. Maybe the show in Jersey was added at the last minute, or maybe the skating-rink appearance was booked quickly. Besides, Run and D's producers figured that Jay wasn't an active part of creating any music, that he was in the group simply to help Run-D.M.C. perform their songs in public, and that even if Jay couldn't come to a show (like at the Fever), they could easily tap someone like the Fever's in-house DJ, Kool Kyle the Star Child, to take Jay's place: DJs—unless they were like Grandmaster Flash, whose name came first in his group's name—were basically interchangeable. But again, why Jay did not attend the group's first shows is unknown.

Run and D entered the Fever, passing the giant bouncer Mandingo and a metal detector, and met Sal, a cheerful young Italian guy with a mustache and a chain that read "King of Disco Fever." On the second floor they faced people laughing at their outfits. Since their publicity photo had not been widely circulated to the public, denizens of the Fever simply viewed them as two kids in funny old-fashioned jackets. " 'Cause they didn't know who the fuck we were," said D.

They passed a bar on their right, a photo booth, the dance floor, and more people laughing. Their confidence slipped. D soon faced his Pumas while Run's eyes landed on his own black-striped Adidas.

People in the Fever wore custom-made leather outfits, sparkles, rhinestones, knee-high boots, pointed shoes, button-up shirts, slick wet jheri curls, and jewelry. Some snorted blow off little coke spoons. Still more scowled at the passersby. "Seventy-five percent of the Fever was coked the fuck out," Melle Mel once said.

Backstage, Run and D felt self-conscious about their plaid jackets and about Jay's absence. Then someone announced, "Here they are, Run-D.M.C.! These guys have a new record out. From Queens, New York: Run-D.M.C." They walked onto the ten-by-twenty-five-foot stage and heard people in the crowd grumble about them being from Queens.

"They were hating," said Hurricane, the same way they did at most parties, when they'd grab the mike and say, "Bronx is in the house, Brooklyn's in the house, uptown's in the house," and neglect to mention the city's largest borough.

In front of the club's famous sign—black with red and white letters calling the Fever home to Flash, Hollywood, June Bug, Kool Kyle, Kurtis, Sequence, Starski, Sugar Hill, and Sweet Gee—Run and D faced this silent, disapproving crowd. "They were really mad that motherfuckers from Queens were getting big," D said.

A few people laughed derisively, and they felt like bolting from the stage. But Kyle played "It's Like That." D noticed specific audience members frowning, and both he and Run pointed their fingers right near their faces. "You should have gone to school!" D yelled at one. "You could have learned a trade!" he raged at another. But the song fueled antigroup sentiment. While the crowd grumbled, Kyle quickly dropped "Sucker MCs," and a few ladies moaned, "Ow! That's the jam!"

After the show, D wanted to leave the band. Run told him not to fret. They'd fine-tune the act. D went home gnashing his teeth, vowing, "I'm gonna take *all* these kids out!"

Within days, he saw Run in a black blazer and matching Lees. Run told D to get a solid-color jacket. D made his all blue, wore it with black Lees and black-striped Adidas. Run then said, "You got to wear a hat!" D reached for a Kangol Applejack. They decided that plaid jackets weren't the best idea.

They settled into wearing black sweatshirts and matching jeans onstage, and Russell liked their no-nonsense look until he picked Jay up for a show one night, saw Jay emerge from his home in a *Godfather* hat, black leather suit, and unlaced white-on-white Adidas, and realized that Jay's everyday street-tough regalia would make for a memorable image. Russell told Run and D, "Y'all not gonna have a uniform, but that's what you're gonna wear there." They'd still wear sweatshirts and jeans for some shows, but if they were going to play a bigger theater, alongside some of the genre's most popular stars, or if they learned reporters would stop by to interview them about their single, D remarked, "we'd put the leather suits on."

Bussell booked them to play the Fun House downtown on August 5, 1983. Run mentally prepared for another run-in with the old school. "Back in the days, people didn't really let him get on the mike," said Hurricane. "So that ignited the flame. Then once he got on, he had to deal with the Bronx." In the audience that night were numerous members of Zulu Nation, a former street gang from the South Bronx that had turned into a large, loosely knit, and unofficial association composed of members from every borough who enjoyed break dancing, spray-painting graffiti, or creating rap music. In the dressing room, Run and D worried about whether the Zulu Nation members in the audience would jeer them as the crowd at the Fever had. Russell had already stopped by the Roxy to hand Roxy DJ Afrika Bambaataa (leader of Zulu Nation and creator of "Planet Rock") a copy of Run-D.M.C.'s single and to tell Bambaataa, "It's a lot like your record 'Planet Rock.'" Russell was cool with Bambaataa and Zulu Nation, but Run and D were nervous about performing their new routine, "Here We Go," patterned after a phrase they'd seen in a children's book ("Dum ditty dum ditty-ditty dum-dum"). Everyone who heard it enjoyed the song, but D noticed Run was anxious. "You know, the competition," said D. "He was always nervous though. Cats used to call Run 'nervous nipple.' In a way, he was schizo, whatever; this motherfucker was fucked up."

D was also anxious. He sat with a fifth of Southern Comfort, chugging it down quickly, hoping to find confidence in it. Behind the curtain, Run and D bickered over who would go out first. "You go out there," Run said.

"No, you go out there!"

Without warning Run shoved D through the curtain. D was

suddenly onstage so he improvised: "One, two, three in the place to be." He swaggered across the stage as Run quietly emerged and stood behind him. "He is DJ Run," D said while pointing, "and I am D.M.C. Funky fresh for 1983!"

Run was in awe. "D had the courage to go out there like that. Him doing it with all the lights on was amazing." Jam Master Jay started cutting up Billy Squier's "Big Beat."

As more stations started playing "It's Like That" and "Sucker MCs," Run-D.M.C. performed in other states. Many concerts were for radio stations that wanted a free show in exchange for more airplay, but Run-D.M.C. didn't mind: they liked seeing new places, staying in hotels, riding in fancy cars, and performing for fans. "It was fun," D.M.C. remembered. "A bag of weed, a couple of forties, and a car, and we were happy."

Russell soon had Run-D.M.C. flying on planes to open for major-label funk acts the Bar-Kays, Cameo, the Dazz Band, the Gap Band, George Clinton and Parliament, Midnight Star, and Zapp. From the beginning, some funk acts took exception to them being on the tour. Many were used to touring with rappers like Kurtis Blow and DJs like Grandmaster Flash, who were grateful for the slot on the bill and emulated them, dressing up before hitting the stage. Run and D wouldn't change for anyone—they wore sneakers and basic black leather suits (no rhinestones, shoulder pads, or fringe sleeves like those favored by the funk stars or the rappers who toured with them and emulated these groups), and kids seemed to love Run-D.M.C. "Let's just say, Bar-Kays," Run explained. "They have five thousand hits. The place is packed. They're headlining. We only got two records. We come. We gotta go on early, get a small portion of the stage. We perform. All the kids go crazy and scream and we do well and then they gotta go on and it's not as exciting 'cause they're on their way out and we're on our way in."

When promoters in certain towns had them headline (since local radio played their record day and night), some funk acts were even more resentful. "We used to go out onstage and bust they ass!" D told writer Bill Adler. "After we finished, the crowd didn't want to see these jerks jumping around with jheri curls, singing and playing the drums."

Some nights, however, self-doubt threatened to overwhelm Run. "Run used to be extremely nervous, damn near used to throw up before shows," said Profile label mate Spyder D, who also performed as an opening act on these tours. "I used to be like, 'Run, you the hottest motherfucker in Kentucky,' or wherever we were." But Run hid this when funk players scowled at him. If one of them muttered, "Y'all niggas ain't shit," road crew member Runny Ray recalled, Run's attitude was: "We ain't shit? All right. Whatever. Wait till we go on then, when we get off you tell me about it."

After their show—Run and D running around onstage performing "It's Like That" and "Sucker MCs"—the same spiteful funk guy would wait right near the entrance to backstage. "Yo, you niggas was hot," he'd say. "You niggas are def!" Soon, some funk groups refused to follow their set. "Niggas were like, '*Damn, I don't even want to go on after you,*'" Ray explained. "'*These niggas done rocked my damn crowd!* The crowd's on *their* dick now! *They done did "Sucker MCs"!* Yo, I don't even want to go on after that. Yo, let *me* go on first and *then* they go on.'"

CHAPTER 9

Rock Box

In late autumn 1983 Profile Records wanted another song, so Russell and Larry told Run-D.M.C. to come to Greene Street Studios. This time, Run called Jay. "Bring the turntable."

In the studio, they wondered how to follow "It's Like That" and "Sucker MCs." Russell told the group, "Take 'Hard Times' and do it up-tempo."

Russell had contributed lyrics about current events and Larry had helped write music for the previous "Hard Times" in 1980. But they felt Kurtis Blow's carefree delivery made it sound like a "Breaks" sequel. Kurt's version went largely unnoticed, but Russell still wanted to foist it on Run and D now. "We needed another single real quick," D explained.

Run felt a bit disenchanted with his former mentor. Runny Ray remembered him saying, "We hot, Ray! Yo, he's terrible!" Since Run-D.M.C. had achieved success, the feeling seemed to be mutual. It was a small industry and almost impossible not to hear Kurt was unhappy with them. As Kurt told it, the group originally asked him to produce "It's Like That," and he told them he was too busy promoting his album *Tough*, which at the time had sold a mere 300,000 copies. Kurt wanted to prevent the Sugar Hill Gang from stealing his audience. If they'd wait until he regained his status, he claimed to have told them, he'd gladly produce the song. But they did it without him and used *his* band, Orange Krush, so Kurt felt left out of the group's success, after having helped start Run off in the business.

Run and D didn't understand what Kurt's anger was about. Kurt had mixed "It's Like That" and never given any indication of being upset with them. They chalked it up to jealousy and had no interest in covering his material. "Run didn't like it that much," said Ray. "He knew he was busting Kurtis Blow on his ass." Regardless, they recorded "Hard Times," setting their shouted tag-team vocals over another intimidating drum track and a few more crescendos from a synthesizer, delivering a reliable "It's Like That" rehash to satisfy fans of the original.

For their B-side they returned to beats and rhymes. D wanted to tell backbiting has-beens the feeling was mutual with a new lyric he started writing after the crowd at the Fever jeered. "The good news is that there is a crew. Not five, not four, not three, just two." The rap would cause beef, but D didn't care. "Not the Furious Five, not the Cold Crush Four, not the Treacherous 3, us two are the best," he said. "If you go back to every record back then I was talking about all them motherfuckers. 'The good news is that there is a crew' and 'all things won't be the same.' I was battling them!

"When Run put me down," D continued, "even though I was high and laid back my goal was to get in the middle of the Bronx and battle the whole Furious Five myself, battle the whole Cold Crush Four myself, and battle Kool Moe Dee and the Treacherous Three myself. 'Run, sit over there. Jay, put this beat on.' Myself."

For the B-side of "Hard Times," Run also wanted to compete

with groups that rapped about their DJs. "Everybody was talking about Flash and his DJing, so 'Jam Master Jay' was about what Jay did and that he was the master of the game," said Larry.

Jay suggested they re-create musician Cerrone's disco-era "Rocket in the Pocket," a favorite at parties with Two-Fifth Down. Run agreed. He also loved Cerrone's noisy, snare-heavy break.

At the board, Larry decided to try a few ideas inspired by the Art of Noise's electronic song "Beat Box." With the English group in mind, he programmed Jay's beat on a Roland 808 and Run's crisper-sounding DMX drum machine. When he finished, Larry asked, "What do you want to do, Jay?"

Jay mixed the hard-hitting three-note horn blast from the break "Scratching," followed with the Cerrone vocal chanting, "Rock it," added other horns from "Scratching," then dropped the beat and rubbed the cut while Run and D rhymed together.

He worked quickly, creating a collage that matched anything on Flash's groundbreaking 1981 single "The Adventures of Grandmaster Flash on the Wheels of Steel." But instead of well-known pop riffs and sound effects, Jay used well-timed scratches to make a drum machine sound as funky as an old-school break.

Russell felt the result—Jay and Larry's attempt to re-create "Rocket in the Pocket"—was the most peculiar song he had ever heard. He led the group to Disco Fever at five in the morning and had the DJ play it, to see if people would dance to it. When the song started, Russell stepped onto the dance floor. Couples who had been dancing happily felt the song was too aggressive, and left the dance floor. A famous rapping patron lifting cocaine up to a nostril spilled every flake. The coke-snorting rapper griped, "What *was* that shit?"

Joey's new song, he replied.

"Well, let me know next time you play it so I'll be prepared."

Jam Master Jay was even prouder than Russell. The song after all was about how great Jay was on the turntables, how superior to any other DJ. At home, before heading to the grocery store, Jay told his cousin and fellow DJ, Doc, "I did my first record. There go the tape. Listen to it and tell me what you think."

In his absence, Doc played it. "And I kept playing it."

Jay returned. "How you like it?"

Doc gushed, "Yo, this is one of the best fucking records I ever heard! Yo, Jay, you're on your way, kid. You're it, man. This is it. This gonna be the hottest record on the streets this summer."

Only two months had passed since "It's Like That" and "Sucker MCs." In December 1983, Profile released their second single. People were used to their sound now, and liked Run-D.M.C. "It was just an instant success and went right on the radio and people bought it right away," label president Cory Robbins remembered. "Then I told my partner, 'We really should make an album with these guys.' Why not? I mean just a few more songs. Because we already had four."

Robbins called Russell, but Russell, he explained, told him, "What? Are you crazy? Rap albums don't sell!" Russell might have objected to an album because some artists received more money for individual singles than for submitting a completed album to a record label. But Robbins did not elaborate.

The group was just as opposed to the idea, so Robbins told them, "Look. Maybe it'll sell *something*. Maybe it'll only sell 25,000 or 30,000 copies, but it's *gonna* sell something. You're gonna make these songs *anyway*. You might as well make an album and let's see. You know? I know no rap album has ever really sold before, but we're halfway there already; we have four songs, so let's just do it!"

They kept saying, "Oh, no, rap is not about albums. It's about 12-inches. We shouldn't do this."

"Well it doesn't really pay *not* to do it," Robbins reiterated, "even if it sells only 30,000 copies. It's worth doing it."

Profile gave them a $25,000 advance for an album, Russell remembered. Fifteen thousand went toward recording. The remaining $10,000 was split between Larry, Run, D, and Russell. Whether Jam Master Jay received any payment for this work remains unknown.

Run would tell D to write about a particular subject. D would fill pages in his notebook. Russell would tell D, "Bring your rhyme book to the studio." In Greene Street Studios, D sat and waited while Russell and Larry thumbed through pages, deciding which lyrics to use. "They would pass over any references to violence, guns, and shit like that," D said.

Musically, Larry wanted everything to have the same feel. "Just different lyrics on top."

Run, D, and Jay helped create beats, but Jay mostly waited on the sidelines until Larry asked Russell, "Does this song feel like it really needs a scratch?"

While recording "Wake Up," Run and D watched Russell and Larry include the sound of a toilet flushing. Like Jam Master Jay, they were also on the sidelines, hearing Larry pitch ideas and Russell intermittently tell his coproducer, "Aw, that shit, that sound weak."

After laying their rhymes down, Run and D got out of the studio quickly, but Jay stayed behind, learning from Larry. "We would go in, lay our verses, and break the fuck out," said D. They were leaving one session and saw Jay with a drum machine, playing one snare drum repeatedly. They returned eight hours later, and Jay was still there.

Run asked, "What the fuck you doing, Jay?"

"I got to get this snare right."

Run and D weren't writing songs. When Larry played a beat, they'd get in the booth and say a routine. "We would rhyme over the whole ten minutes and then they would edit," D recalled. But Russell wanted every lyric to have a hook. Once this was created, he then stayed on them about "staying inside the theme, stay inside the theme, hook, hook," said Larry. He'd listen to their rap, sensing exactly when they needed to let the music ride. When they left Russell would ask someone to cut the tape with a razor, and paste certain parts in a different order.

"They were stressing because sometimes you can't get it right," said Ray. "We'd get there at 7:00 at night and leave at noon the next day." If they felt they had a great vocal, Larry would stop the music, and he or Russell would say they could do better. The tape would be rewound and they'd take it from the top, Larry pressing the Record button when they reached a certain word. The group felt this process of "punching in" drained certain songs of spontaneity and life. "They didn't really like being punched in all the time," Ray said. "When you're rapping, then 'Hold up, we're gonna punch you in on this.' They wanted to just flow on."

Another session found Russell and Larry telling them to record a song called "30 Days." An attempt to inject a little sex appeal into the group, the song was cowritten by Run's father, Daniel, and J. B. Moore of "The Breaks." Said Moore, "Russell called me up and said he needed something very specific for '30 Days.' It needed some sort of spark to it and I came up with what I think is the best single lyric: 'I hear they say it's been raining men / this is a one-time offer won't be made again.'" Run and D felt the song was wack but recorded it anyway on the off chance that Russell's idea might work.

Another evening, they had to wait for Brooklyn rock band Riot to finish their session before entering the recording room. While hearing this band's thunderous metal, Russell told Run-D.M.C. and Larry Smith, "We need to make a rock record."

Riot left, and they had the studio. D told them, "If we're gonna do that shit it's got to be hard." He pounded his fists against a wall to create the beat. "He knew 'boom . . . bap . . . boom-boom bap,'" said Run. "He would always say that when he was drunk, so we put [the beat] down."

After programming the pattern, Larry grabbed his guitar and recorded a chunky bass line. Run said, "Dag, that's the deffest guitar I ever heard in my life." Larry then added bells they thought would evoke Bob James's "Mardi Gras."

In the booth, Run and D rapped a routine about ruling the rap genre, humiliating rival rappers, and being just as legendary as rock groups like the Beatles, then went home feeling they'd created another hard-core hit. Russell stayed behind, saying he wanted a metal guitar on the song.

Larry nodded. "Let me get my friend to play on it." He called Eddie Martinez, a Hollis resident and one of the better guitarists Larry knew. Recently Larry had helped Eddie land a gig touring with Blondie. Now Larry told him, "Eddie, come play this for me." Eddie, inspired by Hendrix, could provide the bluesy emotional guitar the song needed, Larry felt.

While waiting for the guitarist to arrive, Larry told Greene Street owner Steve Loeb about the record.

"You're out of your mind!" Loeb said. "How could you possibly do that?"

"Niggas play rock 'n' roll, too," Larry quipped.

Eddie arrived. They played him the rhythm track. They recorded one riff, rewound the tape, then had Eddie play along with it—multitracking his part. "He played the line, then played the harmony with himself, then played the solo," Larry recalled. "It was three or four takes."

Run and D were shocked when they heard the song.

"It was wack," Run felt.

D agreed: "We thought the record was fake at first. We didn't mind the guitars coming in during the chorus, but me and Run were like, 'Y'all letting the guitars play through the whole shit; that's fake; that's not b-boy; that's not how it's done on a tape.' "

They essentially felt Russell was trying to ruin them. "The guitar line was fine," said Run. "It was the *screaming* guitars over our vocals which made it crazy."

They tried to suggest changes to the record. "When we rhyme

take the shit out," D told their producers. "Every time there's a break bring the guitars back in."

Run kept repeating, "Them guitars are louder than D's voice. I can't hear D."

Russell and Larry ignored them. The guitars went unchanged. "They were a little upset, but Russell and I had the final word," Larry explained. "What could they say?"

At Profile, Russell played "Rock Box" for Cory Robbins. "And it was so weird," Robbins said. "It just took getting used to. Now it seems so normal, but the first time I heard it was like, 'What is this,' and not necessarily in a good way. I was confused. 'What is this?' And 'Wow, will the R & B stations play this? I don't know.' Then I kept playing it over and over. You get used to it, and go, 'Wow, this is pretty good.'

"But it was so radical. I'm sure people can say that about Jimi Hendrix, too, the first time you heard him. But now you hear him on an oldies station and it sounds totally like part of your life. Or Led Zeppelin. At one point Led Zeppelin was the hardest of the hard, and now you can hear it as background music in a store. You get used to everything. But that's how 'Rock Box' was. It was so different, so aggressive, and just *so* different from a rap record. Now you listen to it and it's like, 'Oh yeah, that's "Rock Box." ' It's like an oldie." Pause. "It *is* an oldie and it sounds so sweet. There's nothing radical about it now, but nobody made a record like that before they did." Profile would release "Rock Box" as their next single.

CHAPTER 10

Taking the Throne

In February 1984, "Hard Times" b/w "Jam Master Jay" was still on the black singles chart, so they were going on *Soul Train*. But instead of merely moving their lips while their records played, something the show's producers had guests do because of union contracts, Run-D.M.C. entered a New York recording studio with a copy of their record and on it re-recorded a few crowd-rocking chants ("Throw your hands in the air!") whenever an instrumental break began.

On the *Soul Train* set in California, Run and D lip-synched for the camera, just like any other guest. But when the prerecorded chants came in, producers, who didn't recognize these new lyrics, were shocked, wondering for a second if Run and D weren't violating union contracts by performing live. When producers realized the group had recorded new vocals to fill their set with some spontaneity, they relaxed. After their performance, Run-D.M.C. took the obligatory stroll across the set to stand near *Soul Train*'s legendary deep-voiced host, Don Cornelius, for small talk. Cornelius, who wore a suit and had greasy jheri curls, said, "One of you is Russell's brother. Uh . . . Can you guys come back and do another number for us?" They did, and felt great about being on the February 18, 1984, episode.

Then after their debut record, "It's Like That" and "Sucker MCs," and their second single, "Hard Times" and "Jam Master Jay," Profile Records released "Rock Box" as Run-D.M.C.'s third single in March 1984. "Going from the sound of 'It's Like That' and 'Hard Times' to 'Rock Box' as the next record was such a departure," said Cory Robbins. "But, man, it worked. We got that record played and it went crazy!"

Run and D had worried that "Rock Box"'s metal guitar would alienate their black audience and that these rap fans—some of whom already resented the group for hailing from Queens—would begin to believe Run-D.M.C. was a sellout group, trying to cater to a white audience with minimal lyrics and heavy metal. But Profile released two versions of the song, and DJ Red Alert of influential New York radio station KISS-FM embraced the version with guitars on his high-rated program. And when black neighbors in Hollis started telling Run and D they loved the song, D said, "Me and Run looked at each other like 'What the fuck is going on?' We didn't know."

With "Rock Box" climbing the black singles chart, Russell decided it was time to film a video.

He had Run, D, and Jam Master Jay travel to their mixed-crowd hangout Danceteria. Director Steve Kahn filmed comedian Irwin Corey, known for long-winded, polysyllabic expositions, in a black suit and matching string tie, lecturing about rap's purported similarity to classical music. Midway through his talk, however, Corey noticed Run-D.M.C. behind him, in gleaming black leather, matching turtlenecks, and hats. Run waved his hand dismissively, as if

Corey were foolish. Then the music began. Larry's Cadillac arrived out front, the passenger door opened, and an improbable number of friends exited the vehicle. Run and D, in the nightclub, hollered lyrics in Irwin Corey's befuddled face: "To all you Sucker MCs per-petrating the fraud! Your rhymes are cold-wack, keep the crowd cold-bored!"

As the video continued, white girls danced near b-boys in a crowd as Run and D held microphones onstage. A towheaded white boy in a denim jacket ("for white people to identify with," Russell later explained) shoved his way to the front. White girls in short skirts danced on a giant turntable. Irwin Corey partied with young people. The group gave the white boy—now wearing a black hat—brotherly high-fives before Jay winked at the camera and they walked away.

With the exception of Michael Jackson—whose *Thriller* sold over 20 million copies—MTV didn't air many videos by black artists. "MTV had this belief that all they could play was rock 'n' roll and they forgot that the black community created rock 'n' roll," Russell said. "What they meant by 'only rock 'n' roll' was there were no black people."

Michael Jackson was in heavy rotation, but Jackson—high-water pants, leather jackets, dancing shoes, and shimmering glove—was more of a crossover artist. Still, Russell submitted "Rock Box" to MTV for consideration, and felt he had all the right elements: a song people liked, a group with a strong image, a guitar that comfortably fit the network's rock format, a well-known co-median, an endearing little white boy, and the city's most up-to-the-minute nightclub, Danceteria. "It wasn't like MTV stood up and said, 'Oh my God it's Run-D.M.C.! Let's give them everything in the world!'" said Russell's then client East Coast DJ Doctor Dre (not the West Coast producer who uses the same stage name but spells it "Dr. Dre"). "Russell and them worked their asses off."

To Russell's delight, MTV liked the song and started playing their "Rock Box" video, making Run-D.M.C. even more famous.

"Just in terms of masculinity and assertiveness there was a level of redefinition," said Bill Stephney, who hosted a show at radio station WBAU at the time. "At that time, we're talking about Prince, Michael Jackson, Eddie Murphy with a curl and leather, Cameo with codpieces, Luther Vandross, Freddie Jackson, and Lilo Thomas. Then all of a sudden you have these young brothers with regular around-the-way haircuts, Caesars, shell-toe Adidas, leather blazers, and pants with the *Godfather* hats you could buy in the Jamaica Mall. D.M.C. had the sort of Cazal-like glasses. They looked like brothers around the way and made the everyday the look of stardom."

Bun and D were sharing a bill with the Fearless Four for an early 1984 show at a club in New Jersey. Backstage Run-D.M.C. saw the Fearless Four with braided hair, attired in leather suits and white boots, and heard one member complain, "Man, y'all come just like y'all come off the street!"

Run answered, "That's how we coming, boy! That's how we living! Going out like b-boys, *troopin';* not like the rest of you soft-assed rockers."

Kurtis Blow, who was producing the Fearless Four, attended another of Run-D.M.C.'s concerts during this period. Blow was still in demand—his asking price to produce a record had risen to $10,000, and he asked for and received $30,000 for an album—but Run-D.M.C.'s version of "Hard Times" was on its way to becoming number 11 on the black singles chart while Kurt's original had gone no further than number 75.

Backstage, Run stood near his jheri-curled former mentor while Jam Master Jay scratched on turntables in front of the audience.

"Look at this, Kurt," Run said before D stepped onstage.

Jay scratched part of "Jam Master Jay." "D.M.C. . . . D.M.C. . . . D.M.C. . . . ."

D stepped into view and the crowd roared.

Backstage, Run yelled, "Look, look, look! He called D out."

"Wow, that's how we used to do it, Joey."

"Watch *this* though!"

Jay let more of the record play: "D.M.C. and Jam Master Jayyyy . . ."

D pointed at his belt buckle to dramatically indicate that he was D.M.C., then at Jay on the turns.

Kurt cried, "Oh my God! He's cutting the name! That means who's out onstage!"

Run tapped him, screaming, "Watch *this*!"

D stood near the front of the stage, arms crossed over his chest. Jay turned off the music. Audience members clapped their hands in rhythm.

"Now watch this," Run repeated.

Jay scratched: "Run Run-Run-Run Run . . ."

Kurt screamed, "Oh my—!"

"I'm not going yet," Run said. "I stand here. He does it until the crowd is frantic."

Jay kept scratching the word until the crowd started yelling Run's name. He finally stepped into view and strolled toward the mike. Halfway there, he turned and faced Kurt, who was watching him. Run thought, "Now watch *this*." Grabbing the mike, leaning back like Led Zeppelin's lead singer, Robert Plant, he screamed, "Now it's about that time, for us to say that we're—"

Jay let the record go: "Run-D.M.C. and Jam Master Jayyyy!"

"And we'd be standing there in a triangle-type pose," Run explained. "This thing went from 'Kurtis Blow' to calling *three* guys out."

The old school realized their days at the top were numbered, and Melle Mel—lead rapper on the Furious Five's string of hit singles for Jersey-based Sugar Hill Records—had come a long way from his days as king of rap. Heartfelt lyrics like "Superappin' " and "The Message" had given way to flamboyant leather costumes, knee-high boots, shoelaces tied around his calves, big sunglasses, and braids. Mel was also recording dance music songs like "White Lines" without Flash and other members of the Furious Five.

D and Jay, who still went to the Fever to see Cold Crush and other groups perform, started hearing Mel didn't like them. "We would hear 'He said this, they said that,' " D remembered. "They were a little mad at us. Here are these guys from Queens blowing the fuck up. They were big on tapes and with shows and on flyers but we were blowing up."

Mel, they heard, viewed their tag-team style as derivative of how the Furious Five rapped on their singles. Mel also didn't appreciate lyrics to "Jam Master Jay" lumping him in with the old school. "He was mad at what we were doing," D learned. "We'd act like we owned the shit. We weren't giving them any love. We were taking his shit. Like 'Fuck y'all, y'all fake!' The fucked-up shit was that we were emulating them. Everything Run-D.M.C. did was inspired by Flash, Bambaataa, Cold Crush, and Fearless Four."

At the Fun House, during a concert hosted by WBLS's Mr. Magic, Mel didn't seem too friendly. During their performance, they were later told, Mel stood in the audience frowning at them. "They were always hating," said Runny Ray. "Grandmaster Flash and all them niggas. And Kurtis Blow, too! 'Cause Joe and them would always headline and niggas used to be like, 'Well why *they* got to headline? *I* wanted to headline. Well I'm not going on.' "

Run didn't know exactly why Mel was angry with them and figured D's theory—the old school resented a new group for achieving success in a genre that older performers had pioneered—explained Mel's anger. At the Fun House, he and D watched Flash mix records and the Furious Five come out in their costumes. "We were trying to emulate the rock R & B groups, 'cause they were dressing up," said Flash. But D felt his former idols looked and sounded terrible, and if Run-D.M.C. was more successful, these old-timers could blame no one but themselves. " 'Cause when they made their records they were buggin' the fuck out," said D. "They weren't doing what they did on the tapes." But Run-D.M.C. couldn't help feeling there was more to Mel's anger.

One night Run decided to join D.M.C. and Jam Master Jay at the Fever. "We went to the Fever a million times," D explained. "Run probably went about four times. We were sitting there, getting high, smoking weed, sniffing coke, doing what we did back then." Melle Mel—muscle-bound from working out—stepped to Joe "and just let it all out," said D.

According to D, Mel said, "We were mad at y'all. It wasn't just 'cause y'all were from Queens. I was mad at the way y'all rapped. Y'all were folding your arms. Y'all were just so determined. And when I listened to the lyrics on 'Sucker MCs,' I thought y'all were talking about me!"

On that song, Run had rapped: "biting all your life, cheating on your wife, walking 'round town like a hoodlum with a knife," and D recalled, "Mel told Run, 'I was runnin' around cheating on my girl. . . . Yo, I used to carry a knife with me, I thought I was somebody.' He really thought this record was about him."

D continued, "He thought he was the 'Sucker MC.' Remember, Mel and Kool Moe Dee of the Treacherous Three were competing for the crown, but Mel was really the king. He was the man."

As Mel spoke, Run listened intently. "Melle Mel was the deffest rapper that would ever touch the mike," Run said. "I was impressed. He didn't beat me up. He just said it. I wasn't scared."

Next came the Treacherous Three.

Run had just gotten home from a show. He kissed his wife and played with his daughter Vanessa awhile before hitting the sack. He was exhausted. "You leave from Boston, you get home, your eyes are hurting," he explained. "They wake you up three in the afternoon, 'You're scheduled, you got to go do this TV show *Graffiti Rock*.' " *Graffiti Rock* was a pilot episode for a dance music series patterned after *Soul Train* that the show's producers hoped to sell to syndicated television stations nationwide. It was also a good forum for Run-D.M.C. to finally let their fans, and a new television audience, see the group perform their popular B-side "Sucker MCs." Run yawned, got up, showered, and got back into his black leather suit. During the ride into the city, he, D, and Jam Master Jay smoked some marijuana, and at the venue they saw kids cheer their arrival.

Jay led the way, sporting a black leather blazer and pants, laceless Adidas, a hat, and a gold chain. Run and D followed, in the same outfit, except D wore bulky glasses, and a red feather on his hat. "We got there, fresh and happy," Run explained.

For months the streets had demanded a battle between Run-D.M.C. and the Treacherous 3. Now they saw Kool Moe Dee facing them. Jay approached the battle rapper, who wore a zipper-covered blue and white leather jacket, blue leather pants, white boots, and a white golf cap. Moe kept his eyes hidden behind large sunglasses and calmly said to Jay, "What's up? How you doing?"

Jay, a creator, but also a fan of the music, blurted, "Oh, my God! Kool Moe Dee! Oh, man! Kool Moe Dee!"

Run was nowhere near as impressed. He thought, "Kool Moe Dee's the best rapper around. I'm gonna figure out how to beat him."

Jay leaned in. "Yo, man," he told Moe, "I just want to tell you: shit you did to Busy Bee was crazy." Moe had upstaged Busy Bee in front of a crowd in a nightclub. "I know how you get down. I know you do your battle thing but, uh, this is for TV, man. This is gonna leave an impression on people. So, don't do what you do. All right? I'm just asking you not to do what you do, 'cause we not doing it like that."

Moe nodded.

"You know my group and you know how my group is," Jay added. "We not in it for that. We just doing this for the TV thing."

Moe shook Jay's hand. "All right, cool." He would lighten up and not turn the *Graffiti Rock* episode into a battle. But then he saw Run's facial expression. "And the look on Run's face is like, 'I can't *believe* Jay doesn't have confidence in us and is giving this guy the one-upmanship,'" Moe recalled. "Run really didn't like that too much."

D eyed the set: a gray floor with white starbursts painted on it; dancers in corny break-dance outfits on elevated white metal platforms; a big old-fashioned bubble-letter tag on the wall that faced the camera—a green, red, yellow, and orange version of the famous *Soul Train* logo that read "Graffiti Rock." "That shit looked crazy," he said.

The creative staff also seemed a bit old-school-heavy: Bambaataa was music consultant, and the Treacherous Three would perform the theme song, cohost, rap before each commercial break, and perform their latest Sugar Hill single. As the only people from Queens on the set, Hurricane recalled, Run-D.M.C. "definitely stood out from everybody else. Queens still didn't get mad respect from the Bronx."

"We were like this: we representing Hollis, motherfucker. We went in there with some attitude."

T he show's producer and host, Michael Holman, was light-skinned with a short Afro. His black jacket had leather pads on the shoulders. His jeans and shoes were beige, and he wore Cazals. "We thought it was kind of corny 'cause they wanted to talk about hip-hop," said D.M.C. After the Treacherous Three performed their opening, they watched members of the studio audience in front of the camera talk like characters from blaxploitation movies. "How you rock your hat, man?" one said.

"Well I rock my Kang-ol."

Run and D had just come to rap and felt this was fake. Soon, Run, D, and Jay stood across from the Treacherous Three. Holman's plan was to go back and forth with the Treacherous Three at the show's end.

Kool Moe Dee said, "Okay, for the TV shit, I guess we could do a stage version to show what a battle actually is. How are we gonna do the battle? Is it gonna be authentic? Are we gonna have the crowd respond?"

"Oh, we're just gonna show what the back-and-forth is," said Holman.

D.M.C. nodded, thinking, "Oh shit, we're gonna be battling the Treacherous Three!"

Run meanwhile took it all in. "We do our part. They do their part. They come up with this thing called the battle rap, we're gonna win."

Onstage, with cameras rolling, Moe held his mike. "One two one two," he began. "On the mike at this time, the coolest of the cool. They call me Moe Dee in the place to be. Jam Master Jay, one for the treble, two for the bass; come on Jam Master, let's rock the place." Behind the turntables, Jay let the record go. Moe rapped: "When it comes to rap, I'm the epitome: the rapper's idol and my title is Kool Moe Dee."

Run said a rhyme from their upcoming "Rock Box": "They call me illest and iller there's no one chiller. It's not Michael Jackson and this is not *Thriller*. One def rapper, cold know I can hang: I'm Run from Run-D.M.C., not Kool from Kool and the Gang."

Special K of the Treacherous Three did a party rap, and then D yelled, "Well, I'm D.M.C. in the place to be and the place to be is with D.M.C.; and by the time I'm through you will agree no other MCs rock the house like me."

Moe stepped up again. "Well I'm the coolest of the cool, they call me Moe Dee, and ain't another rapper who's as bad as me."

Run followed with a routine he'd been writing: "Now party people, I'm so happy I don't know what to do 'cause I'm the MC with the rhymes, cold down with the crew. Rock from Africa to France and then to Kalamazoo and every place that I play I hear a yay, not a boo."

Special K got on one more time.

Then D stopped being polite " 'cause them motherfuckers was talking about their braids and trying to speak sexy." He shouted: "D-M-C, that's who I am, I love to perform, but I'm not a ham! My mother said 'do it' . . . I said 'yes ma'am'! And I can *do* it because I know I can!"

The show ended with the bands standing near each other and singer Shannon (who had performed her dance hit "Give Me Tonight"), but everyone knew Run-D.M.C. had finally ended the old-school era. " 'Cause that was the first time that people saw the image," D said. "They felt the difference. We were making it cool to be educated and not a drug dealer.

"We were just as rough as them," he continued. "We made not being gangsta 'gangsta.' Being educated and going to school, getting straight A's, you're not a punk."

CHAPTER 11

Russell and Rick

The wrap party for *Graffiti Rock* was held at Danceteria, and at the club, Russell ran into old friend Jazzy Jay. Jazzy was a member of the Soulsonic Force, the group that joined Afrika Bambaataa on his hit "Planet Rock." The short, athletic-looking DJ was also featured on a new record Russell liked and kept hearing. On this record, "It's Yours," a rapper named T La Rock used big words to describe the actual process of recording the song, and Jazzy scratched a number of horns and singers' voices over a hard drumbeat. At the wrap party, Russell asked Jazzy, "How you made this record?"

Jazzy introduced him to its producer, Rick Rubin, a chubby white twenty-one-year-old New York University film student. Russell couldn't believe that this long-haired fan of Run-D.M.C. and rock music had created the compelling bass-heavy single, but once they started talking, he learned that Rick liked the same records and understood that rap music had to sound hard.

For his part, Rick couldn't believe this was the man credited on over a dozen of his favorite rap records. "Back then, Russell used to wear sports coats, penny loafers, and argyle socks," Rick said. "He used to care what the industry thought of him. I used to tell him as long as the music was good, they'd have to deal with him."

Rick grew up in Lido Beach, Long Island. He loved the Beatles and played his guitar to albums by punk pioneers the Ramones. During high school he enjoyed the Ramones-like Sex Pistols, L.A.-based punk band Black Flag, the metal group AC/DC, Aerosmith's blues-based sound, and early Sugar Hill singles.

Rick enrolled at NYU and moved into a dorm building downtown in 1981. He started a rock band called Hose that specialized in plodding renditions of Rick James's "Super Freak," released a Hose record on his own label, and was a regular at the downtown reggae club Negril. Rick loved to watch DJs scratch and wished more rap records included the sound. "He would roam around looking for new artists to sign and connections to make," party promoter Lady Blue remembered. "The club was connection central in those days. All the deals went down at the club."

In places like Danceteria or the Underground, Rick—who dressed like a Ramones member with a black leather biker jacket, a T-shirt, and faded jeans—stood right in front of the DJ booth, nodding his head while Jazzy Jay scratched. Rick soon introduced himself and invited Jazzy to help with a remix for the Sex Pistols. Jazzy entered a recording studio and did a mix, and while nothing came of it, Rick and Jazzy kept hanging together, and Jazzy took him to real jams up in the Bronx and to clubs like the Fever and Broadway International. "I think I was kind of a novelty," Rick Rubin said. "They appreciated the fact that I was such a fan and knew so much about the music."

At NYU, Rick continued to promote the Hose album he had released on his own label. With copies of the album in hand, he convinced some nearby record stores to distribute it. One day he told his roommate Adam Dubin, "Come on, let's go for a walk, I'm gonna go check my inventory."

Rick stopped in at downtown shops like Rat Cage Records and 99 Records, searched the bins, counted how many Hose albums each had in stock, and told owners he'd return with more. "And he explained the whole punk rock thing was about doing it yourself. You don't need CBS Records or any company to put your album out," Dubin remembered. "You can have them, but you don't *need* them."

Rick soon started scratching at his own parties, and telling people about his respect for Grandmaster Flash. At these events, white college students bombarded him with requests for Top 40 hits like Lionel Richie's "All Night Long," and Rick would tell them, "Yeah, yeah, no problem," but "then he'd put on the Treacherous Three or something," said Dubin. Rick quickly went from inviting rappers from the South Bronx to his events, and having them rap over beats on his new drum machine, to telling Jazzy in a club one night, "I just made a beat. I want you to listen to it." The beat was the rough draft of "It's Yours." Rick added, "I'm thinking about going in the studio with this."

Now Russell Simmons was speaking with Rick Rubin in Danceteria, at the wrap party for the *Graffiti Rock* pilot episode that featured Run-D.M.C. battling the Treacherous Three. Russell was learning that Rubin loved Run-D.M.C.'s first album as much as Russell loved the raw sound of "It's Yours." "Rick hooked up with the only guy he could not miss in the rap world," said Adam Dubin. "Russell *was* the rap world because all the bands were his." It wasn't hard to get to know Russell back then, he added. "If you went to Danceteria, there was Russell. If you went to the Roxy, there was Russell."

Russell soon visited Rick's dorm room at NYU, where Rick attended film classes, aspired to a career in music, and told himself that if all else failed, he could go to law school and become a lawyer.

Rubin's dorm room was a mess but he had equipment: turntables, amps, speakers, and crates of records. Russell learned that in addition to making hard beats, Rubin deejayed as "Double R" for a white rap group called the Beastie Boys, who patterned themselves after the Treacherous Three.

Russell said he wanted to meet the Beastie Boys. He also listened to some of the beats Rick had on his DMX drum machine and felt they were hit records. Rick then stopped by 1133 Broadway, where Russell ran Rush Productions out of two rooms. Rick asked Russell to help promote T La Rock's "It's Yours" around the country. They wound up discussing how the industry worked. Rick claimed his distributor didn't pay him for the T La Rock record. Russell claimed he went underpaid for hits he produced. "So we started hanging out, and he started taking me up to the Disco Fever and Harlem World, and I used to hang out in his office, and we just became friends," Rick explained.

During spring 1984, Russell was excited. He'd been seeking a white rap group with the right sound since 1980, and now long-haired Rick Rubin led three white boys up to him at Danceteria. Russell didn't like the matching red jogging suits and do-rags Rubin had bought down in Chinatown, but knew he could change that.

Rick introduced the trio as Ad Rock, Mike D, and MCA. "Hearing that was Run's brother bugged me out," said Ad Rock. "That he was a manager and managed Kurtis Blow bugged me out. Then I was actually talking with him and he was a different person back then. It was interesting."

Russell still smoked dust and drank excessively. "This guy would be out drinking, like, twelve screwdrivers and going to three clubs every night," said Beastie Boy member Mike D. But Russell signed on to manage Rick Rubin and the Beasties.

One day that spring Rick Rubin stopped by Rush Productions' office and played Russell a tape of rapper L.L. Cool J's song "I Need a Beat." Russell cried, "It's a hit, I love it!"

Rick asked, "Well, do you know what I should do with it? How's this gonna work?"

"This is really good," Russell said. "Maybe we should put it out on Profile."

Rick had already been there, and Profile executives had rejected the song. "Look, all you do is complain to me about how they don't pay you and it's terrible and it's frustrating and it's a waste of time," Rick said. "Why don't we just do it ourselves?"

"No, no, I've got a bunch of artists, and I'm hoping to get a production deal with a major label at some point and this would get in the way of that," Russell explained.

"Well, let me. How about if I make the records and run the company and do all the work and you can be my partner?"

Russell said, "Okay." He'd put up some money. But he wanted to meet L.L.

"He's kind of fucked up, Russell," Rick warned.

"What do you mean?"

"You'll see."

L.L. (born James Todd Smith on January 14, 1969) started rapping at the age of nine. By 1983, he and a friend named Cal rapped as a duo called the Freeze MCs. They met Hollis-based DJ Finesse, who knew Run from neighborhood house parties and jams in 205th Street Park and who hoped to form his own group and achieve as much success as Run-D.M.C. L.L. and Cal started recording demo tapes in Finesse's basement. One day, L.L. and Finesse recorded without Cal and easily filled three ninety-minute tapes. Finesse told L.L., "Okay, I ran out of tape. Are we finished yet?" L.L. kept rapping.

L.L. wanted to make it in music, so he reportedly dropped out of high school. Like Run, L.L. was known for battling at jams, growling, "Yo, you want to battle? Boom. Right here, right now." His technique was to let a challenger say half a lyric, then interrupt with a humiliating punch line. "It reached the point where brothers around the way hated him," said Finesse. At block parties, L.L. embarrassed MCs until hosts surrounded him and said, "Move away. You are not invited here anymore." He was everywhere, said producer Larry Smith. "He would perform in the backyard if necessary." And at home, L.L. bought every rap single he could and studied them all. Run-D.M.C. was among his favorites, but for demo tapes he also recorded a Melle Mel–style message rap called "Heritage." And for another song, Finesse recalled, "He *sang* some shit on the demo tape and *he can't sing*." Then after his mother bought him a small $200 drum machine with her income tax check, L.L. had Finesse tap out drumbeats while L.L. rapped articulate lyrics like "I Need a Beat."

While creating demo tapes in 1983, L.L. learned that Run-D.M.C. would play the United Skates of America roller rink in Jackson Heights. In the crowd, he watched them perform their early singles. When they were done, he approached to challenge Run. "Yo, we could do this right now!"

That day, Run answered, "Yo, when you get a record deal, step back to me."

L.L. glared at him for a second, then said, "Yeah, all right," and left to go home and write more battle raps.

After hearing "It's Yours," L.L. sent a demo to Rick Rubin and called every day to ask if Rick had heard it yet. Rick didn't, but Beastie Boy Ad Rock did. "I wasn't going to school or doing anything at the time," Ad explained. "I was just staying at Rick's dorm room. So I would mess with his drum machine and turntables. I had nothing to do." He rifled through a box of tapes, found L.L.'s demo, and played it. He enjoyed every note. "L.L. was mathematical and used very big words," he said of what drew him to the tape. "It's funny because you learn all that weird shit in school and forget it the day you leave. But he had all those words and an attitude. He sounded like Kool Moe Dee [of the Treacherous Three] and he was good." Ad Rock and Rick Rubin soon had L.L. in a studio. L.L. had one hundred songs, choruses, and verses memorized. The producers had ten beats on Rick's DMX drum machine. Midway through one Ad Rock had programmed, L.L. decided, "I like that one."

Rick told him, "Okay, let's make a song over it." The result was the aggressive number "I Need a Beat," which Rick Rubin played for Russell in his office at Rush Productions.

After hearing Rick play the tape, Russell asked D if he would like to come meet his client, producer Rick Rubin. Since Run had married his high school sweetheart, Valerie, and then had a daughter Vanessa in 1984, Run didn't hang out much. D, who usually tagged along with Russell and who also enjoyed "It's Yours," agreed to accompany Russell to NYU dorm building Weinstein Hall that night. In Rick's dorm room, D met the heavyset white kid with long hair and dark glasses, heard a few of Rick's jokes, and liked him immediately. "Rick was just a cool pizza-eating white boy with rock 'n' roll, rap, and punk records," said D.

Rick's dorm room was small and cramped with two beds. Two desks shoved together held a pair of Technics turntables and a mixer. Two chests of drawers on each side held industrial-size Sterling-Vega speakers. Power amps were strewn about the room. "There was no place to put books or anything having to do with school," Rick's roommate Adam Dubin recalled.

Thumbing through albums in milk crates, D.M.C. saw half of Rick's collection consisted of Kurtis Blow, "Rock Box," "It's Like That," Treacherous Three, and other rap music. The rest were punk rock and hard metal bands like the immortal Ramones, Aerosmith, the Dictators, Motorhead ("Ace of Spades"), AC/DC, and Minor Threat. D, who was getting deeper into rock, liked Rick even more. "Big dirty white boy in college," D joked. "It was a sight. He was

National Lampoon, John Belushi. I don't know how they let him in there." D soon started heading to Rick's dorm room without Russell to hang out, and during one visit Rick said, "Listen to this." Rick played him L.L.'s tape. "This guy, he's from Farmer's Boulevard, right over by you. You know him?"

D heard the rapper call himself "Ladies Love Cool J." He didn't recognize the name but liked his "computerized pitch," and the raw beat Rick had recorded in the studio. "Whoa," D said, and when "I Need a Beat" ended. "Who is this young kid?"

Rick Rubin arranged for L.L. to stop by Russell's office. In the waiting room that day in 1984, L.L.—attired in "Fearless Four [lace-up] boots and straps around his legs like some break-dancer," Russell recalled—approached Reggie Reg of the Crash Crew to gush, "Yo, Crash Crew! My grandma got your record. Yo, I like that one 'Breaking Bells' and I want to do it over."

"Yeah, kid, sure," Reggie said.

Then Russell met L.L., took one look at L.L.'s outfit, and asked, "Where you from?"

"Hollis," L.L. claimed, though he was actually from St. Albans.

"Where the fuck did you get those pants?"

As the meeting continued, L.L. said, "I want to make records like Run."

"Do you like them?"

"They're selling," L.L. replied.

Then L.L., his former DJ Finesse said, signed a deal that granted Rush Productions 50 percent of the money. "Management, producer, talent scout, whatever hat there was, Russ had it on," Finesse claimed. "People automatically say it's highway robbery, but Russell was putting that money right back into what he was doing. The 50 percent from L.L. Cool J went into Run-D.M.C." L.L. received 40 percent, Finesse added, while his new DJ Cut Creator accepted 10.

Another day, Run stopped in to see Russell at his office and was shocked to discover Russ's new artist was the kid who had challenged him at United Skates of America after one concert in 1983. "You looked up and there he was with 'I Need a Beat' and Russell and them had a new project," Run said.

Russell wanted L.L. to open Run-D.M.C.'s concert at the Encore. L.L. arrived for the show with braids, spiked bracelets, and knee-high boots. D stammered, "L, take those shits off! Find some sneakers!"

Run laughed at his appearance. "He was a little corny at the start," Run felt. "He didn't know how to dress. He came in with the Melle Mel style. 'I thought that's what y'all do.' He had on boots and spikes."

The embarrassed young rapper quickly changed his image. "He didn't know," D explained. "He was thinking, 'I got to do what these cool motherfuckers are doing.'"

On another occasion, Run stopped by Russell's office and saw L.L. with a Kangol hat and a tracksuit. Run, who sometimes dressed the same onstage, felt L.L. was imitating him. Said D, "Everybody saw Run. Run saw Run and he checked L.L. for it."

As Run's friend Runny Ray told it, Run said, "I can rhyme better than you, L. Whatever you can do I can do better."

"I'm better than *you*," L.L. replied.

"Nigga, you ain't better than me!"

The two rappers started battling with lyrics.

"They started out with these two-line rhymes and pretty soon one guy would say a line and the other guy would crack back and rhyme his insult to the other guy's line," said publicist Bill Adler, who worked in the office.

L.L. wouldn't let Run finish, so Run interrupted him, and they followed each other from room to room, then out in the hall, then inside again, denouncing each other for twenty minutes. "Since Russell and Run are brothers, everyone thought Run got the special treatment," said Larry Smith. "L.L. worked a little harder to try to bring Run down." When someone asked who started this, Run admitted, "I did!"

Though they didn't always agree with their manager, Run-D.M.C. admitted that by June 1984, all of Russell's ideas had worked: using the "Action" beat, asking Run to mention the band Orange Krush on "Sucker MCs," deciding that Jay's look would be the band's, adding metal to "Rock Box," remaking "Hard Times," and recording "30 Days," a song Run and D truly disliked. Though their fourth single, "30 Days" (after double-sided efforts "It's Like That," "Hard Times," and "Rock Box"), was in the black singles Top 20, they tried to avoid playing the song in concerts, but crowds down south kept yelling, "Yo, play that '30 Days,' man!" Run and D would whisper, "Come on, that shit is *weak*," but crowds kept chanting: "30 Days! 30 Days!" So when Russell said he had a new idea, after his suggestions for songs had helped their debut album, June 1984's *Run-D.M.C.*, become the very first Gold-certified rap album, Run-D.M.C. and Jam Master Jay listened attentively.

Russell had recently met a young black concert promoter named Ricky Walker, a thirty-one-year-old from Orlando, Florida, who had already worked with the funk group the Commodores, the Jacksons' 1979 world tour, and the Kool Jazz Fest. Walker wanted to book Run-D.M.C. for his "New York City Fresh Festival" package tour, and Russell said he'd deliver not only Run-D.M.C., but all of the talent.

Russell was by now managing Whodini, a Brooklyn trio with two popular songs on radio (one about WBLS's Mr. Magic, and "Haunted House of Rock"). Like Run-D.M.C. they wore hats onstage (in this case the big sombrero that rapper Jalil Hutchins wore with his suit jacket and shoes), but London-based Jive Records was promoting Whodini as "the sex symbols of rap." Now Whodini was about to release their second album, *Escape* (filled with Larry Smith–produced numbers like "Five Minutes of Funk" and "Freaks Come Out at Night"), and Russell was working to convince radio to play their single "Friends." Russell traveled to WBLS one night and cornered a DJ in a room. "Russell was cursing some DJ out for not playing a Whodini record, I mean, literally cursing him out," said Kool Moe Dee, who witnessed this. " 'How the fuck you not gonna play this record?' He was talking about how hot the group was, how hot the record 'Friends' was, and how could they not play this record. 'It's got a positive message! You motherfuckers!' He was literally going berserk."

Russell then added the Fat Boys to the Fresh Fest lineup. Another Run-styled trio from Brooklyn, the Fat Boys wore black leather blazers, sneakers, chains, glasses, and hats (raccoon fur models with tails) and specialized in crowd-pleasing Kurtis Blow–produced numbers like "Can You Feel It," "Don't You Dog Me," and "Jailhouse Rap." "They were funny fat greedy guys," Runny Ray remembered. "But they were cool, though. D.M.C. loved them niggas."

Russell also asked Brooklyn group Newcleus to warm the crowd up with their Top 10 novelty single "Jam on It," which featured sped-up Chipmunk voices, and had crews like the Dynamic Breakers, Magnificent Force, and Uptown Express dance on a second stage.

Run-D.M.C. and Jam Master Jay earned $5,000 a night. Whodini, Kurtis Blow, and the Fat Boys received $3,500 each. Russell, managing most acts, earned $1,200 per show.

But Run started introducing their set, near the end of the three-hour concert, by stepping onstage without music, with mike in hand, and yelling: "You've seen a whole bunch of great acts out here tonight. But I want y'all to know one goddamn thing. This is my motherfucking house!" As D.M.C. sipped from his forty-ounce bottle of Olde English 800, Run leaned over the front of the stage, tilted his head, cupped one hand near his ear, and yelled, "Whose house?"

CHAPTER 12

Kings of Rock

During the autumn of 1984, Run-D.M.C. left the Fresh Festival tour during weekends to begin recording their second album. Rick Rubin had asked Russell to let him work with them, and Russell had agreed, as they all wanted something different for their next single. Run and D wanted a harder sound and felt Larry might not be the man for the job. "Larry was a great R & B musician," Run explained. "Rick was more thugged out. Larry's a great musical genius and Rick was more rock 'n' roll." Rick had also created the b-boy classic "It's Yours."

In Rick's dorm room, Run and D would watch as Rick showed them his favorite movies, new punk rock songs, and ideas on the drum machine. Rick wasn't like Russell. D.M.C. felt Russell was rebellious because he found it could earn money. Rick was like that because that's how he felt. Where Russell and Larry drowned their beats in R & B music, Rick listened to D say a rhyme to a beat he pounded on a wall with his fist, and encouraged him to capture that raw feel on their songs. Having Rick onboard, D felt, would make recording a lot more fun. Run meanwhile viewed Rick as "a new guy Russell added to the roster," someone who could program the ideas Run now had for their music.

Run and D.M.C. brought a new routine to the studio. Jam Master Jay helped them create its drum pattern. Run and D entered the booth and faced the mikes, and Rick Rubin—seated near an engineer at the enormous mixing board—rolled tape. Run yelled, "One two one two, and I say . . ." Then Jay hit a button on the drum machine and started the beat. D said, "Party people, your dreams have now been fulfilled." As they rapped, Jay kept pressing buttons, stopping the music, restarting it, adding dramatic pauses, and playing it live. "No punches on the microphone," Run said. "We weren't able to the way Jay had set it up. He did it like he was scratching." They finished recording, and felt they had another hit on their hands. "It was a hard beat," said Runny Ray. "All the other shit was real commercial. This was real b-boy."

But their bodyguard Hurricane—who had rapped in Hollis with Davy DMX's group Solo Sounds and hesitated before letting Run rock at those bygone park jams—thought Run borrowed one of his ideas. "The way Run starts the record, 'One two one two, and I say . . .' That's how I used to start my [Solo Sounds] parties. When he said that, I said, 'Wow.' " Hurricane didn't think it was cool.

D.M.C. disagreed. "That came from every old-school tape there was. 'And I say . . .' That was the b-boy shit."

Kool Moe Dee of the Treacherous Three also bugged out. " 'Together! Forever! Together! Forever! Run-D.M.C. and we're tougher than leather!' When they did that I was like, 'That's straight out of 'At the Party'! 'Together! Forever! Together! Forever! And this is the way we rock all together! Do it!' *That's a Treacherous Three routine. What are you doing?*"

Back on the Fresh Fest tour, Run-D.M.C. saw the new song

"Together Forever (Live at Hollis Park)" become another quick-selling hit.

At this point, said Ray, "Whodini were kind of a problem because they always used to hate." Once "Friends," "Freaks," and "Five Minutes of Funk" entered the black singles Top 5, Whodini wanted to headline over Run-D.M.C. "Jalil was the hater really," Ray felt. And soon Jalil teamed up with Kurtis Blow to battle Run. "He was funny, though," Ray felt. "Jealous. Like, 'Run-D.M.C. sounds def, they're hot, they're playing their shit more than mine,' you know what I'm saying?"

During one backstage battle, Run heard Jalil let loose a few rhymes calling him wack, and then Run let him have it. Kurt went for his, and Run let him have it too. They tried three or four times, but Run used twice as many put-downs to insult them both. "Run got tired of that after a while," said Ray. "Like, 'Yeah, you better than me, whatever.'" But Run also noticed Russell's new artist L.L., along for a few shows, seemed to be waiting in the wings for a chance to battle.

In Miami, most of the acts spent seventy-two hours sniffing coke. Day and night blurred into a nonstop party interrupted only by two shows, and at daybreak one morning D stood on a hotel balcony with a slimy dealer, who pointed toward a nearby body of water and said, "See that building right there? See that boat right there? That's the feds. And that boat, this is where they bring the stuff in." D.M.C. didn't want to hear this. But then he learned some security guards did drugs and fell into the habit of telling them, "Yo! Here's three hundred dollars. Whatever you get tonight, make sure you get me some and come see me after the show."

It was fun but sad. In Hollis, he had told a few of the guys who joined him at "the building" that they couldn't stay high forever. They'd have to get their lives together one day. But during the Fresh Festival tour, the summer of 1984, twenty-year-old D.M.C. saw middle-aged black men—some working as road managers and security for other acts—sniffing, drinking, and trying to pick up young groupies backstage.

In mid-September 1984, Russell had them take a quick flight to Jersey and play a concert for MTV. At the Capitol Theater in Passaic, a film crew waited, and this fit, clean-cut rock singer named Lou Reed, hosting the concert and wearing a black T-shirt with a Harley-Davidson logo, said MTV had asked him to choose his own guests. He really loved "Rock Box," so he chose Run-D.M.C. Reed was thrilled that they would be on his episode of the network's series *Rock Influences*.

Onstage, they saw three thousand white people in the audience, some of whom had never heard rap, never attended schools with black kids, and never heard black music on local stations. They performed "It's Like That" to polite applause. Then they did "30 Days" and some rock fans booed. They did "Rock Box" and saw some audience members run up and down the aisles, cursing, and saying it sounded terrible. Run—sensitive as he was—held his tongue and kept rapping. Times like these Run and D wondered whether they should really be rapping over rock music. If black kids were not yelling "sellout," whites felt they had no business using metal.

They returned to the tour, playing twenty-seven shows that would earn a whopping $3.5 million, and kept flying to Manhattan during weekends to work on the second album. In the studio, Russell and Larry (and Rick Rubin suggesting a few ideas to his new pal Russell) were creating the music without them, and were in a big rush. They wanted this done with and in Profile's hands, so they could be paid royalties for the first album. Russell and Larry also wanted to keep adding rock songs to Run-D.M.C.'s repertoire.

Run and D would usually leave right after recording vocals, but with Larry and Russell micromanaging recording sessions—creating songs without them present and bringing in other songwriters—they wanted to leave even sooner. Run also wanted to get out of there, since he was near Hollis and could see Valerie and Vanessa, hear about how they were doing, play with his kid, read her a bedtime story, and enjoy a rare home-cooked meal. After recording vocals, Run would say, "I'm ready to leave!" But Jay would answer, "Nah, you can't go nowhere, nigga! We got to finish, you know what I'm saying?" Most times, Run unhappily stayed in the studio and kept following more of Russell and Larry's orders.

An album began to take shape, but Run and D wished they could have more input into how it sounded, especially since the result would feature their names on the cover. "We didn't actually do the second one together," D explained. During one weekend session, they watched from the sidelines while Larry Smith programmed a big beat and Larry's Puerto Rican friend Eddie Martinez played metal riffs louder than any on "Rock Box."

"So what raps you got, D?" Russell asked.

D handed Russell his newest composition notebook and watched him flip through pages. Russell's eyes lingered on a five-page rhyme. "Russell read through it and got all the way to the end," said D, and seemed to like a lyric that went: "I'm the king of rap! There is none higher! Sucker MCs call me sire!" After suggesting that D change "king of rap" to "king of rock," Russell had them enter the booth. D rapped nonstop over the entire track, and during the playback Russell listened to the lyric that excited him and said, "We're gonna put this in the front." Russell had an engineer hack the tape with a razor blade and paste D's lyric so that it opened the song. By the time he was done, Russell had requested three hundred edits on this song "Kings of Rock" alone.

While they were recording *Kings of Rock*, Russell started discussing his new white group, the Beastie Boys, with D.M.C. "Yo, when you meet these guys, they're gonna bug you out," he told D. "These white guys are ill." During one session, Russell led the white trio in. D took one look at their red do-rags and red Adidas warm-up suits and thought, "I must be on *Candid Camera*."

Everyone shook hands and then Run and D got back to work. The Beasties watched them record. "Larry Smith was behind the board and we were like, 'That's fucking Larry Larr who drove off in his Cadillac?' " said Ad Rock. "And there's Russell passed out behind the couch."

Rick Rubin also attended more recording sessions. "We were surprised," said Runny Ray. "Like 'Oh shit!' He'd always try to put his little two cents in. He'd sit at the board talking about 'No, do it this way.' Larry wanted them to play it one way, but Rick would want them to do it another way."

Run accepted that Russell wanted his new friend to help create new Run-D.M.C. songs; D.M.C. initially welcomed Rick, figuring he had a lot of rock records, and great ideas for rock-rap: "We needed him 'cause he knew what to put." But D's opinion changed when he saw Rick start trying to tell them how to record their b-boy songs, said Ray. "[Run and D] were like, 'What is this nigga doing here?' "

But Rick and the Beastie Boys continued to attend recording sessions for the next Run-D.M.C. album, and Jam Master Jay took the Beastie Boys under his wing. Packing them into a car one night, he drove them out to Long Island and introduced them to Chuck D, a college student and rapper who hosted a rap show on Adelphi University's radio station WBAU. Chuck was skeptical at first but later explained he "couldn't doubt their legitimacy 'cause they were down with Def Jam and Run-D.M.C., and the beats were right." Jay asked Chuck to let them say a few raps during an episode of his radio program. Chuck agreed, and liked what he heard. "And the

Beastie Boys started playing the radio show as they got the buzz from Jay and then D and then Run," Chuck said.

During another session, the Beasties watched Run-D.M.C. record "Slow and Low." Instead of rock or keyboards, they set this to nothing but a Roland 808 drum machine.

Larry added sound effects but Run-D.M.C. felt it sounded too much like "Together Forever," and decided not to include the song on the album. "They were like, 'Oh, we're not gonna use it,' " Ad Rock recalled. At the time, Rick Rubin and the Beasties were working on their first rap album, and, Ad explained, "Our sound right then was desperately trying to sound like Run-D.M.C."

When the Beasties expressed interest in recording "Slow and Low," Russell Simmons and Rick Rubin felt it was a great idea. Russell had had little success trying to make the Beasties popular with black audiences. One night he had arranged a show with Kurtis Blow at the Encore in Queens and had a stretch limo take the white trio to the nightclub. But an all-black crowd saw their red Adidas suits and frowned, then jeered when the Beasties took the stage. "They got booed because the black crowd didn't appreciate that they were some white boys trying to act like Run-D.M.C.," Profile artist Spyder D remembered. When one Rush Productions employee said, "Yo, this crowd is hostile," Spyder replied, "You can't wear an Adidas suit in the Encore. They would have been better off looking like they were from NYU."

But Russell hadn't given up. If anything, he'd worked even harder to break the group, his friend, publicist Leyla Turkkan, explained. "Russell was obsessed with them," she told a reporter. "This was back in those Danceteria days when everybody was really high on coke. All he could talk about was the Beastie Boys, and I just didn't believe it was gonna work." Russell kept having the white trio play Disco Fever "for three people who weren't watching," Beastie Boy Ad Rock recalled.

As Run-D.M.C. continued recording a second album during the fall of 1984, Russell told the group, "Yo, we need more 'songs.' We don't need a bunch of 'Sucker MCs' records." Tony Rome—L.L.'s road manager—told them, "I got your socially conscious record that y'all should do." He handed them his lyric "You're Blind," which started out like old Melle Mel, with raps about tenement buildings and skyscrapers. Run thought it was cool enough to use.

Then Russell told them, "Go make a record called 'You Talk Too Much.'" They envisioned something as hard-hitting as Whodini's hit "Big Mouth," but Larry buried Run and D's scathing insults and chorus ("Shut up!") in synthesizer riffs and alienated Russell by adding a funk bass without consulting him.

Rick Rubin went from suggesting rock records to sample or replay, to actively contributing ideas to their rock-rap songs. D didn't mind, but also did not want Rick trying to tell them how to sound b-boy. When he drank, D would tell his friend Ray, "Yo, they bringing this white boy in. He don't know what the fuck he's doing." Ray used to laugh, thinking D would end up punching Rick or something.

Larry Smith was also disgruntled. "See, I didn't hang with Rick," Larry said. When Rick arrived at a session, he'd immediately be "in Russell's ear" with his ideas, Ray said, and Larry felt, "Damn, Russell. You were just talking to me, and now you over here with him?"

They recorded "Jam Master Jammin'," a tribute to their DJ, but the rock-style bass line—played by Run-D.M.C's Larry-approved first DJ, Davy DMX—was dour. Jay scratched a boring sound effect ("Whoo"). Someone then decided Davy DMX's rock riff wasn't forceful enough, so Rick—who usually sat and practiced a few riffs on an electric guitar while Russell and Larry worked with Run-D.M.C—plugged his guitar in and got ready to play a melody that evoked the metal group AC/DC. "He couldn't do solos or anything," said Adam Dubin. He was good at punk-style bar chords and choosing what sounded good but "wasn't a good guitar player." Even so, Rick played his riff alongside one by Davy DMX. "That was foul," Runny Ray felt, especially since Rick's sounded identical.

Another weekend, Run and D heard Russell say, "L.L. got an idea for your record." The idea was "Can You Rock It Like This," a rant about reporters, fans, and groupies, set to another guitar-heavy track.

Since their epic battle at Rush, Run and L.L. had continued to butt heads, said Ray. "Every time they'd meet they had a battle. Run was the instigator. L.L. was like, 'All right, nigga, whatever. You got your shit.' But Run would keep instigating and then it would make L.L. rap." Run would say, "You ain't deffer than me. Your shit is weak." Crowds formed. "Then L.L. would say his shit and everyone would say 'Run is better' 'cause everybody was on his shit. Run-D.M.C. was on the radio, and Run had records out: 'You're def, you're def; nigga, you're def.' "

L.L. arrived at Greene Street that day despite the fact that Run didn't want him involved, said Runny Ray. "I don't even think he should get royalties," he remembered hearing Run say. "I think we should just pay him and let him go." And when L.L. tried to coach them on how to say the lyric, Run asked his brother, "Why we got to do his record?"

" 'Cause we need another song."

"Well why we got to do *his* shit?"

L.L. kept coaching, Ray added, and Run snapped, "Don't tell me how to do them. I'm' a do it my way."

Larry stood up from his chair. "Certain times I would just walk out the studio and leave."

Jay told Run to relax, but, D said, "Run wasn't too happy with L.L. telling him what to say. But we laid it. You know what? That particular day they were friends."

The group left the studio with mixed feelings. "*King of Rock* was uninspired," said Run. "It wasn't as good. The best record was 'Kings of Rock.' Some of that other stuff was just okay. And we did 'Can You Rock It Like This.' We obviously didn't write that ourselves. 'You're Blind.' We didn't write that. 'You Talk Too Much' wasn't half as good as 'It's Like That.' "

Larry felt the same. "If you notice, Rick Rubin's on there," he said of the album's production. "That's when Russell and Rick's relationship started gelling, coming together."

Russell liked "Kings of Rock" and "You're Blind" but felt they all should have taken more time and made it as unique as their debut. "A lot of the problem was economic," he later wrote; "we had to deliver the second album to Profile in order to get paid for the first."

Right after Run-D.M.C. finished recording their second album, Rick Rubin and Russell Simmons publicly launched Def Jam Recordings by releasing L.L. Cool J's November 1984 single "I Need a Beat," and placing a triumphant ad in *Billboard* that announced, "The purpose of this company is to educate people as to the value of real street music by putting out records that nobody in the business would distribute but us." Rap fans flocked to the single, which cost $700 to produce and quickly sold 100,000 copies, while Run-D.M.C. waited for Profile to release their still-untitled second album, which they had mixed feelings about because Larry Smith and Russell had drowned their beats in commercial music. (Even though Rick Rubin was present during sessions and Russell liked Rick's "It's Yours" production, Russell and Larry stuck with the tried-and-true musical sound that had helped Run-D.M.C.'s debut sell over 500,000 copies.) Profile president Cory Robbins heard their song "Kings of Rock" and decided to make it "king, singular," and that it would make a good album title. And when they planned to shoot a video for the title track, Robbins ("a big Dave Letterman fan") suggested including comedian Larry "Bud" Melman, who appeared on the highly rated talk show *Late Night with David Letterman* (then airing on NBC) every weeknight.

One winter day in 1984, Run-D.M.C. and Jam Master Jay bundled up in black leather coats and rode toward upstate New York during a snowstorm. Cory and Russell had agreed to pay the wizened old comedian's manager $1,500. As cameras rolled, Melman (in blazer, white shirt, and black-framed glasses) blocked the entrance to a building. As Run and D (in their black leather blazers, pants, and turtlenecks) ran up some steps, Melman said, "This is a rock-and-roll museum. You don't belong here." They shoved him aside, then pushed through two doors. "I'm the king of rock, there is none higher!" D yelled.

Both rappers stomped on Michael Jackson's sequined glove, smashed Elton John's sequined glasses, set a black hat onto a bust of the Fab Four, then crossed their arms, looked at a television set airing footage of Little Richard and Chuck Berry, and shook their heads. When Jerry Lee Lewis appeared on-screen, playing piano, they turned the set off. The video concluded with the duo nodding approvingly while viewing "Rock Box" footage on another set. Although "King of Rock" hewed closely to the "Rock Box" blueprint—metal, funny lyrics, white guest stars, and a story—some MTV executives were offended. " 'Cause of the rock-and-roll museum," D explained. "They didn't like us pulling the plug on Chuck Berry. We had the audacity to dis rock and roll legends." But Rus-

sell defended the "King of Rock" video during meetings with network executives. "We're not moving it," Russell told them. "This
shit is art." Then D attended an informal gathering at MTV to "explain the glove-stepping thing. I had to bring a glove and demon-
strate what I did." The network relented, realizing the mock
destruction was in line with rap's self-aggrandizing, competitive
spirit, making Run-D.M.C. bigger than ever. "We took the crown
from the Bronx and Manhattan," D.M.C. said happily. And as the
single became a hit, fans took to calling Run-D.M.C. the kings of
the rap genre. But Kurtis Blow called Run the day *King of Rock* was
released to stores in January 1985. "I was just in record stores in
Harlem," Kurt told him. "Niggas said it's wack." Days later, Kurtis
spoke with D when Run left Run-D.M.C.'s dressing room after a
concert. "Kurtis Blow happened to catch me one minute when Run
wasn't around and said, 'Yo, D, man, you got to stop saying you're
the fucking king!' " D claimed. When Kurtis left the room, D
thought, "Whoa. What should I do? Should I really stop? Out of
respect?" Run came back in, saw D's expression, and asked what
had happened. D told him. Run was livid. "What!" Run yelled.
"Motherfucker!"

Run charged through the crowd, ran up to Kurt, and yelled,
"Motherfucker, you leave fucking D alone! You don't play my man
D like that! Number one, he says what he wants! You fake!" The
crowd was stunned. "That was probably the day Run came out
from under Kurt's shadow," said D.

Run, who was twenty at the time, disagreed. "I had stopped being the son of a Kurtis Blow a long time ago," Run said.

King of Rock (released in January 1985) emerged as another
record-breaking Run-D.M.C. hit—the first million-selling rap album—and *Rolling Stone*, the biggest rock magazine on earth, raved
about every note. D's claim of being the king of rock was outrageous, but "damned hard to refute," the review noted, and while
other rappers might be better in some areas, "Run-D.M.C. attacks
on all fronts." The review described Run-D.M.C. as a "hip-hop

Black Sabbath," questioned whether rock fans would accept their music, and stressed, "these guys are no mere pretenders to the throne."

Suddenly, Run-D.M.C. was the most famous rap group in the world. That they wore maroon jackets with prominent gray Def Jam logos in public caused the million fans that bought *King of Rock* to express interest in the company. "That was just to show that we were down with Def Jam," said D. During interviews for *King of Rock,* they'd talk about how great Def Jam was, promoting the label as much as their own music. " 'Cause it was his brother's company," Runny Ray said of Run. Jam Master Jay also helped Def Jam during this period by agreeing to give opinions about new records Rick Rubin and Russell planned to release. Of the three members in Run-D.M.C., Jay was the only one who had really hung out with neighborhood toughs, regularly attended parties in other boroughs and embraced new sounds, kept his ear to the street and learned about sounds and trends and the audience's changing tastes. "Jay was the barometer for Rick Rubin and Russell," said Hank Shocklee, part of the circle of DJs at WBAU. "So, with everything, if it didn't go through Jay, they weren't messing with it! Or if Jay didn't like it and they did mess with it, it fell off real quick."

Russell in turn worked to make Run-D.M.C. even more successful by arranging a surprising new deal. One night in February 1985, after 1:00 a.m., D.M.C. heard someone ring the doorbell at his parents' house in Hollis, where the laid-back twenty-year-old rapper still lived. D threw the door open and saw Russell with a rotund film producer named George Jackson, who had attended a Fresh Fest concert in California two months before and tried to interest Russell in the idea of filming a documentary about the tour.

Russell extended some papers. "Yo! We're gonna do this movie. You got to sign here. We'll be starting in three months." D was shocked; there had been no talk about a Run-D.M.C. movie. But he happily invited them in and got his parents out of bed. "It was me, my mother and father, and Russell, George Jackson, and another producer," D remembered, all standing and discussing the deal in his kitchen. Then he signed the contract.

Run was in his basement when Russell and Jackson caught him later the same night. "They just came with contracts and I signed them," Run recalled. For the film *Rap Attack*, Russell would be paid $15,000. Rick Rubin would receive $15,000. Run-D.M.C. and Jam Master Jay would share $15,000. Jay was euphoric, telling his Hollis Crew pal Hurricane, "Yo, kid, we're doing a movie. It's wild. I can't believe they're shooting a movie."

The movie, quickly renamed *Krush Groove*, supposedly sprang from a conversation producer George Jackson had with Kurtis Blow at the Disco Fever nightclub one evening. One Blow confidant claimed Jackson had approached Blow with black director Michael Schultz of *Car Wash* fame in tow to say, "I want to make a movie with you and I want to call it 'The King of Rap.' "

Producer George Jackson soon became interested instead in fictionalizing the story of Russell's success in the music industry and his cocreation of Def Jam Recordings.

Run-D.M.C. didn't mind, because they wanted to leave Profile Records and commercial-sounding production for Russell's new label and the hard-core sound Run-D.M.C. inspired and Rick Rubin brought to L.L.'s single "I Need a Beat." But since they couldn't join Def Jam—because of their contract with Profile—Run-D.M.C. had to compete with L.L. Despite the fact that *King of Rock* sold ten times as many copies as L.L.'s single, Run-D.M.C. saw the young rapper smirk at them when they ran into each other. And when they did concerts, L.L. was in the front row, studying their performances and, people claimed, taking notes. They didn't mind this, since Run-D.M.C. supported and hoped to be on Def Jam soon, but they also showed rap fans they were still the roughest rap group in the business with a new b-side that found them turning a line from the children's book *Hands, Fingers, Thumbs,* which Run read to his daughter Vanessa before bedtime, into an unforgettable routine, Jay cutting up Billy Squier's "The Big Beat" while both rappers shouted, "D.M.C. and DJ Run, dum, diddy dum, diddy diddy dum, dum."

Then, with Jam Master Jay already assisting Def Jam (by suggesting refinements to artists' images and ideas), Run-D.M.C. decided to become more involved with the label by bringing it a group called the Hollis Crew (their old friends Butter and Cool T), and producing their single "It's the Beat," which evoked L.L.'s articulate approach with lyrics like: "The force that invades every musical tone. It sounds so def when the beat's alone. It's not the funky fresh rhymes or the cuts galore. It's the beat! Word! And that's for sure!"

At Profile, Cory Robbins didn't mind seeing Run-D.M.C. wear Def Jam jackets in videos and photos or work on the Hollis Crew single for Def Jam. And if Def Jam records evoked Run-D.M.C.'s "Jam Master Jay" single, it was because "Rick Rubin was doing them," said Cory. "But, um, that's *okay*. Many records sound similar. I didn't think they were rip-offs."

But then Run-D.M.C.'s historic success with *King of Rock* attracted interest from other major labels, and Russell allegedly signed Jam Master Jay (not included in the group's contract with Profile) to Def Jam. "Russell was gonna sign Jay and put him out separately and Profile kept refusing to put Jay on the covers at first because they didn't want to blow him up and not have him signed," said Profile artist Spyder D.

Then Run-D.M.C. started telling friends they wanted to be on Def Jam. *"Badly!"* D said. "But we couldn't 'cause Russell always had problems with Profile. We signed a multialbum deal and sealed our own destiny. But what could you do? We had fun doing what we were doing. Although Def Jam should pay me for advertising 'cause Run-D.M.C. endorsed Def Jam and put in work in the beginning."

When major labels began to ask Rush Productions if Run-D.M.C. would be willing to sign a better deal with them in mid-1985, Run-D.M.C. saw Rush employees feud with Profile so acrimoniously that representatives from both companies could not be in the same room without shouting at each other, Spyder D recalled. "Because of money, renegotiations, and the threat of Run-D.M.C. slipping off to Def Jam.

"It hurt my career because I couldn't get Russell to speak to Profile about my album," Spyder continued. "They couldn't have a conversation without a shouting match about Run-D.M.C."

Run-D.M.C. on Def Jam would make the new label bigger, Spyder explained. "If Russell could have had his way they would have been gone from Profile." But Profile would not let Run-D.M.C. go because their songwriting abilities created a valuable catalog that would continue to earn money, through reissues and performance fees, even if the burgeoning rap genre faded from popularity.

Russell, however, continued to dream of having Run-D.M.C. serve as the centerpiece for a new rap empire he now felt he could build. Only twenty-eight years old, he had already made history by coproducing Run-D.M.C's Gold-certified debut and Platinum-selling second album, and less than a year after he co-created the record label Def Jam, Hollywood was already creating a major motion picture about his life. If he could bring Run-D.M.C. to Def Jam and land a distribution deal with a major label, which he and Rick Rubin were actively seeking in 1985, Russell felt there would be no limit to the heights to which he could take this musical genre. The only obstacle, however, was the contract he'd had Run-D.M.C. sign after every major label rejected "It's Like That" in 1983. (Though Rush Productions received payment from Profile, then distributed it to Run-D.M.C., both Russell and Run-D.M.C. had signed agreements with the label.) "The Profile contract was almost like they put the lid over the coffin and said, 'You're here for life,' " producer Larry Smith claimed. "And if Run-D.M.C. had gone to Def Jam, Profile wanted to be paid every cent they had.

You gotta realize two smart men ran Profile. Cory Robbins and Steve Plotnicki were smart to *not* let Run-D.M.C. go."

That spring of 1985, Run-D.M.C. kept hearing about interest from major labels. Def Jam released singles by L.L. Cool J, the Beastie Boys, rapper Jimmy Spicer, and Beastie member MCA and engineer Berzootie. Rick Rubin and Russell Simmons offered Def Jam music to major labels. Larry Smith and Russell grew further apart. Larry reportedly alienated Russell by selling his part of publishing rights to certain songs to another label even though Russell had included these specific publishing rights in an offer for another deal. Larry also signed on to serve as music supervisor for an upcoming movie called *Rappin'* even though Russell had met with its producer, Menachem Golan, to discuss collaborating, and decided not to work on *Rappin'* with Golan's movie studio, Cannon Films. And as Run-D.M.C. worked on a Hollis Crew single for Def Jam, and filmmakers were preparing in May 1985 to start shooting *Krush Groove*, a work that would show Run-D.M.C. signing to a Def Jam–like independent label, Profile executives suspected Russell of trying to sneak Run-D.M.C. onto Def Jam.

CHAPTER 13

The Silver Screen

For the opening scene of *Krush Groove* Run, D, and Jay had to get into blue coveralls and shower caps, and scrub cars at a car wash. Jay stood behind a nearby set of turntables while break-dancers mounted car roofs and spun on their heads. In the next scene Run stood facing his real-life father, playing a reverend, said he wanted to quit his job and make music, and heard his pop give him a tongue-lashing. Then they hung in their trailer while director Michael Schultz filmed a scene where Russell's character, Russell Walker, and Rick Rubin, playing himself, tried to convince a bank to give them a loan to start Krush Groove Records. In the scene, both of them kicked one of L.L.'s lyrics: "An insurmountable beat, subject of discussion. You're motivated by the aid of percussion. There's no category for this story. It will rock in any terri-tory." The bank rejected them, and Russell borrowed the money from a suit-wearing cigar-chomping older gang-ster. Run and D then reappeared in a red-lit studio: D wore an Adidas tank top, Run wore a Kangol, and they yelled their recent hit "King of Rock." Then Krush Groove started selling the record from their cramped one-room office.

At this point, Russell and Rick Rubin sat near suit-clad Andre Harrell at a table. Jay ushered a woman out of the room after her audition. L.L. and his DJ, Cut Creator, wanted in, but Jay said, "No more auditions." L.L. wouldn't leave, so Jay shoved his hand into the front of his athletic warm-up jacket as if going for a piece. "I said no more auditions!" The others said it was all right. L.L. and Cut then entered. L.L. growled, "Box," and Cut pressed Play on a huge portable radio. L.L. then stole the show with a lively performance of his new Rubin-produced single, "I Can't Live Without My Radio."

In the middle of all this, Run had to compete with the Russell character for Sheila E. at Danceteria. Since no one wanted her Prince-like sound, Run and D tried to teach her how to rap by saying a few lines from "Slow and Low." At Manhattan Center, they rocked "It's Like That," then saw her sing "Holly Rock." Then jheri-curled Kurt performed his go-go inflected "If I Ruled the World" with Mel-styled grunts, a tuxedo jacket, a cane, two DJs, and a revue of dancers.

As *Krush Groove* continued, Run had to look angry and disaffected when Sheila chose sweater-wearing Russell over him. He left the Krush Groove label and recorded the angrier "Can You Rock It Like This" for a rival company. Then he rode to Danceteria in a limousine, ignored his brother, and left with his new white manager and white girls. Then he met Russell backstage at a concert and mouthed off about Sheila. Russell Walker slugged his brother so hard, Run and Russell fell to the floor fighting, lying on top of each other and sliding across the floor of the room.

Run and D got to sit out the parts where loan sharks beat the shit out of Russell Walker, but Run had to go to a rooftop and hear

Kurtis Blow lecture him about how his ego was out of hand. Then Run told Sheila's character he accepted her decision (choosing Russell Walker over him), and hurried to the Fever to hand Russell money to pay the loan shark back. Then Run and D watched the Disco 3—the Fat Boys' name before the Brooklyn trio was discovered in a talent contest—finally get their big break by winning Krush Groove's big talent show at the Fever. After their victory, Run-D.M.C., Kurt, Sheila—everyone in the film—got together to sing the theme song. And while credits rolled, the Fat Boys and L.L. started a *Soul Train* line.

With Schultz directing, filming *Krush Groove* was a pleasant experience for Run, D, and Jay (who had just purchased a shiny black Lincoln Continental), but Run didn't like the part where he had to betray Russell's character. Jam Master Jay disliked when Schultz had Sheila E. slap Run, thinking it made Run look soft.

Russell Simmons didn't like that Schultz went with Blair Underwood to play Russell Walker, over Fab Five Freddy, or the soft dialogue, either. He kept pushing to add slang. Michael Schultz meanwhile didn't like Russell saying "motherfucker" every twenty seconds: "Look, let's put a little English now and then, so the uninitiated will know what we're saying." He also didn't like young, bearded Rick Rubin trying to tell him how to shoot a film. At one point, about to film a scene with Run and Underwood, he heard Rubin cry, "*No!* That's *not* how it goes! *This* is how it goes!" Rubin launched into a speech, but Schultz said, "Excuse me, Rick. Come with me for a minute." With an arm around Rick, he led him across the theater, stopped walking, then said, "Rick, I appreciate your enthusiasm. But there can be only one director. And I'm the director, so don't ever do that again."

Rick gushed, "I'm really sorry, but it was really making me mad because once you put it on film that's the way it's gonna be and it's gonna be wrong."

Schultz returned to his post by the camera. Someone asked, "What should we do?"

Schultz almost sighed. "Do what Rick said."

There were other tensions on the set, one source claimed, because Run-D.M.C's management kept trying to pressure the filmmakers into firing Kurtis Blow, who was producing much of the film's sound track. Sheila E. reportedly avoided mixing with the rest of the cast, while Prince, riding high off the *Purple Rain* movie and sound track, sat in a mostly empty balcony, watching production of *Krush Groove*. And L.L. Cool J didn't like his attitude: "Prince and his boys thought that we were making 'Sheila E. Goes to Hollywood' when the film was really about my homeboys Run-D.M.C. and Kurtis Blow."

The audience of extras at the Manhattan Center meanwhile didn't like Sheila E.'s "Holly Rock" song. While Run did all the acting, D hung with pals, ate that wonderful food they had lying out, and enjoyed receiving new Adidas suits, Kangols, and Lee jeans every day. "It was cool to me," he said of those twenty-six days. "I didn't have to say shit. I just had to be D. During the movie I'm really writing rhymes that whole time."

CHAPTER 14

The Kid with the Hat

M ay 31, 1985, days after *Krush Groove* wrapped, they were back on the road, headlining the "second annual" Fresh Festival barely five months after the original had ended. Once again, Whodini and the Fat Boys joined them. So did Shabba Doo and Boogaloo Shrimp, dancers in the two *Breakin'* movies, the Double Dutch Girls (who skipped rope to Prince songs), the Dynamic Breakers, young singer Chad from *Krush Groove*, and the tour production manager's son, Jermaine Dupri, who breakdanced and moonwalked. Kurt was supposed to be on the tour but reportedly complained about not headlining, so Rush Productions yanked him from the lineup and replaced him with Grandmaster Flash, whose instrumental single "Larry's Dance" and its sampled voice chanting "L-L-Larry" kept crowds happy.

Though the film would not be released to theaters until October, the *Krush Groove* sound track was in stores and L.L.'s hard-core single, "I Can't Live Without My Radio," was receiving heavy radio airplay. Now, when Run walked toward the stage and passed L.L., who was leaving it, there were a few tense seconds while they smirked at each other. L.L. now wore a Run-like hat and tried to grow sideburns like Run, but kept alternating between being a fan and wanting to take Run out.

Thus, more backstage battles. They'd compete for hours. But their competition was escalating; battles moved onstage. "I heard that one time Run and L.L. were doing that 'Anything you can do I can do better' and going back and forth at some arena," said Chuck D, then of WBAU. "So Run took off his hat and threw it across the stage and L.L. couldn't do that. 'Cause L. wasn't taking off his hat." L.L. wore his hat so much that people wondered if he was self-conscious about the size of his head. "And that's how Run beat him!" Chuck continued. "That shit was incredible."

When they stood before the audience on this second tour, Run, D, and Jay saw a sea of white faces. "It was maybe 80 percent white," said D. Many white fans in the audience were attracted to Run-D.M.C. concerts because they had seen Run-D.M.C.'s rock-driven videos "Rock Box" and "King of Rock" on MTV and had enjoyed Run-D.M.C.'s fusion of rock and heavy metal. Run-D.M.C. left the tour about a week after it began. MTV invited them to film another special, but this one on their own. On Wednesday, June 12, they took a day off from the tour, traveled to New York, and performed a few guitar-heavy numbers for cameras in the rock club the Ritz. *Run-D.M.C.: Live at the Ritz* aired on June 30. Then they were back on the network as part of what many considered the biggest rock concert in history.

One night in July, they were exhausted after a show and an after-party in Savannah, Georgia, but Rush Productions called to say they had to fly to Philly first thing in the morning to play Live Aid, a festival Boomtown Rat member Bob Geldof hoped would raise money for starving people in Ethiopia. In newspapers, a controversy played out about promoters not inviting Run-D.M.C. or many other black performers (out of sixty acts, only three were black), but rock promoter Bill Graham, also involved with booking acts for Live Aid, called Rush to invite the rap group onto the bill. Traveling to the show, Run-D.M.C. heard everyone talk about how the entire world would be watching.

At JFK Stadium in Philly they saw Tina Turner, Sade, Madonna, Black Sabbath, Led Zeppelin, Paul McCartney, the Who, the Beach Boys, Elton John—the list went on. Bill Graham—a big burly white guy—led them to a dressing room with their name on it and thanked them for coming. A few rock stars came to ask for autographs for their children. They signed a few and then went onstage. It was hot that day, over a hundred degrees, and people in the crowd were fainting. They would have only twenty minutes to set up Jay's turntables *and* perform three songs. And they were playing for a white crowd that didn't know or care about rap (which explained why promoters had Run-D.M.C. open the show when their album was selling better than those of a lot of the rock legends).

The edge of the stage was far from the crowd, so Run and D couldn't make eye contact with audience members. They had to squint while performing and only had time to perform "King of Rock" and another song—not the three they had hoped to play—for one hundred thousand people in the crowd and millions watching the show on their television sets. After the show, they left town to rejoin the fifty-five-city Fresh Fest tour.

*O*n August 3, 1985, two months into the second Fresh Fest tour, Run-D.M.C. traveled to California to become the first rap group to tape a performance for the rock-oriented *American Band-*

stand show. By now they had two gold albums and had placed five singles in the Black Top 20. In California, Russell and Rick introduced them to photographer Glen Friedman, an intense young white guy who came from the world of punk and had recently impressed Russell and Rick with photos of the Beastie Boys. "We just all got along; we just clicked immediately," said Friedman.

Before heading to the *Bandstand* set, Run, D, and Jay followed Friedman out of the downtown hotel Le Mondrian. It was early in the morning and Run-D.M.C. and Jam Master Jay agreed to pose for pictures in front of a church across the street. Run wore a Run-D.M.C. shirt, D wore his white Izod shirt, and Jam Master Jay wore Fila, still in style at the time. "What I wanted to capture was the way I perceived them," said Friedman. "From the way I heard their music." He placed them very specifically so the composition was right, told them which direction to face, asked them to lift their chins a little, and used a wide-angle lens he had brought over from his days shooting skateboarders. But soon Friedman looked a bit frustrated. "As you can see in almost every photo of Joe, like usual, he's always running his mouth. He's always talking. Even when we're trying to take photos, it's whatever he wants to say. That's what's important."

On the *Bandstand* set later that day, Run-D.M.C. walked out and saw a white audience go crazy. Dick Clark introduced them then they played "King of Rock" and the recently released Rick Rubin version of "Jam Master Jammin'." Backstage after the show, everyone wanted Clark to pose for pictures with the group. Clark smiled a few times, but everyone wanted Clark to cross his arms in a b-boy stance. Clark agreed to try it. Run, D, and Jay beamed in the photo with him, copies of which their publicists quickly mailed to every newspaper they could.

Run-D.M.C. returned to the second Fresh Fest tour in August 1985 but left again, to spend one day performing for another wholesome project—a song called "Sun City." Producer Arthur Baker and guitarist Steven van Zandt (who played guitar for Bruce

Springsteen's legendary E Street Band) wanted to denounce the South African resort Sun City's policy of not letting black citizens attend concerts. Van Zandt also wanted to name the performers the guitarist alleged still played there despite the abhorrent policy, a list that included some of rock's biggest acts.

By late August 1985, the Fresh Fest tour was winding down. Run and D thought their boys the Hollis Crew—Butter Love and Cool T—would see their August 1985 single "It's the Beat" put them in the big time. The single, Def Jam artist DJ Doctor Dre added, was also "how Run-D.M.C. was gonna be on Def Jam, through the Hollis Crew record. But Rick and them said you couldn't market and sell Hollis Crew." The Crew had talent but some Def Jam executives felt they lacked a hook for the media. "I mean there's nothing 'rock' about them," and everyone was changing their focus: if a record sounded good didn't matter as much as whether white people would like it. "Run-D.M.C. had now become a television thing on MTV and was starting to build that little bridge across the water, to becoming a pop group," Dre explained.

Run was frustrated. He felt Def Jam wasn't promoting the Hollis Crew single enough. D also felt Def Jam "put it out and forgot about it." Cool T and Butter meanwhile looked forward to recording an album. "They were writing every day," said Ray. "But Russell was fronting on them. Just let them do that one shit and that was it."

Russell then asked Run and D for help with the Beastie Boys. Madonna's manager had called Rush Productions to ask for a group Russell didn't manage to accompany her on tour. "And he was like, 'Well they're busy right now,' " Ad Rock recalled. He offered Run-

D.M.C. but "wanted like $100,000 a show or something crazy and they were like, 'No,' so he's like, 'Well the Beastie Boys will do it for $500!' " Once Russell landed the Beasties a spot on Madonna's national Like a Virgin tour, he felt the white trio needed more material. That's when he contacted Run-D.M.C. "They just said, 'We need to give the Beasties something,' " D.M.C. remembered. "Like, write a record. We were gonna write something but the Beasties said, 'You're not gonna use "Slow and Low"?' We said 'No.' They said, *'We'll take that one!'* They liked it." Run-D.M.C. offered to write something new, but "They were like, 'No, *we want that one!*' "

In Chung King Studios—"the House of Metal," an inconspicuous facility on the sixth floor of a building near Chinatown and Little Italy that had graffiti on the walls—Rick Rubin replaced Run-D.M.C.'s Roland 808 track with a huge guitar chord and bells that evoked "Rock Box." The Beasties substituted Run and D's names with their own and changed a line that said "D sees real well 'cause he has four eyes" to "White Castle fries only come in one size."

Run and D.M.C. didn't mind helping Def Jam but put their foot down when they heard what L.L. planned for his debut album. Already, L.L. patterned much of his album after Run and D's recent "You Talk Too Much." Song titles included "You Can't Dance" and "That's a Lie." He also included Russell ad-libbing on "That's a Lie" (something Russell had done on a Def Jam single by producer Jazzy Jay—not Jam Master Jay—called "Def Jam," which had become a hit on New York rap radio shows, but hadn't done on any Run-D.M.C. songs or albums). But L.L. reportedly heard a brand-new, unreleased track Run-D.M.C. planned to include on their next album. Jam Master Jay had decided to abandon the group's earlier sounds—the slick live music feel of Russell and Larry Smith productions and the slow, bass-heavy, sparse sound Rick Rubin had brought the group. Jam Master Jay instead programmed a brand-new beat—the one that drives Bob James's classic song "Take Me to the Mardi Gras"—into his drum machine, then mixed the actual record over the pattern. Jay kept mixing the record on his turntable until the entire drum machine track featured the dreamlike chimes.

L.L. wanted Rick Rubin to use the same Bob James record on his own song "Rock the Bells."

When Run heard the title, he immediately became suspicious. "The Bells" was the nickname many DJs had given the Bob James record. When he was DJing in his attic and wanted his assistant Runny Ray to pass him that record, Run, like many other DJs, would say, "Yo, give me 'The Bells.' Let's rock 'The Bells.' You got 'The Bells'?"

Run confronted L.L. and reportedly yelled in his face. Then, D said, Run told his brother, "Russell, if you let that happen you're fucking up!" At the last minute, Rick removed the Bob James break from L.L.'s song. "That's why it's called 'Rock the Bells' but didn't have any bells on it," D said happily. "L.L. was gonna have Rick put 'Mardi Gras' in and Russell was torn between two lovers."

*B*un, D, and Jay continued to write new material while on the road. On the tour bus, they kept playing and enjoying Doug E. Fresh and the Get Fresh Crew's 1985 single "The Show/La-Di-Da-Di," which had come from nowhere to redefine the sound of rap, making it more lively and energetic. On the A-side, vocalist Slick Rick and Doug used a tag-team approach that evoked old-time comedy teams, and Doug also re-created famous beats with his mouth. Their B-side, meanwhile, had Slick Rick rhyme with a Cockney accent over Doug performing the beat from James Brown's "Impeach the President." Run, D, and Jay loved both songs, said D. "And we tried to be like that in our way."

It started with Jam Master Jay. Onstage one night, he leaned into the mike over his turntables and started doing the human beat box. Then Run started doing it. Finally, during another show, D rapped, and Run exploded with the beat box. Backstage, Run said, "We gonna do that shit again tomorrow night, D." And soon, "We're gonna make a beat box record!"

Run was also inspired by Prince's single "Raspberry Beret," a psychedelic song in which Prince described meeting a woman at his dead-end job in a five-and-dime store, and screwing her in a barn during a thunderstorm. On the tour bus, Run decided to say his new rap "You Be Illin'" in a similarly conversational tone. "Just the whole feeling," he explained. "The way he was speaking on that record was very sassy and 'groovy.'"

By fall 1985, Run-D.M.C's third album took shape, one they wanted to produce themselves: "'Cause we were getting better," said Run, and because they were tired of other people programming some of their beats and taking full production credit. They were also tired of following orders, recording other writers' songs, throwing in rock guitars, and being told to promote a wholesome image while Slick Rick and L.L. were allowed to be profane or more aggressive. They were also confident in the material they improvised onstage each night, which represented, D said, "what *we* were doing. It was coming from the heart." No one could say, "Let's do it over," in front of a crowd, he added.

While they toured and wrote songs, Russell and Rick made the rounds at major labels. Seven Def Jam singles (two by L.L., two by the Beasties, and one each by Jazzy Jay, Jimmy Spicer, and the Hollis Crew) had sold over 250,000 copies. Every major turned them down, but then Al Teller, head of Columbia, expressed interest. Said Doctor Dre, then with the Def Jam act Original Concept, "The Def Jam deal with CBS all happened based on the fact that the Beasties were signing to Def Jam and opened for Madonna, so CBS smelled something. And Russell promised them Run-D.M.C."

On September 2, 1985, after playing fifty-five arenas in just as many cities and helping the second Fresh Fest earn over

$7 million—twice as much as the original—Run-D.M.C. finally returned to Hollis. And in October they learned that Columbia and Def Jam had signed a historic deal that called for Columbia to manufacture and distribute albums and singles from Def Jam. "L.L. Cool J had no bearing on whether that check was being signed," Doctor Dre explained. The Beasties' debut and the promise of Run-D.M.C. were "the two reasons the deal happened. When Russell couldn't deliver Run-D.M.C. over to CBS," Dre speculated, "his credibility was shot."

On October 25, 1985, Run and D saw *Krush Groove* arrive in 515 theaters. The film earned a quick $3 million that weekend and emerged as the number-one movie in America. Run-D.M.C. was bigger than ever, but the media focused on L.L.'s cameo and his contribution to the 500,000-selling sound track, the unassuming "I Can't Live Without My Radio." Then Def Jam quickly released L.L.'s debut album *Radio* with Columbia's major distribution, and Run-D.M.C. saw it quickly sell a million copies (twice as much as the *Krush Groove* sound track). Suddenly, L.L. looked like he was doing just as well as they were. Though word of mouth said he had only one or two good songs on *Radio* (and Run-D.M.C. albums typically arrived in stores with at least four or five), the media kept describing L.L. as the new "prince of rap," comparing him to Run, and congratulating L.L. for selling over a million copies of his Columbia-backed debut album. "So L.L. looking just as good on paper as Run-D.M.C. created rivalry," said Hank Shocklee, the outspoken producer who had met Run-D.M.C. up at college station WBAU.

D enjoyed the *Radio* album. "It was b-boy like us. It wasn't Kurtis Blow or Hollywood . . . it was the street." But he knew Run-D.M.C. was facing serious competition.

So did Jam Master Jay. "*King of Rock* wasn't as good as we wanted. It wasn't the best Run-D.M.C. could do."

Run saw L.L. go from posing near him in photos (wearing the same hat) to making the hat his signature. Run told D, "Damn, I can't wear the Kangols no more. I can't wear this. This shit reminds me of L too much." Now, in pictures for fanzines like *Right On*—the rap equivalent of *Tiger Beat*—Run stuck to the black velour hat. And that winter, watching TV, all he saw was L.L. He had to turn it off. Same with the radio: L.L.'s voice was everywhere. "Oh, my God!" he exclaimed. The media were treating Run as if he were Richard Pryor and L.L. was Eddie Murphy. "He said he was inspired by me," Run explained. "He said he wished he had the sideburns." Even so, fanzines like *Black Beat* and *Right On* promoted L.L. as Run's successor, as the new heartthrob that *also* appeared in *Krush Groove*. "Now you got this new kid that's got muscles taking all Run's pussy," D.M.C. laughed. "Bottom line, he was stealing Run's shine."

L.L. had larger company Columbia Records backing him. He was the darling of Def Jam, with Russell actively promoting his work. He also tapped into a female audience with love-rap B-sides like "I Want You" and "I Can Give You More." "He was a real threat to Run," said D. And *Radio* was selling faster than January 1985's *King of Rock*. "That was the biggest beef," Doctor Dre noted.

Run had overlooked what he viewed as L.L.'s arrogance. He had let L.L. write "Can You Rock It Like This." He had let Russell include L.L. on the bill at their shows. But when L.L. asked Rick to use "The Bells," the "embracing of L.L. in the beginning started to become more of a competition," Dre remembered. Run-D.M.C. returned to the studio.

CHAPTER 15

Proud to Be Black

In early 1986, Run-D.M.C. started to record their third album. "The first two records were just, 'Get on the mike, rhyme, I got a record,'" said their bodyguard Hurricane. The group worked in Chung King, with the Beastie Boys stopping in some nights to keep working on their own debut album.

Run-D.M.C. didn't want anyone but studio co-owner and engineer Steve Ett helping them create the new songs. But Russell was going to executive-produce, and with Larry Smith gone, he invited his Def Jam partner Rick Rubin to help. Though Rick and Russell were present, Run and Jay took over. "You could look at Run-D.M.C. perform and realize they were the real producers," Run explained.

They wanted greater creative control because they didn't like any of the ideas they heard from Profile or Rick Rubin, said their friend Doctor Dre. Everyone wanted them to record rock-rap that would cross their album over to a white audience, but Rick and Pro-file had differing ideas about what rock actually sounded like. Rick wanted an AC/DC sound. "They wouldn't just be a rap group try-ing to do rock songs," said Dre. " 'Rock Box' was cool but more funk than rock." Profile, he added, wanted esoteric "pop metal" like that heard on MTV, and created by bands like Whitesnake and Def Leppard. Run-D.M.C. wanted neither. "So Profile felt threat-ened by *Raising Hell* because Run and D wanted to return to the roots of 'Sucker MCs' and that feeling, and make sure they had the street," said Dre. "There was a certain point where Run-D.M.C. weren't sure."

Run came up with the main ideas; D wrote most of the lyrics; Jay created beats and arrangements and told a reporter, "No one of us has the formula. We all have it."

Run, D, and Jay knew how they wanted to sound, and one day they quickly knocked out four songs. After finishing each one, Run snapped, "Okay. There's nothing else to do to this." They didn't want strings, hand claps, or people singing choruses. They'd play completed works for Rick and Russell, who'd look at each other, nod, and agree that nothing else needed to be done. Once a song had song structure and sounded like it was created with cheap equipment—something Rick strove for, since a rugged, back-to-basics sound satisfied listeners tired of overproduced, chorus-heavy rap—their executive producers were happy.

Away from the studio, Run relaxed in his basement, playing UTFO's latest album. UTFO (an acronym for Untouchable Force Organization) was a Brooklyn quartet most famous for the humor-ous single "Roxanne Roxanne," but doing R & B now, with their ballad "Fairy Tale Lover." "He was talking some good stuff," Run said, referring to rapper Kangol Kid, who used a singsong delivery to compare himself to fairy-tale characters. Run felt he could use this in rap, make it harder, and make fun of those characters. He started a lyric called "Peter Piper" with a line that mentioned Jack and Jill: "Jack's on Jay's dick."

In Chung King, Jay brought out the Bob James track he'd created. They rapped, and Jay scratched the dramatic "I Can't Stop" horn blast over their voices. For "Dumb Girl," about a materialistic and confused young woman, Jay used nothing but an empty drum track and a slow sampled voice chanting, "Dumb."

They created another hit while hanging in Hollis one night. They were at "the building," where D used to sneak cigarettes, when their old friend Butter Love rushed toward them. "Yo, Run! Yo, Joe! I just seen your brother Russell dusted up on Hollis and Two-Fifth."

Run said, "Yeah, right!"

"Yo, he's up there right now!"

They walked toward Hollis Avenue and saw Russell on the corner.

D asked, "Yo, what's up?"

Russell quickly whispered, "Yo, guys, here's what y'all do. You need to make a record about your Adidas and you're gonna talk about where y'all been and you're gonna start by saying 'My A-didas.'"

D said, "Sounds good to me." Already, rappers had talked about Bally shoes (the Get Fresh Crew's "La-Di-Da-Di") and Gucci (Schooly D, a newcomer from Philadelphia, chanting, "Looking at my Gucci it's about that time"). And D himself had for years rhymed about b-boy lifestyle accoutrements like Pumas and British Walker brand shoes. But Russell kept them out there for two hours, raving about the idea.

In Chung King they played a bouncy swing beat on the drum machine and rapped about where they'd worn their Adidas sneakers while Jay again scratched the "I Can't Stop" horn blast. Their experimentation continued with "Perfection," in which they invited a sixteen-year-old drummer to play a beat as jaunty as the one on "La-Di-Da-Di," and recorded a lighthearted falsetto-driven rap about things they owned (a favorite topic of rappers who created the genre during jams in the South Bronx in the mid-1970s, and of rappers a quarter century later who continue to claim they own possessions many might never afford).

Another night, Run let Jam Master Jay hear a few rhymes from "You Be Illin'." Their friend and roadie Ray started banging on a table with his fists, creating a beat while Run rapped. Run told him, "We'll use that shit," as Ray kept playing a beat, and Jay hummed a piano melody. In the recording room, musicians translated their ideas into sax and piano riffs that went against the hard-core aesthetic the group had told Russell and Rick Rubin they wanted (but also gave the third album a heavy-music-and-chorus commercial moment that pop radio stations might react to), and D saw Run rap solo on the entire song.

In the past, D.M.C. didn't mind if Run recorded longer verses on songs like "Sucker MCs." They were still both appearing on records and sharing stages during performances and videos. But after "You Be Illin'," D wanted his own solo moment. "And I got a little souped. I said, 'I'm gonna go home and write the baddest rhyme I ever wrote.'" In the studio, he let Run hear his lyric before adding, "When I say, 'hit it, Run,' you're gonna do the beat box every time." Over a fast drum machine, Jay scratched the "I Can't Stop" horn, and Run beat-boxed during each break. They called the song "Hit It Run."

They were happy creating hard-core, but Rick and Russell eventually wanted some rock-rap. Run and D had a few of their usual boasts written and recited them over a churning metal track. Since one lyric said they were "raising hell," Russell decided the phrase would be the song title. Run bristled at the suggestion. To him, it sounded like "some white people stuff."

Then they saw a Cold Crush Brothers–style routine turn into more rock-rap. In Run's basement one night, D watched Run mix "I Can't Stop" on his turntables, and heard him say, "D, we're gonna use these beats." D recited a new rap he set to the rhythm of Toni Basil's lyrics on her new wave hit, "Mickey." But where Basil had chanted, "Oh Mickey, you're so fine, you're so fine you blow my mind, Hey Mickey," D rapped, "It's tricky to rock a rhyme, to rock a rhyme, that's right on time, it's tricky!" Rick Rubin heard the idea and said it would be cool if they said the rhyme over a track that used portions of the Knack's popular "My Sharona."

And through it all, the Beastie Boys were "lurking," Run recalled. "They would come and hang out. And the Beasties knew they were getting ready to do their album," said D.M.C., implying that the Beasties were absorbing ideas to then apply to their own new songs. "But it was all good," D.M.C. added.

A nother day at Chung King, Doctor Dre led WBAU producers Chuck D and Hank Shocklee into the studio and toward Russell. By now, D.M.C. had heard a tape by Chuck on WBAU, and felt Chuck was rap's next big star. The tape, a promo for Chuck's radio show, was called "Public Enemy No. 1." Chuck had written its rap after conversing with his friend Flavor Flav (born William Drayton), who had his own show on WBAU. Flav needed a job, so Chuck provided one at his father's furniture store in Queens, helping Chuck deliver orders in a truck. They were driving toward a customer's home one afternoon to deliver furniture when Flavor told Chuck that a rapper named Ron D—a member of the unsigned Long Island group Play Hard Crew—had heard Chuck on the radio and wanted to battle him. "Man, they want to like take you out!" Flav added.

"Take me out for *what?*" Chuck asked. "I ain't battling."

There were people who considered Chuck to be a has-been, since his first single, "Check Out the Radio," as part of the group Spectrum City, had flopped in the early eighties. So Chuck wrote a battle rhyme and set it to Fred Wesley & the J.B.s droning break beat "Blow Your Head."

After taping Chuck's promo off WBAU, D.M.C. traveled to

Manhattan to tell Rick Rubin, "Yo, there's this guy and his side-kick. These motherfuckers are ridiculous." Rick Rubin heard D's tape of "Public Enemy No. 1" and offered Chuck D a contract with Def Jam Records. "He liked the whole Melle Mel approach that everybody thought was kind of old at that time," said Chuck D. While Chuck considered whether to sign with Def Jam—thinking, "I don't know about making no records"—Rick tried to get his hands on a clearer-sounding tape of Chuck's song. Since the song aired on Dre's radio show on WBAU, Doctor Dre arrived at Def Jam's 298 Elizabeth Street offices with a tape. (Rick and Russell had bought the building shortly after signing Def Jam's distribution deal with CBS in late 1985 and had moved into it with new employees by January 1986.) In an office, Dre saw Rick sleeping on one side of a rolled-up mattress on the floor. Russell slept on the other side. Both had presumably been working all night on Def Jam projects. Dre played the tape for Rick, but Rick went back to sleep. "And then Russell rolled over, got up, and said, 'Are you crazy? This is the worst shit I ever heard!' Russell went to the machine, took the tape out, opened the window, and threw it out."

"Yo, what are you doing!" Dre yelled.

They argued until Russell ordered him out of the room. Near the door, Dre turned and said, "You know what? You don't know your ass from your elbow. I don't care what anybody says. Man, you've lost it." Rick, who slept through Dre's playing of the tape, never said a word.

Despite Russell's reluctance to sign Chuck D to Def Jam, Rick Rubin kept offering a contract. Then Rick told Def Jam employee (and former WBAU program director) Bill Stephney, "Yo, if you don't sign Chucky D you're fired!" Stephney was stunned. "For what?"

"Because you should be able to sign him; that's your man."

But Chuck had heard artists from many labels complain to him about going unpaid. "So we said, 'Why would we want to get involved with some bullshit like that?' " Hank Shocklee recalled. Although Stephney promised that Def Jam would treat them well, Chuck still hesitated.

But Chuck did go to Chung King with Hank Shocklee to offer Run-D.M.C. a song for their next album. The song was called "God Bless U.S." "It was a political rap about the state of the world done to a Chuck Berry beat," said Hank Shocklee. Russell rejected it. Hank remembered him saying, "Rap is not supposed to be talking about some political shit. Rap is supposed to be on some party shit."

But Run and D wanted to tackle the issue of race, so Russell invited a lyricist to help write lyrics. Doctor Dre and T-Money of Original Concept were in the studio that day observing and laughing at the outside songwriter's ideas. "That ain't gonna work," Dre said of one. "That ain't gonna work," of another. "That ain't gonna work," of a third. Finally, in an adjoining room, Dre and T-Money created an elaborate hard-core beat on a DMX drum machine. Reentering the studio, Dre said, "Yo, we got a record y'all should do." The heavyset DJ played Run-D.M.C. the tape he had just recorded. D.M.C. said, "Yo, we got to do *this*! We need a songwriter!"

"Well, I know the cat to do it," Dre told him.

Dre called another Original Concept bandmate, Rapper G, and requested a cross between James Brown's "Say It Loud (I'm Black and I'm Proud)" and the Isley Brothers' timeless "Fight the Power." G banged it out. The next day, back in Chung King, Dre said, "This is how it goes," and played the tape. Everyone was excited.

"Wow."

"Yo! We got to do this, we got to do this!"

Rapper G recorded a reference vocal (which suggested how Run-D.M.C. should perform certain phrases). Dre recorded the beat on a studio reel. Russell heard the new song, "Proud to Be Black," and told Dre, "Aw, that was cool."

The third album was finished, but D and Jay wanted another hard-core cut. They arrived at Chung King early on the afternoon of March 7, 1986, and looped the Aerosmith break beat "Walk This Way."

"We were just gonna do the normal 'I'm D.M.C. on the mike' and call it a day," D recalled. But Rick Rubin walked in, heard the beat, and asked, "Do you know who this is?"

D said, "No. Poison Ivy?"

"This is Aerosmith! *Toys in the Attic* by Aerosmith! It would be really great if you did this record."

"We are," D said.

"No, let's make the whole record. Do a remake. Take the lyrics home and learn them."

Run and D.M.C. hated the idea, D said. "We were like, 'Y'all takin' this rock-rap shit too far! That shit's gonna be fake!' "

But Jam Master Jay—who agreed with Russell and Rick's ideas about hooks and story raps lending commercial value to their otherwise formless rap boasts—said it would be cool.

D disagreed with him. "You know, they're trying to ruin us."

In D's basement, Run and D had pens and pads ready. D put the record on a turntable. They had never heard anything but its opening beat. "It was the scariest moment in our lives, to know what was coming after these guitars," D said.

They heard the guy singing, and Run wanted to cry. He couldn't hear what the guy was saying. "I had no lyric sheet," he recalled. "What is he saying? 'Backseat lover on the hiding 'neath the cover'?" Then the guitars played what they perceived to be hillbilly music, and they felt even worse.

D reached for the phone and called Rick. "We were crying again," he said, and when Rick answered, he yelled, "Yo! This is fake! This is hillbilly bullshit! You're gonna ruin us! Everyone's gonna laugh! Y'all buggin'!"

Rick said, "Calm down. Y'all got to do this record."

D hung up.

They returned to the studio the next day with what they thought was the lyric. Run did a huge chunk by himself though he really felt like screaming, "Garbage! What the hell are you doing?"

D also did his verses alone.

Neither put much energy into his vocals. They wanted to leave, but Jay walked in and said, "Y'all motherfuckers better get back in there and do this record with some energy like Run-D.M.C. It's gonna be a big record. I'm telling you. It's dope."

They reentered the booth, shared sentences, gave it a little more energy, then went home angry and hating the song. "They didn't want to sell out," said their bodyguard Hurricane. "They just wanted some hard-core beats and rap. 'Rock Box' was a different kind of rock. It was still hard-core. 'Walk This Way' was straight-up rock." Rick and Russell forecast that the song would unite white and black people, but D didn't care. "I just want to be dope on the mike," he thought.

The next morning, Jam Master Jay called D to say: "You got to come back and do the lyrics over."

"No, we did them," D replied. "What do you mean? We did them!"

"Well, now you got to come back and do it over the right way. Rick says Aerosmith is gonna be here."

On March 9, 1986, they traveled to Magic Venture Studio in New York. "They didn't like it," said their roadie and friend Ray. "They didn't like Steven Tyler. They didn't like none of them nig- gas." They arrived and saw Jay near his turntable, showing Aero- smith's long-haired lead singer, Steve Tyler, how he cut their beat up. "And them niggas freshly came out the rehab," Ray joked of Tyler and Aerosmith guitarist Joe Perry.

Tyler—wearing a headband and shiny shirt with shoulder pads—looked perplexed. "So, when are you gonna hear me?" he asked.

D stopped sipping from his beer. "That's the key. You don't get to hear your voice."

Rick Rubin sat at the giant mixing board. He'd already programmed a quicker version of Aerosmith's beat in his drum machine. He had the thin guitarist play the song's riffs, then the singer wail the chorus. Jay meanwhile coached Run and D on how to perform this song. "Y'all trying to do a record like they did it. Do it like Run-D.M.C. would do it!"

Rick kept the music at an earsplitting volume, so they had to shout. Rush Management publicist (and former journalist) Bill Adler, in the room with other employees and friends, stood up and asked Rick to turn it down, but the producer screamed, "No!"

D was a little buzzed when Rick said they should go into the booth. But Jay was right. They had to do it their way, not soften up. "That's when we did the switching off, and trading lyrics," D explained. They passed the rock guys (each reportedly paid $8,000 to be there). "I take the first lyric, you take the second, I'll take the third, and we out," D told Run.

Then in the booth: "C'mon, Joe. Let's go. You go on that side. I'm here. Yeah." They did their verse, then saw Rick send Tyler in to shout all over their rhymes. After five hours' work, the song was finished. Everyone posed for a photo near the board like one big happy family. "They were so happy about it," said D.M.C. "Jay was like, 'Yo, this gonna be big.' But Run and me were like, 'These motherfuckers buggin' out. That shit's gonna flop and "My Adidas" is gonna be dope.'"

Around them, however, the older executives who managed Run-D.M.C.'s career continued to be most excited about Run-D.M.C.'s remake of the Aerosmith song, and how it could cross them over to a white audience. Run, D, and Jay were asked to film a video for the song.

The first scenes of the video involved Run-D.M.C. and Aerosmith's Steve Tyler and Joe Perry rehearsing in adjacent rooms. Tyler, holding a mike, heard Jay scratch the song's familiar guitar riff and looked confused. And before he could sing, Run and D yelled the lyric. Tyler responded by using his mike stand to smash a hole in a wall just in time to shove his head through it, and screech the chorus. As in other videos, Run and D faced a white guest star with disapproval and folded arms.

From there, the action moved to the brightly lit rock arena Park Theater in Union City, New Jersey. Onstage in a flamboyant, frilly outfit, Tyler performed for a cheering multiracial audience, and was about to sing when Run and D smashed through the back wall of the stage and started rapping again. This time, Tyler and Perry stopped what they were doing and watched these guys in sweatshirts, jeans, and unlaced Adidas. Aerosmith and Run-D.M.C. then danced together. As filming continued, Run gave Tyler a kick in the ass, Runny Ray recalled. "When they were doing the dance," he said, "that was real. Run was tired. He didn't want to do that video. But they made him."

Jam Master Jay went along with whatever Rick and Russell wanted. But Run and D were wary of how Profile would market the album. The whole point of producing *Raising Hell* themselves had been to recapture their black audience, not to do more rock-rap that might alienate rap fans and black radio stations that didn't want their rap set to rock. Run and D.M.C. called Profile directly and said "My Adidas" and "Peter Piper" should be the first single. "If y'all don't do it, we're gonna give it to radio and fuck everything up," D told them. A few executives and people close to them tried to persuade them that their audience wanted, expected, even *needed* to hear "Walk This Way" first, so they could all make a lot of money, but Run, D.M.C., and Jam Master Jay—who had agreed to record the Aerosmith song as a concession to Rick and Russell and pop radio but still wanted the group to be known for the competitive hard-core sound Jay brought to songs like "Peter Piper" and "My Adidas"—stood their ground. "We fought hard to make sure those two records were the first single," Run explained, and they finally won a battle concerning their career.

CHAPTER 16

The Mainstreaming
of Hip-hop

In June 1986 Russell and Rick were operating Rush Management and Def Jam out of 298 Elizabeth Street, a three-story building in downtown Manhattan. "It was not any kind of fancy place," said Rubin's friend Adam Dubin. "There were crack vials in the street and it was one foot from the Bowery so there were a lot of bums and drug addicts all over the place. And across the street, many drug addicts would be getting their food from a church that was a soup kitchen. It was just a run-down street." Rush Management was on the first floor. Def Jam's overcrowded offices were on the second. Rick Rubin lived on the third. The basement would supposedly hold a new, state-of-the-art recording studio.

Run-D.M.C. and Jam Master Jay used to stop by to visit Russell, Rick, or Run-D.M.C's former road manager Lyor Cohen (young, tall, white, with black hair, now working for Russell at Rush) and listen to the plan for the third Fresh Fest. Run-D.M.C. was excited. They had a great album finished, and Profile Records had already received advance orders for 600,000 copies. And at Def Jam–Rush, everyone said they loved "Peter Piper" and "My Adidas," and predicted "Walk This Way" would be the biggest thing on MTV. In fresh new outfits, new hats, and new Adidas, Run-D.M.C. met with Lyor Cohen, who reported that promoter Ricky Walker, creator of the Fresh Fest, wouldn't be involved with the new tour. Lyor (pronounced "Lee-Or") had handled negotiations, and disagreed with Walker over how much Rush should earn from each show, so Rush would do the tour without Walker. The new tour also wouldn't feature the Fat Boys (a group always managed by Charles Stettler, the music executive who discovered the group at a talent show), Kurtis Blow (who was moving to California to pursue a career in film and had severed ties with Rush Management after appearing in *Krush Groove*), or breakdancers. It would feature mostly Rush clients—Run and D, Whodini, L.L., and the Beastie Boys—and be called the Raising Hell tour.

Bun-D.M.C. didn't say anything about the Beasties being on their tour. They liked the group's new song "Hold It Now, Hit It." Instead of their usual ass-dragging drums and stiff rock chords, "Hold It Now" featured funny lyrics over a track that evoked "Rock the Bells" and "Peter Piper": "Now I just got home because I'm out on bail!" one line went. "What's the time? It's time to buy Ale!" For its chorus, Rick used samples, a blaring Kool and the Gang horn, Kurtis Blow on "Christmas Rappin'" yelling, "Hold it now," Slick Rick's "La-Di-Da-Di" cheering, "Hit It," a DJ scratching a whistle over bongos, and a sample of funk singer Jimmy Castor calling, "Yo Leroy!"

Run and D thought the Beasties were cool, and onto something with this new song. But Run and D also felt the Beasties and other Def Jam artists were imitating their sound, benefiting from an association with them, and, in some cases, riding their coattails. "Listen, 'hip-hop body rocking doing the do' from 'Hold It Now, Hit It' is rhymes from off of 'Together Forever,' " said Run. " 'Pulsating, dominating up above, cold chillin' and I'm willin', my name's Run love.' That's my flow."

Then there was L.L. Cool J, Def Jam's other big act. Run felt L.L., eighteen now, was still imitating Run-D.M.C. Run had seen L.L. perform "I Can't Live Without My Radio" and "Rock the Bells," on the March 22, 1986, episode of *Soul Train*. Run's mother, Evelyn, by his side, turned to him and said, "He's imitating you guys." And when Run-D.M.C. stopped by Def Jam's building in the city, they heard many of the young employees gossip about how L.L. had stopped by and told everyone that during the tour he would "take Run out and take the crown," said Bill Stephney, the former WBAU employee turned Def Jam publicist. " 'Cause obviously at that point, Run considered himself the king."

In the Raising Hell tour, Timex Social Club, not signed to Rush but known for their rhythm and blues song "Rumors," opened with two songs. Then the Beasties did their fifteen-minute set, including "Slow and Low" and "Hold It Now, Hit It" (then on the black singles chart). Then L.L. Cool J did a few *Radio* numbers, Whodini performed some of *Escape* and *Back in Black*, and Run-D.M.C. performed hits from their three best-selling albums (the double-sided single "My Adidas" b/w "Peter Piper" and *Raising Hell* were both released by early June 1986).

On June 21, 1986, a month into the tour, Run-D.M.C. played Philadelphia's Spectrum Arena. Lyor Cohen held a video camera. With Lyor taping his every move, Run went onstage and introduced Run-D.M.C.'s "My Adidas," then in the black singles Top 5, by yelling that he wanted the crowd of twenty thousand to remove one of their Adidas sneakers and hold them above their heads. Five thousand people did as told. Six days later, thirteen thousand excitable fans showed up to see Run-D.M.C. sign autographs at an Adidas outlet in Baltimore. The mob was so large that local authorities decided it'd be safer to close the entire mall. Along with his videotape of the June 21 concert, Lyor Cohen sent Adidas a report about the large crowd Run-D.M.C. attracted to the outlet, in the hope that the sneaker company would be interested in making them the first nonathletes signed to an endorsement deal.

As the tour continued that summer, Run and L.L. Cool J continued to go at it. Run-D.M.C.'s bodyguard Hurricane felt they were like heavyweight boxers Ali and Frazier. Said Run, "He was young, hot girls were going nuts, and I was not having it. I was trying to beat him. I was trying to make sure this kid didn't steal my shine. The crowd was cheering *very loud* for him. I had to keep him off my tail."

On tour, Run and L.L. couldn't be in the same room without arguing, and Jam Master Jay and D.M.C. stayed out of it. "I used to hang with L 'cause he would always have girls following him around," said D. And L.L. stopped by D's house one day to proudly show him his new red Audi and cry, "D! Look! I got a car, man!" After shows, D and L would hang out and talk about their careers. "Even though a lot of people thought he was arrogant, he was funny," D said. "He was normal and he kind of looked up to me 'cause I was the only guy that would talk to him sensibly. He and Run talked about competition and the business and fame. When he talked to Russell and Rick it was about music and trying to get money. When he talked to me it was just talking, being normal, and I think he needed that balance in his life."

But Run continued to resent L.L.'s new stage show. L.L. already wore a Run-like hat, tracksuit, gold chain, and sneakers. His DJ Cut Creator's glasses, gold chain, and strong, silent presence evoked Jam Master Jay. Now L.L. had a new group member, E-Love, who wore a multicolored Adidas sweatshirt, the same black mobster hat as Run-D.M.C, and a fat gold chain, and folded his arms onstage. "Oh, the fucking arms," D.M.C. chuckled. "You notice how E-Love used to stand there and just be looking like, 'I'm Bad'? That was L.L.'s D.M.C., of course. He was biting everything. He had to go make fucking love records," D said with amusement. "You know what I'm saying?"

The more Run watched L.L. take the stage with his DJ and E-Love, the angrier he felt. Finally, Run told L.L., "That's your D.M.C.! You trying to bite? Right? You trying to bite?" He kept telling him this, but E-Love continued to carry a huge radio onstage, then put it down, fold his arms, and nod (like D.M.C.) while L.L. rapped. "He needed a sidekick," Run sighed. "E-Love was his D.M.C. That was cool. I fought him."

Having three people—one with folded arms—evoked his stage show, Run felt. "Maybe that's why my mother said that," he reasoned, " 'cause he was trying to come out of them Melle Mel clothes and look like me."

Another night, promoters wanted L.L. to close the show. After L.L. ended the concert, he approached Run-D.M.C.'s amiable roadie, Runny Ray, backstage to ask, "Ray, how was I? Was I good? Did I rock the crowd? Was I def?"

Ray, supportive as ever, said, "Yeah! Hell yeah, it was def! Nigga, you rocked! You rocked!"

"Did I rock harder than Run and them?"

"Hmm, no, not that much," he said. "But you rocked though." Ray remembered having this same conversation on numerous occasions. Then L.L. started going onstage to yell, "Hollis is in the house" even though he was not from Run-D.M.C.'s neighborhood. Run accepted this, but was infuriated when L.L. started asking the crowd, "Whose house?" L.L. wanted them to say "L.L." but the crowd was accustomed to Run asking this. To L.L.'s chagrin, they would yell: "Run's house!"

Doctor Dre, on the tour as DJ for the Beastie Boys, remembered, "Run-D.M.C. was the headliner, and L.L. would go out and do their show before they'd come out." Dre saw L.L. do this every night, and thought, "What is wrong with you? You don't do that!" Saying "Hollis in the house" wasn't like using the standard, non-specific crowd-pleasing shout, "Everybody say Ho!" L.L. was taking specific things he knew Run-D.M.C. would come out and perform once he was done, said Dre. "It's not good. You have to respect people, especially when you're on their tour."

Backstage, Run was furious. He watched swaggering young L.L., his stocky DJ Cut Creator, and thin, silent E-Love enter L.L.'s dressing room. Run ran into the room, got right in L's face, and yelled, "Stop saying you're from Hollis! You ain't from motherfucking Hollis! This ain't yo' house, motherfucker! I know you're coming for my crown!" L kept doing it, D recalled, and Run kept barging into his dressing room to yell, "This is my tour!" Soon Hurricane and other Run-D.M.C. road crew employees started getting into arguments with L's crew while trying to separate Run and L.

y the Fourth of July, Jam Master Jay called his cousin Doc in Brooklyn to say, "We're fighting every day, man. It's getting really crazy out here."

In addition to backstage drama, Run-D.M.C. was contending with jealous tough guys in every town. "Because these successful MCs are coming to *your town* where you've been living all your life," Jay's cousin Doc explained. "And these guys had been trying to get at 'Mary Sue' for the last five, ten years and couldn't get 'em. But these new rap guys step in one day, so of course there's jealousy. And that's the worst, when you have to fight your own people for your success. They call it 'crabs in the barrel.' Every positive black man trying to be successful has another trying to pull him down."

Five weeks into the tour, *Raising Hell* matched *King of Rock*'s sales of 1 million. One night when Run and D left the stage, a Rush Management employee asked if they had heard about "Walk This Way." They didn't know what he was talking about.

"They put 'Walk This Way' out last week," the man explained. Run asked, "Huh?"

"Did you hear it's the number one most requested song in Boston?"

"On what station? The black station or what?"

"No, it's a whole other thing going on." Radio station WBCN in Boston played it first, then yanked it after white listeners called in to shout racial epithets and label the rap version of an Aerosmith classic sacrilegious. But then, when the song emerged as WBCN's most-requested song of the week, the station immediately started playing it again. "You're up to 1.5 million in sales."

Run told D, "Man we'll go platinum like regular."

"We were like, 'Aw, they're buggin',' " D.M.C. recalled. "We didn't care."

But within a week, someone told them *Raising Hell*'s sales had climbed to 1.8 million. "How?" Run asked. Other influential stations and MTV had sat up and taken notice.

"They did whatever they wanted with it and made it a smash," Run said. "We looked up and it was selling more. Then next thing you know this thing caught on and took us beyond our dreams in sales."

Run-D.M.C. were busy touring and hadn't even been told the song would be their next single. Though "Walk This Way" became the first Run-D.M.C. single to appear on *Billboard*'s pop chart (at number 4), and continued—along with the Raising Hell tour—to attract more Americans to rap music, D.M.C. worried that its classic rock sound would disaffect the black audience they wanted to recapture. He feared that fans would cry "sellout" until he heard "Walk This Way" included in mixes of hip-hop records aired every Friday and Saturday night on New York rap station WRKS (KISS-FM). "Red Alert started playin' it," said D. "That's all we cared about: what the motherfucking b-boys were gonna think. Our whole shit was 'All right, they want to go after white people with "Walk This Way," let them. Just don't let it fuck with our b-boy Cold Crush shit. If it would, then we don't want that shit. That's why me and Run were like, 'We got to put out "Peter Piper" and "Adidas" so people don't get thrown off.'"

With *Raising Hell,* they had created an album's worth of classic material (humor on "Perfection," metal on the title track, black history on "Proud to Be Black," and hard-core on "My Adidas," "Peter Piper," and "Hit It Run"); but now, with the song on rock radio, all reporters wanted to ask about was "Walk This Way." "They didn't like that," said Runny Ray. "Reporters were trying to bring back Aerosmith. That's why."

Soon, someone from Rush Management called to say, "Y'all at two million," D recalled. "We had to fly home and do a photo shoot to put in *Billboard.*" The magazine announced that *Raising Hell* had become the first multimillion-selling rap album. For a photo that would run with the caption "Two Million," D and Run stood near each other and each held two fingers up like a wartime sign for victory. But they didn't really care. They were too busy planning the next album, asking each other, "What are we gonna do? Let's make some more beats."

The tour kept going, and on July 18, 1986, they rode the tour bus to Manhattan to play Madison Square Garden—the biggest arena in town—and earn about $100,000 for two hours' work. Someone from Rush let them know, "Yo, this guy named Angelo Anastasio's gonna be coming." Anastasio was a young executive from Adidas who wanted to explore the possibility of making Run-D.M.C. the first nonathletes to endorse the popular footwear brand. An Adidas endorsement deal would be big, but Run-D.M.C. didn't alter their behavior in any way. On the tour bus after a concert at the Spectrum in Philly, they drank heavily. Run-D.M.C. didn't think partying before their concert, with the Adidas executive in the audience, would jeopardize an endorsement deal. They weren't that shrewd or concerned with earning money from side projects. The potential Adidas deal was an idea from Rush Management, and if it went through and they did get money for endorsing sneakers they already enjoyed wearing, they would appreciate the deal and the prestige it brought the group. But Run-D.M.C. were focused primarily on creating music that satisfied their fans. Run-D.M.C. were happy that fans had reacted positively to the hard-core sound Run, D, and Jay had created for many of *Raising Hell*'s songs, and happy about being able to keep earning money by performing for adoring fans nationwide.

Run-D.M.C.'s tour bus reached Manhattan before dawn. The group checked into a high-end hotel, and opened fresh bottles of Olde English 800. The sun was rising when D told his boys, "Yo, it's time to go to bed." He closed his eyes but woke up after only two hours to head to the Garden for a sound check. At the arena, D.M.C. accepted a morning beer from one of his friends and practiced a few songs. Then he returned to his hotel room to drink some Olde E, smoke some weed, then order numerous cheeseburgers, fries, and desserts from room service. Then Run-D.M.C. headed to the Garden. Walking down Eighth Avenue, searching for an entrance to the sprawling complex, they saw lines of teenagers waiting to get in.

With an hour to go before they took the stage, Run left the dressing room and went to look at the crowd. Standing backstage where they couldn't see him, he was stunned. The place was packed. Hurricane sidled up to him and said, instead of telling the crowd this was Run's house, as Run always did, why not say, "I beg your pardon, but this is my motherfucking Garden." Run thought it was a great idea.

Onstage, Run, D, and Jay heard deafening applause and watched a huge light swing over the audience. D saw rows of people stretch all the way to the Garden's far-off rear wall. Run held the mike. "Tonight I walked in here and they wouldn't let me in the back door," he began. He tossed nearby security guards a dirty look. "And I said, 'I beg your pardon . . . but this is Run's motherfucking Garden!'" The crowd roared. They did a few songs and then Run once again started "My Adidas" by demanding, "Hold your Adidas in the air!" This time, twenty thousand people obeyed. Even Run was awed by the sight of so many three-striped sneakers being held aloft, swaying from left to right.

As soon as they left the stage, the affable, Ferrari-driving Angelo Anastasio asked, "You guys want an endorsement deal?"

Later that night Run entered a limo by himself. He would head home to his wife and his two-year-old daughter, Vanessa. He considered how he was only twenty-one and about to have Adidas create a Run-D.M.C. clothing line. "Russell and them pulled it off," he said. He told the limo driver that he'd have his signature on a sneaker, and about the lines outside the Garden, the nonstop applause during every song, the sneakers waving. Everything was going his way, he said. Like a dream come true. "I was out on the Raising Hell tour. It was crazy. It was a big time in my life. The deal called for us to make our own line of sneakers. We had our own line before anybody." The car stopped in Hollis that night. Run thanked the driver and gave him a $100 tip, then went inside. The next morning he visited his father, who held up his copy of the morning newspaper. With silent amazement, Run looked at a photo of himself holding a mike and rocking the Garden.

They signed the deal with Adidas and received gold Adidasshaped medallions to attach to their chains. Even their bodyguard Hurricane got one, but his was small, so he turned it into a ring. And everyone received piles of Adidas sneakers and athletic wear. The media reported on a seven-figure deal and about how, instead of the usual blue box with white stripes, Adidas would package the new Run-D.M.C. sneaker in black boxes that featured the group's red and white logo. They were the envy of everyone in the rap music industry. But Run and D knew the deal wasn't as lucrative for them personally as some media reports claimed. While reporters implied they were swimming in millions, D said, "They basically gave us a little bit of money and put most of the money into the tour."

CHAPTER 17

War and Peace

Between concerts during August 1986, D and his Hollis Crew boys hung out on Run-D.M.C.'s bus. Run and Jay partied with the Beastie Boys on the white group's tour bus. "Run was around a lot, actually," said Ad Rock. "They were very funny people, those guys." On their bus, the Beasties held one party after another and listened to demo tapes of the Beasties' first album in progress.

Run and Jay soon started "giving them a lot of advice about what they need to do for the album," said Doctor Dre, then DJing for the Beasties. "'Cause Run, D, and Jay—Jay a lot more—knew what the Beasties needed to make it go."

D.M.C. began to feel two of the Beastie Boys didn't like him much. He didn't understand why. He always thought the Beasties were cool. He had let them attend *King of Rock* sessions, let them have the song "Slow and Low," and let them hang out while Run-D.M.C. recorded parts of *Raising Hell*.

Ad Rock wasn't the problem, he felt. It was the other two. D.M.C. wondered if they were angry with him for not partying on their bus, drinking Budweiser with them, playing Nintendo, or rushing to join them in a photograph or homemade video they were filming.

He first began wondering whether they disliked him when Run told him some disturbing news. Run was high, D recalled, and told D that he'd been sitting around smoking weed with the Beasties. "He just out of nowhere said, 'The Beasties said your fucking rhymes are corny,' " D recalled. D was confused. Then Run added that the Beasties were gonna say this to his face, too. "Then why the fuck they imitating me?" D thought. "They're fucking clones! I was like, 'Damn,' " D recalled. "I was *hurt*. How could they say this? They up in my face every day; we're fucking showing them the ropes, opening the door for them, putting them on, and they're gonna say that."

On Run-D.M.C.'s tour bus, D played some of his own music and told himself, "None of my rhymes are corny." And when the Beastie Boys tried to say what's up, he'd only nod. He waited for them to criticize his lyrics to his face, as Run claimed they would. "You know . . . I love Run but it's like Run's nuts," said Ad Rock. "If he said that, that's nuts. D.M.C. is not Chuck D; he's not 'whoever'; he's not Nas. But he's D.M.C. from Run-D.M.C. He's one of the heroes of all time. We would never say that. There would be no reason to say that. I hope D knows that."

The Raising Hell tour continued. The Beasties approached Jay one day, anxious because their DJ, Dre, was leaving. "W-what should we do?" one member asked.

Jay calmly replied, "Cane. Hurricane can do it." Jay, Run, and

Russell knew Cane had skills, and asked Dre if it'd be all right if Cane took over. Dre told Hurricane he should do it. "I'm not doing that!" Hurricane yelled. "I'm with fucking Run-D.M.C. You're not gonna get me out here DJing for these white guys acting crazy! I ain't doing it."

But Russell led a choir of people saying, "C'mon, Cane, you can do it, man!" Then Dre came back. "Come on, Cane, be there for me, man. . . . Do it for them, man. Fuck it, just do it."

Cane said, "All right, kid. I'll do it."

Before his first show, Hurricane covered his bald head with a baseball cap and pulled it down low. He further disguised himself with a pair of shades. "So nobody would even notice me," he explained. Onstage, he played "Hold It Now," "She's on It," and "Slow and Low."

After the show, Run, D, and Jay joined the crowd that mobbed him backstage. Everyone said, "Yo, kid, you rocked it," and Hurricane looked proud. Newspapers reported that they were a united family, that Hurricane joining the Beasties strengthened the bond between groups, and races. But Hurricane was still "Jay's man," Ad Rock recalled. He wouldn't ride with the Beasties. "I'm not sleeping near you guys," he told them. Instead, he slept on one of the twelve beds on Run-D.M.C.'s bus.

CHAPTER 18

The Long Beach Episode

They arrived in Long Beach, California, on August 17, 1986, to perform the fifty-sixth of sixty-four concerts. At the Long Beach Arena, they did a sound check, performing a few songs for the sound engineer at his board amid rows of metal chairs in the audience. "I had my forty-dogs on ice, a new suit, and a haircut," D later remembered. "I was ready to have fun!" When they left the arena, they saw drivers standing near vans and limos outside, and heard one person warn, "Yo, it's gonna be ill today! I'm telling ya, it's gon' be ill."

That night they returned to the arena and saw nine cops on motorcycles and nine on foot. Inside, Whodini was backstage. The members of Run-D.M.C. slapped them all five and wished them luck. The show began and Run, D, and Jay observed from the side stage, watching L.L. perform a few energetic numbers. While he performed, a few gang members marched down an aisle, stood in front of the stage, and waved their fingers, curled into gang signs. Then gangsters jumped on the stage during L's set. "Security grabbed them off the stage," said Runny Ray. "But L.L. was shaking like a leaf."

And that wasn't all. During an intermission, a few people in the crowd started fighting each other. Hurricane recalled that backstage "the show's promoters were debating about whether Whodini should go on. The promoters said let them. It might calm [the crowd]. Whodini did about two records at the most and had to stop." The entire crowd started fighting, or trying to escape nearby brawls. "People were trying to come up on the stage again to get whoever was up there," said Ray. "They were beating the sound-man in the audience, throwing chairs."

The houselights came on but the fighting continued. Jalil of Whodini, standing onstage with mike in hand, begged the crowd to stop fighting, but gang members tore legs off chairs and bashed people. Gunshots went off. Eight security guards chased kids in one direction, then ran in the other with eighty kids after them. Some-one was thrown off the balcony. Other concertgoers tried to run but were trapped in the crowd with club-wielding attackers ap-proaching. In anguish, D.M.C. yelled, "Oh, shit! Look at that, Ray! Oh, shit! Damn!"

As the riot continued, D.M.C. stood onstage, helpless, while more of his group's fans were hurt. D.M.C. heard Ray yell, "Oh, shit! You see that? Get the hell out! Yo, homeboy, you better run!" Certain sights stood out. One guy led his girlfriend toward some empty seats; the gang leader saw him do that, ran over, and pum-meled him without mercy. Other people were bleeding. They saw someone club a woman in the head. "I felt like crying," Ray said. "I think I probably did cry. That was the worse show I ever been at."

After ten minutes, security led Run-D.M.C. backstage and into the dressing room. Former Miss America Vanessa Williams, who was in the audience, arrived in their dressing room, in tears. Her body-guard and manager followed, saying, "We don't know what's going on out there!" Then Lyor Cohen, accompanying Run-D.M.C. as road manager from Rush, entered and slammed the door shut. "It's crazy out there!" he said. "Oh, my God. They're killing each other."

A security guard's radio said, "We're losing it! We're losing it!" Then a guard entered, sweating, wide-eyed with terror. "Yo, don't lock the door."

"Why not?" D asked.

" 'Cause when they come back here, I'm coming in with y'all!"

Jay and D looked at each other before tearing legs off chairs and holding them up like clubs. Security shoved the group Whodini into the room. Rapper Jalil numbly said, "We went out there and they just started fightin', man. We were in the middle of our song. And I looked up and I seen a guy come off the top of the balcony down to the floor. I know he got to be dead."

Gangsters tried to get backstage, but guards held them back by erecting a barricade in a narrow doorway. At 11:02 p.m., three hours after the crowd began to fight, police arrived. Sixty cops in riot gear marched through the arena with nightsticks. Within fifteen minutes, the place was empty. A security guard said Run-D.M.C. and the other performers could leave. On the way out, Run-D.M.C. observed the arena floor. It was covered with blood, chair legs, torn chains, jackets, purses, food, sneakers, and chairs torn from bolts.

At the hotel, they watched the news on television. Newscasters kept saying rap music caused the riot; forty-five fans were in hospitals; one was shot; four were arrested; five were stabbed. At 2:00 a.m., their management representatives told Run-D.M.C. that they'd have to go to a radio station in three hours to defend themselves against media reports accusing them of inciting violence at the Long Beach Arena. The radio interview was a hastily arranged appearance that would hopefully prevent reporters from tarnishing the group's name and scaring promoters in other cities into canceling shows, which would lead to Run-D.M.C. losing income. The group also learned that with controversy brewing about their lyrics, their next scheduled concert, the next night at the local club the Palladium, was canceled.

Their publicist, Tracy Miller, new to Profile's staff and a Run-D.M.C. fan since 1983, encouraged Russell to have Run-D.M.C. meet with reporters and set the record straight. They organized a press conference, held the day after the concert, and Run told reporters, "Those kids have nothing to do with Run-D.M.C. They're scumbags and roaches and they would have hit me in the head, too." He added that gangs were "running" L.A., and he wouldn't come back "until the local authorities get the problem under control."

The mood on the Raising Hell tour darkened. "I mean everybody was depressed about how fucked up it was, 'cause it was crazy," said Ad Rock of the Beastie Boys. "It wasn't just 'wilin' at a show.' It was some full-scale shit. And it was crazy. So people were depressed. Run and them were banned from places."

Though they didn't actually perform the night of the riot, reporters kept blaming Run-D.M.C. for the violence. "They were trying to blame us for something the politicians and the powers that be can't control," said D.M.C. They kept touring, and urged reporters to "Go check the album." None of their lyrics, they explained, were violent.

But without warning, Kurtis Blow told a reporter they did encourage violence.

Since his 1984 album *Ego Trip*, Kurt's fans had abandoned him, ignoring his 1985 album *America*, his 1986 work, *Kingdom Blow*, and his current single, "I'm Chillin'." When Long Island, New York, daily newspaper *Newsday* asked Kurt about Run-D.M.C. and rap music, Kurt said, "Those lyrics are bad. 'Time to get ill' means go crazy, time to stomp somebody's face off. What Run-D.M.C. is doing is perpetrating, acting like they're tough gangster kids when they're not. And the kids see Run acting that way, so they try to be gangsters."

Run was furious with his former mentor. And D.M.C. felt, "Kurt was agreeing 'cause we were busting his ass. It was a way to hopefully have reporters write us off so he could move back into the limelight. But we were too powerful for that bullshit."

Their fans knew the media had it wrong and continued to support them. And Run found distraction from negative coverage in the studio, working on a demo he hoped Michael Jackson would include on his next album. "Run wanted to do it 'cause Michael was the biggest star in the world and Run wanted to be the biggest star," said Hurricane.

Run and Jam Master Jay created a great track that would have their *Thriller* idol sounding like Jesse D of Staten Island rap-singing group the Force MDs, a rapper who wore a black suit, a glove, and shades, and, Run recalled, "used to skip around and act like Michael." With this new song, Run explained, "We were gonna try to put Michael on a fly beat, have him sing over a b-boy beat."

After Hurricane helped with the demo, Jay told the Beasties' new bandmate, "Go in there and sing the hook."

Hurricane said, "Nigga, I can't sing! Whatchu talking 'bout?"

"Man, just sing it so [Michael] could know what to sing by the time we get there."

With a sigh, Hurricane entered the booth and sang. "Terrible," he sighed. "Just something so he could hear the idea. We sent it off to him." Michael Jackson's people then invited Run-D.M.C. to L.A.

They returned to Los Angeles the second week of October 1986. *Raising Hell* had sold well over 2 million copies. Major rock music magazines credited "Walk This Way" with bringing rap to the mainstream. And *Rolling Stone* was doing a cover story. *Rolling Stone*'s freelance writer Ed Kiersh accompanied them to an appearance at a radio station, where the group spoke out against gangs and defended themselves against charges that they were to blame for the Long Beach riot. Run was happy to have the cover—an honor reserved for rock bands—but also resented the fact that the magazine chose this particular moment to give them the cover. "The only reason I got the cover of *Rolling Stone* was because of the fight in Long Beach," he felt.

Things were still going well for Run-D.M.C. They remained the top-selling group in rap. Technics turntables wanted them to sign an endorsement deal. Adidas was creating a clothing line. Jay and D had diamond rings on every finger and partied in every town. But Run was weary of touring: He liked the money (it bought him a 1966 Oldsmobile and a new Riviera) but he needed a break. He wanted to spend more time with his now three-year-old daughter, Vanessa; he wanted to sit down and write rhymes, to wax his car like a normal guy, to drive wife Valerie to the doctor's office where she worked, to call Jay and work on the next album. Instead, in his swanky $750-a-night penthouse suite at the Stouffer airport hotel on October 9, 1986, he told the writer from *Rolling Stone* they were positive role models with a clean image.

Outside the hotel, preparing to go for a head-clearing drive, Run looked uneasy. While he was telling the reporter Kiersh that Run-D.M.C. were there to urge gangs to form a truce, a black cop cut across a throng of businesswomen and extended his hand. "Boy, is my son a fan of yours! All because of you he wants to be a DJ. I just bought him a mixer."

Eyeing his gun and badge, Run said that's how he had started. "DJing and playing basketball. Give your son the word: DJing is good, it's def. Tell your son you were hanging out with me."

"I will, I will! My son will go wild about this."

The valet arrived with Run's rented black Corvette. Behind the wheel, Run reached for the phone to call Valerie. For ten minutes they talked; then he promised he'd call later that night. "I have to go for a ride to clear the bees out of my head," he told the writer. "Later I'll get in the Jacuzzi. That way I can get my brain together. I have to decide if I want to hang out with Michael. I just don't know, I . . ." He stomped on the gas, tires squealed, and he left the writer behind at around noon.

e saw the writer again at the press conference at all-rap radio station KDAY later that same afternoon, but turned away from Kiersh while shaking his hand. "What type of article is this gonna be anyway?" he asked.

After the conference, Run said he didn't want the writer to join them at McDonald's, where he, D, Jay, and their entourage would eat lunch, and perhaps discuss their true feelings and worries about the media and articles about Long Beach, or enjoy a respite from the controversy. They met again in his penthouse suite, but Run fixed him with a "long, hard stare," sat in a chair by a window, rolled his hat around in his hands, and stared at the city outside. Asked about Kurtis Blow's recent comments to *Newsday,* Run said, "Kurt tried to ruin us. He's so jealous. He never had a Gold album in his life. He's disgusting."

Kiersh continued to question Run exclusively while D and Jay watched the interview from the sidelines. Within minutes, Kiersh then asked Run about "Walk This Way." Run voiced his frustration with people "nagging" him about the song. "Everyone's talking about crossovers. 'Hey, son, didn't you do this to get more radio play?' I hope nobody wants to talk to me next year. I'm ready for a flop."

Jay and D watched him talk. "You know why?" Run added. "If everybody is nagging me about 'Walk This Way,' they can get my dick head." He banged his fist on a table. "You know why? I made that record because I used to rap over it when I was twelve." He warned black rappers not to record rock-rap. "You have to do what's real," he said.

That night, Russell joined Run and D at the studio where they'd meet Michael Jackson. Jay and Hurricane arrived late. Everyone was excited. "We were like, oh shit, Michael Jackson coming, that's dope!" said Hurricane. Mike entered the room wearing a surgeon's mask. "I don't know why he came like that," said Ray. "Like we got germs." He also had a pet chimpanzee named Bubbles with him. He shook everyone's hand. "How y'all doing?" Then he made Russell shake Bubbles's hand.

Run got along with Michael Jackson better than D.M.C. did. Jackson stared at Run's chest and said, "Oh those gold chains are so beautiful. Right, Mary?" ("Or whoever," D quipped: Mary was a cook preparing plates of fried chicken and rice in the background.) "Can I try it on?" Jackson added.

Run removed the chain and handed it over.

"Wow," Michael said while slipping it on.

"He was amazed," D remembered. "Like a little kid."

While Mary prepared their meals, Michael told them he loved "King of Rock," "Peter Piper," and "Sucker MCs." They discussed collaborating on a project but had different ideas about what to do: Run wanted him to record the song they'd submitted; Jackson preferred that they costar in a Martin Scorsese–directed video for "I'm Bad."

While they talked, Ray said, "the monkey was jumping around the table, grabbing things. It was crazy." And Run began to look a little annoyed, said Runny Ray. "At first it looked like he liked [Michael] but after a while, he didn't want to hear what he was saying anymore."

Mary served plates of chicken and rice. They were eating, said

*R*un-D.M.C. at the Thirty-first Annual Grammy Awards in New York City on March 2, 1988. From left: Joseph "Run" Simmons, Darryl "D.M.C." McDaniels, and Jason "Jam Master Jay" Mizell. *(AP/Wide World Photos)*

Members of rap group Run-D.M.C. on the road between Virginia and New York, 1986. (Eli Reed/Magnum Photos)

Joseph "Run" Simmons; his father, Daniel Simmons; and Darryl "D.M.C." McDaniels at Daniel's home in Hollis, September 1986. (Eli Reed/Magnum Photos)

*R*un-D.M.C. and the Beastie Boys pose atop a restaurant in mid-town Manhattan on May 11, 1987. The two groups held a news con-ference to announce their forty-city Together Forever Tour, which kicked off in Hawaii on June 12, 1987. Front row, left to right: Jason "Jam Master Jay" Mizell, Joseph "Run" Simmons, and Davy D. Back row, left to right: Mike D, Darryl "D.M.C." McDaniels, King Ad-Rock, and MCA. *(AP/Wide World Photos)*

In New York City, April 5, 2001. The once-mighty rap pioneers were attempting a comeback with their new album. (AP/Wide World Photos)

Run-D.M.C. arrive for the MTV Video Music Awards at New York's Radio City Music Hall, August 29, 2002. (AP/Wide World Photos)

*R*un-D.M.C. create handprints in cement as they are inducted into Hollywood's RockWalk in Los Angeles on February 25, 2002. The group produced the first rap album to go gold and was the first rap act nominated for a Grammy Award. *(AP/Wide World Photos)*

*T*he casket of Jam Master Jay is carried from his funeral service in Jamaica, Queens, on November 5, 2002. *(AP/ Wide World Photos)*

As police officers guarded the entrance to the studio where Jam Master Jay was killed on October 30, 2002, a makeshift memorial took shape, including an Adidas sneaker, with "R.I.P. JMJ" written on it, in memory of "My Adidas," one of Run-D.M.C.'s best-known songs. *(AP/Wide World Photos)*

Hurricane, when "the monkey kind of, like jumped on Jay, caught Jay off guard. So Jay damn near threw the monkey to the ground, like, Yo!"

Michael cried, "Bubbles!" Then, according to Ray, Michael added, "Money, you can't do that here."

Jay answered, "Well, your monkey tried to bite the shit out of me. What you want me to do?"

Michael cooed, "Come on, Bubbles, come on, baby." He still wanted to work with them.

When Run saw the *Rolling Stone* writer again, he couldn't stop praising Michael. "He's the best man in the world," Run said. He described the meeting and said Run-D.M.C. would appear on Michael Jackson's new anticrack song, and in his video. "The whole thing was just great. Michael kept asking me about rap. I asked him about record sales. And when the fried chicken came, I knew he was cool."

Back in New York, *Rolling Stone* called them in for a photo shoot. "And everybody was making a big deal of it," D.M.C. remembered. They posed for the photo. "And we were like 'Could you hurry up, man? We want to go.' We didn't know when we came in how big it was." But once they saw a few framed covers on each wall—including some with the Beatles—D thought, "Whoa, this is large."

CHAPTER 19

It's the New Style

The Long Beach controversy subsided, and Run-D.M.C. was able to breathe a little easier. Promoters kept booking them for concerts. Their Adidas line was about to arrive in stores. *Raising Hell* continued to sell. Other rappers were releasing records, but Run-D.M.C. was still the genre's most successful and best-loved group. On a personal level, they had money to spend on new cars, fur coats, and jewelry, and—for Jay and Run—to support their families. (Jay and his live-in girlfriend, Lee, were expecting their first child.)

While touring in 1986 Run agreed to write a song for the Beastie Boys album. "It was a family thing," Run explained. He asked D to help: "D, I need you there to help me write this record for the

Beasties. I'm producing it." Since D had forgotten about Run's claim that the Beasties had insulted D's lyrics, and since D liked seeing the Beasties perform intricate routines, he said no problem.

For a year now, Rick Rubin (with longer hair and a thicker beard) had spent many of his nights in Chung King Studios in downtown Manhattan, creating the Beasties' debut. "We just tried to make music that we loved, for ourselves," said Rick. They were taking their time, to ensure the album had diversity. They'd write and record a song, then return six weeks later to create another. "By taking so long, it really gave it a breadth and depth that's different from a typical album, where an artist has six weeks to write their songs for a record."

The Beasties' influences included rappers like Run-D.M.C., the Furious Five, and the Funky Four; punk rock groups like the Ramones and the Sex Pistols; and reggae artists Bob Marley and the group Big Youth. Another influence was rapper Schooly D, and he and the Beasties would popularize a new style called gangsta rap. A former shoe salesman from Philadelphia, Schooly D (J. B. Weaver) filled his self-released singles "Gucci Time" and "P.S.K." with violent and preposterous descriptions of gunplay and lyrics about Philadelphia's infamous Park Side Killers gang. After hearing Schooly's music, the Beasties decided to rap like Schooly on a few songs. The Beasties described how one person shot another in the face on "Scenario," threatened to smash someone's glasses on "It's the New Style," and promised to kill MCs with a "big shotgun" on "Rhyming and Stealing." "We were definitely trying to get that sound on a couple of songs," Ad Rock recalled, so when rapper Chuck D of WBAU offered a lyric called "Too Much Posse," about a Schooly-like gang, Ad remembered, "We recorded it. But our version was terrible."

Sessions usually started with Rick and engineer Steve Ett setting up the beats. While the Beasties wrote rhymes, Rick would program the drum tracks before trying different guitar sounds and samples. "It was a lot of trial and error," said Rubin's friend Adam

Dubin. After the Beasties recorded vocals, Rick then suggested changes. "You know how on the Beastie Boys records, each guy has his part?" Dubin asked. "How they trade off vocals and each guy does his part? Rick would actually instruct them. Not all the time. They also knew what to do. But Rick would tell Ad Rock for instance, 'Okay, now do the higher, more Jerry Lewis–sounding voice on this word.' He'd tell rapper MCA, 'Okay, you do this part.'" Said Ad Rock: "We all just did it together. He was like the fourth member of the group." And where Run and D had producers sometimes micromanaging their sessions, "Not that much thought went into like what songs meant," said Ad Rock.

The Beasties' song "Time to Get Ill" presented a sample-heavy wall of sound that included the guitar chord from "Rock the Bells," Schooly D's voice ("Looking at my Gucci it's about that time"), TV talking horse Mr. Ed singing his name, and someone scratching the theme from *Green Acres*. "That was just like a routine record," Ad explained. "Posse in Effect" used slow drums, the horn from "Catch a Groove," and the beat from rapper Joe Ski Luv's popular "Pee-Wee Herman" single. And for its finale, Rick threw in an entirely different track and a crowd chanting, as crowds in rap clubs did, "Brooklyn, ho!" For this one, they wanted to "make some real b-boy records with some 808." Their song "Brass Monkey" used horns from an obscure break beat and discussed "getting fucked up. That's a summertime jam," Ad continued. "Girls" was a sprightly ditty about women who would cook and clean for them, set to marimba vibes. Def Jam wanted "Slow Ride," and its samples from War's bongo-heavy "Low Rider," to be the single. Then Run and D heard "It's the New Style," a disjointed beat, a guitar chord, a swelling synthesizer flourish (almost like a siren), then Run and D's chant "There it is" (from "Peter Piper"), the Beasties yelling "Kick it," and a funky beat from the B-Boys' lesser-known rap single "2, 3, Break." "We wanted to do a rap song that had two different tempos," said Ad. "Nobody had done that before."

Then they had rock-rap that made "Walk This Way" sound tame. "We had definitely been inspired by Run-D.M.C.," Ad recalled. "A lot of the idea of doing rock and rap came from 'Rock Box' and 'King of Rock.' "

"Rhyming and Stealing" found them rapping about being the most illin'est b-boys over a thunderous AC/DC guitar and slowed-down Led Zeppelin beat. "She's Crafty" was about a larcenous one-night stand and included a Zeppelin guitar. "No Sleep Till Brooklyn" was their "road song," a rap equivalent of Motorhead's *No Sleep Till Hammersmith* that had them yell over the drum solo from Queen's classic "We Will Rock You," and roaring guitar by Rick's new Def Jam signing, Slayer.

But "Fight for Your Right" was their strongest, most commercial rock number. They wrote the song on a napkin, in five minutes, while drinking vodka and grapefruit juice in the Mike Todd Room at the Palladium nightclub. A spoof of metal hits like "Smoking in the Boys Room" and "I Want to Rock," "Fight for Your Right" featured Rick's droning metal riff over crashing rock drums.

"I was amazed," D.M.C. said of hearing the Beasties' then-unreleased album. "It was so much fun. I was like 'Oh wow' at everything they were doing. I liked a lot of the beats, too. I was kind of jealous. I'm a real rock fan, and wanted some of that rock shit they did, like 'No Sleep Till Brooklyn' and the shit where they sampled 'Back in Black.' I was jealous. I ain't gonna lie."

Run had mixed emotions about the Beastie Boys' album in progress. During the Raising Hell tour, he had handed them a few lyrics, like "From an apple to a peach to a cherry to a plum." Now, many of the Beasties' songs seemed to evoke their record-breaking *Raising Hell:* sharing sentences, b-boy themes, certain drum sounds, the Cerrone "Rock it" chant, even their voices from "Peter Piper." "A lot of stuff was inspired by us, period," said Run.

There were similarities between the two Rubin-produced works, but, D.M.C. noted, "The Beasties *also* knew about old school. The Beasties knew about Treacherous Three and Bam-baataa and what they did on the tapes. They knew about break beats. It wasn't anything new to them. We just showed them how to utilize it."

In late October 1986, Run and D arranged to meet the Beasties at what Beastie member Ad Rock called "this weird studio on Twenty-something Street." The Beasties were on time, waiting out front on a stoop and excited about actually writing a song with Run-D.M.C. But three hours later, they were still on the stoop "waiting for these fucking guys to show up," said Ad. "We're just talking and sitting there drinking beers. Then we hear somebody scream-ing. We turn the corner and it's Run at like midnight running down the street toward us, screaming, 'Here's a little story I got to tell, about three bad brothers you know so well; started way back in his-tory: Ad Rock, MCA, and me, Mike D.' "

Run and D shook the Beasties' hands (Jay wasn't with them), and then they all entered the building that housed the recording stu-dio they'd work in this night. Run claimed to have handed the Beasties a new idea. "They don't claim this but I for a fact turned the beat backward on 'Paul Revere,' " he said. He did it, he contin-ued, because he used to turn Kurtis Blow's old record "Do the Do" backward on his turntable and enjoy the unearthly sound reversing the record produced. "So I used to turn that around backward and it sounded so fly and I did that for Rick and the Beasties."

Ad Rock, however, disputed this. "It was definitely *not* Run's idea," he said. "It was MCA's idea." And when MCA did it, "Run and everybody in the room" looked at MCA "like he had just in-vented the wheel," Ad Rock added.

Once the beat was ready, they added scratches that evoked the hectic sound Jam Master Jay had produced for Run-D.M.C.'s 1983 single "Jam Master Jay." But in this case, they added a horn blast with the "Yeah" scratched on T La Rock's "It's Yours." Said Run, "I scratched it with my hand." He probably did, said Ad Rock, but then Rick Rubin replaced it with other scratches. "Me and Rick did all the scratching on *Licensed to Ill,*" he added. Whether these later scratches included ideas created by Run is not clear.

The song was finished, and Ad Rock decided to call it "Paul Revere." The title, he said, came "from that *Guys and Dolls* movie. Like 'I got a horse right here, his name is Paul Revere.' "

Run didn't mind helping the Beasties with their album. For Run-D.M.C., helping the Beasties was akin to helping Def Jam, which they had done during the two years that Russell and Rick Rubin's label had been in existence. They had let L.L. tour with them and write a song; let Rick Rubin produce their albums; let Russell try to get them off Profile and onto his label; written two songs for the Beasties; recorded another Def Jam act's pro-black song; brought the label the Hollis Crew and "It's the Beat"; steered Rick Rubin to Chuck D's demo tape "Public Enemy No. 1"; and even worn Def Jam jackets to public appearances. Now Rick and Russell wanted Run-D.M.C. to help get another new company off the ground.

CHAPTER 20

Def Pictures

It started in the fall of 1986 with Rick and Russell telling Run-D.M.C. they'd be making another movie. "I was probably so drunk I didn't know what was going on," D.M.C. admitted. "I just remember all of a sudden 'we're making a movie.'"

Though the all-star movie *Krush Groove* was based on their lives and included many of their artists and songs, Rick and Russell had received a small percentage of profits from the 1985 box-office hit ($15,000 each for acting in the film). They felt that producer George Jackson, who died in 2001, had made minimal contributions to the film but had received the lion's share of the profits. "So Rick and Russell said, 'Well, this is bullshit! Somebody else is making all the money from rap. *We* should make a movie, put our artists and music in it, make the money, and control everything,'" said Rick's friend Adam Dubin, who worked with Rick during this period. Rick and Russell had also been unhappy with Jackson so expanding the Fat Boys' subplot that the obese trio's comic antics threatened to dominate *Krush Groove,* something Jackson did after negotiating a deal with Warner Brothers, midway through filming of Run-D.M.C.'s first movie, for a Fat Boys vehicle called *Disorderlies.* Rubin convinced Russell they should start their own film studio, Def Pictures, then told an old pal, NYU film student Ric Menello, "You should write this script."

Menello warned, "Man, [filming a movie] is gonna be expensive," but Rick and Russell decided it would be worth it and paid him to turn a story idea by Lyor Cohen and publicist Bill Adler into a screenplay. "It was this romantic-comedy musical, *Krush Groove,* with this little murder mystery thrown in where their friend gets killed and they solve the mystery," said Menello. "But there was no real action in it."

Michael Jackson's celebrated producer, Quincy Jones, heard about the movie, Menello recalled, "and originally offered to get the money and produce it for a few million." But Jones didn't think Rick Rubin, a first-time director, should helm the project, since Run-D.M.C. had acted in only one other film. The screenwriter suggested that they hire Bill Duke, who had directed *A Rage in Harlem,* but Rubin wouldn't relinquish the director's chair.

An executive from New Line Pictures somehow got his hands on a copy of the script (someone connected to the project, never identified, passed it to the film studio). After reading it, the film executive approached the screenwriter. "He explained why New Line could give the film more care than a bigger distributor, and wanted the film based on the script," said Ric Menello. "I told him Rick and Russell weren't making any deals until the film was finished." Rick and Russell decided that Rick, Russell, Run, D, and Jay would handle production costs.

Run-D.M.C. was excited about the prospect of Def Pictures earning them more money. Run and D felt that Profile wasn't paying them what they deserved as a platinum-selling act, and that they should have received more for their starring roles in *Krush Groove* than the $15,000 they had had to split with Jam Master Jay (who also starred in the film). Jam Master Jay meanwhile welcomed the deal because he was a member of the group and received an equal share of monies from performances, but was not officially signed to Profile (meaning he might not be receiving royalties for albums that included songs named after him).

If they put up most of the money for the film, Rick and Russell told the enthusiastic young trio, Run-D.M.C. would have greater creative control and earn more money once they sold the completed film to a larger studio. And in addition to an action-packed movie, Rick and Russell told them, Def Jam would release new Run-D.M.C. songs on a Def Jam sound track album, and have Rush Management publicist and former journalist Bill Adler take a leave of absence from Rush to create an authorized biography that would bear the same title as the movie and the sound track album; and best of all, the book, the movie, and the album would arrive in stores and theaters in unison. The group decided that it was a sound and innovative plan, and a brilliant way to bombard the media with new Run-D.M.C. products and keep them in the public eye, and agreed to divide costs of the film with Rick Rubin and Russell Simmons. "We were rich, we had money; we could do it," said Run.

Now that it was time to record a fourth album, Run began to worry that fans might not enjoy their new material as much as they had enjoyed their earlier works. Run-D.M.C. was the first rap group to go gold, then platinum, and then triple platinum; to have a video on MTV, get the cover of *Rolling Stone*, and sign an endorsement deal. But fear of not being able to match the success of the last album had Run feeling he didn't want to leave his bed each morning. Crippling self-doubts and an exhausting work schedule—touring, recording, and planning to film a second movie that

Run-D.M.C. would help finance with their hard-earned savings—overwhelmed Run to the point where he didn't look forward to participating in any of these projects. He couldn't explain why he felt this way, and it seemed nothing could snap him out of his depression. Everything technically was going great, but he still felt melancholy, and voiced his fears in interviews with Adler, who was hard at work on the authorized biography. "Run was always under a lot of pressure but I think it was always self-induced," said publicist Tracy Miller, who handled Run-D.M.C.'s career from her desk at Profile Records. He was also a perfectionist. "Maybe there was a fear of not matching the success of the last record, a feeling that he had to do that." Run joined Jam Master Jay and D.M.C. in the studio to simultaneously begin a fourth album and record songs for the second movie while the movie script was being written. They decided to produce the fourth album—ultimately to be called *Tougher Than Leather*—without Russell. "Peter Piper" proved Jay could produce hits, so Rick Rubin wouldn't produce either. "We didn't want him to, basically," D.M.C. admitted. "We didn't mind him doing the rock shit but then he tried to do everything and we were like, 'We don't need any help with the b-boy shit.'"

Instead, original DJ Davy DMX, whom Larry Smith wanted, coproduced songs for their new album because, D explained, "Jay and Davy were hanging out." Run and D weren't concerned about Jay's choice, because they didn't have clear-cut ideas aside from wanting to rap over "I Can't Stop" on one song.

So Jam Master Jay and Davy DMX created tracks, and Run and D.M.C. did what they did best: rapped. Their new "Papa Crazy" covered the Temptations' "Papa Was a Rolling Stone." "Ragtime" revisited the lighthearted Doug and Slick Rick–style of "Perfection" (with Jay saying a few rhymes). "They Call Us Run-D.M.C." seemed to be influenced by the Beasties in that the song included the horn from the break-beat "Catch a Groove" (which the white trio had rapped over on their song "Posse in Effect"). Now Run-D.M.C. included the same horn, and "How'd Ya Do It Dee" had as much echo as the Beasties' song. "They came out after us and went to number one and were new and white," said D. "And Run being very competitive didn't know how to handle that information. Jay and me didn't give a fuck." D, happy with the money he was making, just wanted to use more break beats, but Run, D said, was intent on competing with the white trio's success. Run began to feel that the Beasties were mimicking Run-D.M.C.'s sound as much as he had once felt L.L. was imitating Run's look and Run-D.M.C.'s stage show. "But for focusing on that, it fucked Run up in the head."

As sessions continued during 1986, D also wanted to modify their sound. With new rappers Big Daddy Kane, Kool G Rap, and the Juice Crew enjoying success with break beats, many other new record labels offering rap records with more intricate rhyme styles, and new rap groups insulting Run's simpler lyrics (as the Ultra-Magnetic MCs had on their popular single "Ego Tripping"), D.M.C. thought, "We're getting too far away from the fucking basement! Why aren't we doing that shit? That's our shit they stealing! We're busy making fucking rock records to try to fuck with MTV. I want to go back to the park, man!" He told the others he didn't want to record any rock songs, but they ignored him. "I guess they saw the industry was growing, they were looking at *Billboard*, and they were worrying about MTV. They started worrying about the bullshit we shouldn't worry about. 'Cause when you worry about it you start to decline." Before D knew it, he and Run were recording "Miss Elaine," a cheesy rock number that mimicked the theme of Van Halen's MTV favorite "Hot for Teacher."

They were in Chung King when Rick showed up with screenwriter Ric Menello and said, "Here's the guy who's gonna cowrite your film." Menello was then writing the first draft of *Cold Chilling in a Hot Spot*, as the film was called at the time. Rick had told Menello to "make it the best action film you can" and "give it a little *Blues Brothers* comedy." D.M.C. had another vision for the film. "I want it to be like *The Terminator*."

The chubby white screenwriter returned within weeks with a finished script, now called *Cold Chillin'*. Menello had managed to give everyone what they wanted.

Cold Chillin' begins with D.M.C. in a prison cell. A white corrections officer comes to escort D to the warden. He's about to be released from prison. The officer attempts to hit D with his nightstick on their way to the warden because he feels D is acting defiant and not walking quickly enough, but D grabs the stick in midswing, holding it for a second.

In the warden's office, the warden lectures D about staying out of trouble on the outside. The dialogue establishes that D's character was incarcerated after attacking a guy with a broken bottle during a barroom brawl. "So we knew it was self-defense and his being in jail was bullshit," said Menello, "but it was cut because Rick thought it made D seem 'tougher' to be just coming out of jail for something we didn't know about. More mysterious." Still, the fact that his character was innocent explained why the warden in the movie wanted to meet with D before his release from prison. D is released. Outside the prison, Run's character waits by a cool black car while Jam Master Jay sits inside of the vehicle, behind the steering wheel. D hugs Run, who says, "My nigga."

In the black hot rod, the mood of the script changed. Instead of more mature character development, Rubin and Menello decided to include a ludicrous scene in which Jay describes a nightmare about two beautiful women picking him up on the road, then giving him oral sex. "I'm like, 'Yeah!' " Jay shouts. "And then you know what she do? She bit my dick off. Same fucked-up dream for weeks."

D mutters, "Fucked up."

The anecdote, Menello explained, "was based on an actual dream a friend of mine kept having." He also felt it was ironic, macho rappers expressing a Freudian fear of the opposite sex. At the very least it would "explain some of the more sexist stuff later," he said, "like Slick Rick singing 'Treat Her Like a Prostitute.' "

After going from emotional drama—D's release and reunion with old friends—to Jay mouthing a sexually explicit anecdote (a result of Rubin, Russell, and Run-D.M.C. all asking the screenwriter to juggle comedy with action), the next scene shows Run-D.M.C. meeting with their manager, Russell, and saying they want to "lay down some funky joints." Russell takes Run-D.M.C. to see his new group, the Beasties, perform. The Beasties performance detracts from the film's main story—that of Run-D.M.C.—but Rubin and Russell wanted to include the Beastie Boys in the film and figured a concert scene would be a good way to let the film-viewing audience see the group perform a new song (which would appear on the Def Jam sound track) and also introduce even more comedy to the film (since the Beasties follow their performance with a few jokes).

Russell then leads Run-D.M.C. to small label Strut Records, where owner Vic Ferrante wants to sign them. Russell says he'll have to sign the Beasties, too. Ferrante (played by Rick Rubin) agrees. Once they leave, Ferrante tells fat, bumbling label executive Arthur Rattler (played by bearded Ric Menello): "Sign them."

"But why, boss?"

"Nobody wants to watch ten niggers play basketball, now *do they?*"

The line—created by Russell, Menello explained—was an example of the sort of shock value Rick Rubin wanted to include in the second Run-D.M.C. movie, and very different from Run-D.M.C.'s public image as positive rappers. The story picks up once the viewer learns Strut is a front for a mobster's drug ring. When Runny Ray, Run-D.M.C.'s newly hired roadie, happily walks into Strut and interrupts a drug deal, Ferrante shoots him dead. "Why'd you have to kill the guy?" Rattler asks. "Why couldn't you just pay him off?"

"Since I'm not a Jew like you," he answers, "I didn't think of it!"

Ferrante plants drugs on Ray's corpse. Run-D.M.C. eventually suspect Ferrante of involvement in Ray's murder and meet with the police to discuss their suspicions and ask whether the police have any leads in solving the crime. But the cops are not only racist, they believe Ray was a drug dealer and not worth the effort. Run-D.M.C. (by this point Russell's character goes unmentioned in the script) have no choice but to take the law into their own hands: breaking people's fingers, beating rednecks in a bar, and finally buying their own weapons from a local gun dealer to use in their rescue of a potential witness to the murder of Runny Ray. "We wanted the film to be like *Death Wish*," said D. "We wanted it to be real. 'Yo, they killed fucking Ray!' We didn't want to be the 'good Catholic suburban kids.' We wanted to be the motherfuckers from Hollis."

During the finale, Run-D.M.C. learn that a woman they questioned during a quick-moving scene has been kidnapped by Ferrante and his bodyguard. Run-D.M.C. therefore kidnap one of Ferrante's employees—who can also provide evidence to the police that Ferrante killed Runny Ray. Run-D.M.C. then carry their weapons to a prearranged meeting in an abandoned warehouse to exchange hostages, and hope to not only rescue the hostage Ferrante is holding, but also capture Ferrante and turn him over to the police with evidence linking him to the murder. But during the hostage exchange, Ferrante and his black bodyguard, Nathan— who has been seen throughout the script scowling at Run-D.M.C. and defending his racist boss—pull guns out and threaten to shoot Run-D.M.C. After a few bullets fly and every character ducks behind various objects to avoid being hit, Jay confronts Nathan. "Jay was the free person who stood up for his friends like a man should and was loyal, while the bodyguard, Nathan, sold out for money," Menello explained.

"I like you, Jay," Nathan tells Jay while aiming his gun at Jay. "I'm gonna kill ya, but I like ya."

Aiming his own pistol, Jay tells Nathan to drop his gun.

"I've come too far to go back now," Nathan replies. "A black man who wants big money ain't got a choice how he makes it."

Jay shakes his head. "A man always has a choice." (Jay outdraws Nathan in a gunfight.)

D.M.C. finally corners Ferrante. In a traditional action movie, the hero aims his gun at the villain, preparing to shoot, but a supporting character stops him with the reminder that pulling the trigger will make the hero no better than the villain. But in this screenplay, Ferrante yells, "I never thought it would all end at the hands of a nigger." D shoots him in the face. There is no one to stop him.

The script ends with Run-D.M.C. walking backstage after a concert. They face a newspaper headline saying Ferrante's assistant, Arthur Rattler, has provided evidence that exonerates their friend Runny Ray of charges he was a drug dealer. Run says, "You think anybody will care about this tomorrow?"

D replies, "That ain't the point. If we didn't do this, it would've been like Runny Ray never lived." Then D adds, "A wise man once said every man is the father of every child."

Jay says, "Word, I'd like to be every father!"

"Every man is the father of every child?" Run asks. "That's cool. Who said that?"

D quips, "I did."

Rubin changed the title of the film to *Tougher Than Leather,* and Run-D.M.C. adopted the name for their forthcoming album. Then Rick and Russell began talking seriously about getting Run-D.M.C. off Profile. Run and D supported the move. They already felt Profile was "jerking the shit out of them," said Runny Ray. "They wanted to be on Def Jam or 'whoever' really." They complained to friends about money, having to pay for independent record promoters, studio time, extra plane tickets if they wanted friends to join them on trips. During midautumn 1986—when they were between albums and not touring—they were always unhappy with Profile Records or Russell, Ray said. "Run used to always talk about, 'We signed to this nigga; niggas always robbing us and taking our money. We ain't getting our royalties for this record, that record, this album.' Sometimes he'd say Russell. Sometimes he'd say Cory Robbins."

)t was going to be great: a bombarding of the media. A movie, Adler's authorized biography, and a new Run-D.M.C. album. Their songs on a Def Jam sound track. Many Def Jam artists in the movie. More action than *Krush Groove,* and more money once Def Pictures sold the completed film to a larger studio. The only obstacle, Russell and Run-D.M.C. felt, was Profile Records. Profile didn't mind Run-D.M.C. starring in the film—much as Profile hadn't minded Run-D.M.C. starring in *Krush Groove*—but the label suspected Russell was trying to get Run-D.M.C. off of Profile and onto Def Jam's roster of artists. To prevent any other label but Profile from releasing Run-D.M.C. music, Profile reminded Def Pictures that Profile held the sync rights, meaning Run-D.M.C. could perform their music in the film only if Profile agreed. "They wanted it to be a Def Jam sound track and that's sync rights and Profile said, 'No, no, no, if you're gonna put out a sound track to this movie, its gonna be a Profile album,' " said Adam Dubin.

At Profile, Cory Robbins knew Run-D.M.C. "wanted out of the contract at various times" and that it bugged Russell that "they were not on his label," but Profile wasn't about to let Run-D.M.C. go. The group was simply too valuable. The first week of filming, early November 1986, their *Rolling Stone* cover appeared on newsstands, so they were huge. Yet, though their contract was ironclad, Adam Dubin explained, Rick and Russell still tried to get them onto Def Jam. "As I remember it, Run-D.M.C. was signed to Pro-file," said Dubin. "Jam Master Jay was signed to Def Jam so he would appear on a Run-D.M.C. record 'courtesy of Def Jam,' but that wasn't enough 'cause [Rick and Russell] wanted Run-D.M.C." When Rick and Russell allegedly signed Jay to a Def Jam deal is unclear, and Dubin did not elaborate. But Dubin said Rick and Russell saw "other people making money off what they were do-ing. [Rick and Russell] were making *some* money but wanted to make *a lot* of money. So that was also the idea behind making *Tougher Than Leather*."

To get around the issue of not having sync rights, Run and D were handed scripts that called for them to perform "routines." "It didn't say they're doing a song 'cause then Profile gets the music for it," Dubin said. The filmmakers tried using misleading scripts to conceal that Run-D.M.C. would be filmed performing songs de-spite the fact that Profile Records never prohibited Run-D.M.C. from performing their music for film cameras. "They said, 'Per-form all the music you want but [Profile] is doing the sound track. Go do anything. Record anything. It's just that we, not Def Jam, own the right to release any new material by Run-D.M.C.' " A bat-tle with Profile was forming and Run "didn't really want to do the movie," said Runny Ray. "Because of all that bullshit they were go-ing through. All this shit. 'Niggas robbing them.' " While Profile and Def Jam bickered over which record label would release new Run-D.M.C. songs, Run-D.M.C.'s new batch of songs sat unre-leased and the group remained out of the public eye.

CHAPTER 21

Rhyming and Stealing

Filming began on Thursday, November 13, 1986, in front of the aircraft carrier *Intrepid* in Manhattan. But when Run-D.M.C. arrived on the set they saw that the $200,000 they had put up wouldn't get them much. Even *Krush Groove*, which cost $3 million, was considered low budget. But at least with that film they'd been the stars. They had real sets. There were trailers, wardrobe people handing them gear, food lying out. "In comparison to this it was plush," said Dubin. "There were literally no trailers on *Tougher Than Leather*. There was no money for that stuff. The holding area was wherever they could keep them, in their cars."

Still, Run-D.M.C. was delighted to be filming another movie, and even more excited when they heard people talk of a sequel called *The Posse*, which "would've been even more of a spaghetti or B western," said Menello.

But the first day was a complete disaster. The scene called for Rick's character and his father to meet outdoors, since the father's phones were tapped. It rained like crazy. There wasn't enough light. The crew moved impossibly slowly. The director of photography wanted arty shots when they could afford only quick setups and getting it done. Rick casting himself as an actor in the movie turned out to be another disaster. "Either you're the director or the actor," said Dubin, "but to do both on a low-budget film is nearly impossible."

They didn't get the day's work done, and what they shot looked terrible. "Day two wasn't a whole lot better," Dubin said. On Austin Street in Forest Hills, Rick wanted to shoot Runny Ray meeting a chauffeur whose limo isn't working. The driver's money-eyed employer is threatening to fire him until Ray fixes the car. They hoped to finish by midday, but Rick wasted time trying to get an elaborate tracking shot past the front of the car. They were still out there when schools let out at three o'clock and young fans bombarded the set. Rick got his shot, but spent all day on something he should have finished by noon.

"I just thought the whole thing looked rinky-dink from day one, just the way it was being shot and the way things were going," said photographer Glen Friedman. "But Joey [Run] seemed really impressed with his acting skills at the time. Really, everyone [at Def Jam and Rush Management] thought he was a fucking *actor* after *Krush Groove*."

They filmed a homecoming party in D.M.C.'s house in Hollis. The entire neighborhood came out to watch, and D spent more time partying than shooting his scenes. Neighborhood pals wanting to be in the movie kept coming by the set, distracting Run, D, and Jay. Then Run-D.M.C. became impatient with filming and started asking Rick, "How long until you need us?"

Rick would say, "I don't know. We're setting up the shot. It'll be like an hour."

Since they had completed their new album, Run-D.M.C. would pile into their cars with friends and disappear to McDonald's and other hangouts. They'd never return on time. Everyone had to wait and money was wasted. "They were all just partying," said Adam Dubin, who worked on the set. "I just remember forties of Olde E all the time all over the place."

To keep Run-D.M.C. in line, Rick had young production assistants accompany them, but to no avail. "Here's a kid with a walkie-talkie and a bunch of their friends and everybody's smoking pot and drinking in these cars and we're radioing to them: 'Okay, we need Run-D.M.C. back on the set,'" Adam Dubin recalled. "And they're like, 'We're five miles away and hanging out at so-and-so's house.'" It happened all the time. The young assistants couldn't control all three members of Run-D.M.C. More time was wasted.

D would also often show up on the set already drunk, and Run would show up high on weed. They wouldn't remember their lines and would improvise, but deleted information crucial to the plot. "We were dazing a lot," Run said flatly. And since the screenwriter wasn't around—Menello was working at his day job at NYU or helping to film music videos for the Beastie Boys' first single—no one said, "Well, if they say that, they got to make sure to say this, too."

They started filming in Def Jam's offices at 298 Elizabeth Street, taking up most available space with cameras, wires, lights, and equipment. Employees were kicked out of their offices. "They had no money," said Bill Stephney, then working for the label. "It disrupted absolutely everything and sort of took our eyes off the prize, as it were."

During a rare visit to the set, Ric Menello asked Rick, "What if this whole thing falls apart? What if *Tougher Than Leather* falls apart? What if the company falls apart?"

"I'll just do it again," Rick answered. "I'll just do it all over again."

By the third week of filming, the film was over budget and Run-D.M.C. had to pull more money from their pockets to fund production. Rick started filming things quickly. "No elaborate shots," Dubin said. "No tracking shots; none of that stuff. Just shooting to get it done. And at that point, it started to wear on Rick. He was physically drained."

Suddenly, when call time arrived at 6:00 a.m., Rick was nowhere to be found on the set. The crew stood around waiting, since he, as director, was the only one who knew the next shot. They'd call the screenwriter, who'd suggest a shot, but when Rick arrived at 9:00 or 10:00, he wouldn't like the screenwriter's suggestion and had the crew waste more time setting up the shot he wanted.

None of it mattered to D.M.C., who was having a great time—until Rick and Russell asked for a certain scene. Near the finale, D's character enters a room with guns in both hands. Menello's script said the character's grandfather, who had served with the Red Ball Express, owned the guns. "The Red Ball Express was a black unit in World War II that had to prove themselves to white people," Menello explained. "They were very heroic. They had to bring fuel through the battle lines to the soldiers." Menello felt mentioning the unit would position Run-D.M.C. as carrying on its tradition of "courage under fire."

But D saw these fake guns, and was furious. He knew Russell wanted to protect their image but felt it was a sham. "We had bull-shit Lugers," he said. "We wanted nines and .45s."

He reluctantly agreed to carry the fake guns in and even use the guns during the climactic shoot-out but was still very dissatisfied. "Everybody else shooting the automatics, they're shooting German Lugers," Ray laughed.

They finished shooting the ninety-five-minute movie on December 9, 1986, and all concerned were happy it was over. Run-D.M.C. was disappointed and felt that because of collusion on the set, their dream of a movie like *Death Wish* had become a nightmare. They feared audiences would think they were acting fake. Instead of creating something from the heart, Rick Rubin and Russell Simmons had them "going through the motions hoping for success," D felt.

After filming concluded, Run-D.M.C. needed a break. They spent December 18–22 in Japan. At the airport, hundreds of fans in Kangols, sheepskins, velour hats, Adidas, and jeans waited for them. It was the closest thing they'd experienced to Beatlemania. Everyone was polite to them, deferential. Considering the crowded but neat and well-policed streets, D thought, "Whoa! This is paradise."

At dates in small halls in Kobe, Tokyo, and Nagoya, they saw Japanese kids loved their music. Everywhere they went, huge crowds mobbed them, wanting autographs. After posing for pictures with a few Japanese b-boys, Run asked Ray, "Damn, we got these kids out here in the street doing our shit?"

While Run-D.M.C. were overseas, the Beasties' *Licensed to Ill* emerged as the biggest-selling debut in CBS Records history, and outdid *Raising Hell* by becoming the very first rap album to reach number one on the U.S. pop charts. "I watched it grow like *Raising Hell*," said Run. Run felt partly responsible for its success. " 'Slow and Low,' they took my vocals. 'New Style' I wrote some of the rhymes. 'Paul Revere' I wrote a lot of the rhymes and I produced 'Paul Revere.' " But now, everyone seemed to want to talk only about the Beasties. "These niggas were like, 'Huh?' " said Ray. " 'These motherfuckers selling more records than us? Get the fuck out of here.' "

Licensed to Ill's stay at the top of the pop chart started in November 1986 and stretched to fourteen weeks (March 1987), and many reporters who denounced Run-D.M.C. for Long Beach praised the Beastie Boys, who dressed, rapped, and acted like them.

"If a fourteen-year-old white girl in, oh, Alabama had brought home a Run-D.M.C. album in those days, you know, looking at these black guys as rock 'n' roll guys or sex symbols, it would not really have been okay," said Rick Rubin. "Whereas, as stupid and disgusting as the Beastie Boys might have been, that was okay because they were white."

A few Def Jam artists felt overshadowed by the Beasties' success, said photographer Glen Friedman. One day Friedman saw L.L. "practically depressed. These cranky white boys from downtown were taking his spotlight." L.L. was so dejected he neglected to wear his hat, "and in those days he was never seen without a hat," Friedman said. L.L., walking aimlessly down Elizabeth Street, called out to Glen, who was heading to Def Jam's offices. "Yo, Glen." Glen, who didn't recognize L.L. without the Kangol, thought, "Who's that guy with the hamburger on his head?" He squinted and saw it was L.L. "Oh, hey, man," he said. "How you doing?" L.L. sounded deflated. "Yeah, you know, just workin' on the new album."

The Beasties meanwhile were themselves far from happy. In January 1987, with *Licensed to Ill* a chart-topping hit and Def Pictures offering MTV a sitcom starring the Beastie Boys, the Beasties enlisted a journalist to help write their own movie. Rick and Russell mentioned to the group that they would have the Beasties star in a film that they would release through Def Pictures. Once they had a screenplay finished that reflected their view of how they should be presented in a movie, the Beasties arrived at Electric Lady Studios in Manhattan, to tell Rick Rubin (producing a rock album for the Cult) their idea for *Scared Stupid*, which would feature them outrunning ghosts in a haunted house. Rick liked the idea of the Beasties battling ghosts and felt it could make for a great film. "But this is where they found out how bad it is to have your manager also be your record company," said Rick's friend Adam Dubin. " 'Cause nobody's advocating for or protecting you. They were managed by Rush Management, which is Russell," Dubin explained, "and Rick and Russell would make their movie and that's their record company." If the Beasties had had a separate manager, this manager would have negotiated with Def Pictures—Rick and Russell—to get the Beastie Boys as much money as possible for acting in the movie. But since Rick and Russell were both manager and film studio (as well as the record label that would ostensibly release a *Scared Stupid* sound track), Rick and Russell would have felt they were free to determine how much the Beasties would receive. The Beasties tried to negotiate a better deal by offering to help pay production costs—as Run-D.M.C. had done with the recently filmed *Tougher Than Leather*—in exchange for a larger cut of profits, but, Ad Rock said, Rick Rubin told them, "Well, you guys will get a point each on the movie."

The group was incredulous. "A point each?" Ad asked Rick. "What are you talking about? We wrote it, we're starring in it; we're making it."

Rick Rubin reportedly ignored the Beasties' requests for more money, and they began to resent that their manager—Russell Simmons—wasn't stepping in to persuade his Def Jam and Def Pictures partner Rick Rubin to let the Beasties receive a higher percentage of profits in exchange for helping to fund production costs.

The Beastie Boys butted heads with Rubin again while filming a video for their rock-rap hit "No Sleep Till Brooklyn." The song featured a solo by Kerry King, a member of Def Jam's new metal band Slayer, and for the video Rick wanted to use special effects to show the Beasties running around a sixty-foot-tall Kerry King. The Beasties hated the idea, said Ric Menello, who with Adam Dubin had directed the group's first video, "Fight for Your Right." Instead, the group wanted to start the video at the Central Park Zoo. Their idea was "you see a chimpanzee leave his cage, put on a hat, and hold a guitar case; hail a cab, get in, go to the theater, and when the solo came on, play the guitar," Menello recalled. The Beasties and Rick Rubin compromised: instead of a trained chimp or a giant guitarist, they presented a man in a gorilla suit playing the solo un-til Kerry King shoved him aside and finished it.

In the spring of 1987, the Beasties agreed to join Run-D.M.C. for the Together Forever tour to promote the Beasties' *Licensed to Ill* and to keep Run-D.M.C. in the public eye while Profile and Def Jam battled over which label would release the new songs Run-D.M.C. hoped to include in their upcoming movie. A year had passed since Run-D.M.C. released *Raising Hell*, but fans continued to want to see Run-D.M.C. perform *Raising Hell*'s many hits, in-cluding "Walk This Way," and the Together Forever tour brought rap music to huge amphitheaters and American suburbs for the first time. "It was probably Russell's idea," said Ad Rock. "Russell probably wanted to benefit because he would get paid twice."

At first, Run-D.M.C. thought black concertgoers would go buy hot dogs when the Beasties came onstage. "But they stayed," D.M.C. later recalled, "and liked it, too." More whites appeared in the audience. "Beastie Boys must have pulled, on average, a three-to-one ratio, white girls to white guys," Public Enemy's Hank Shocklee explained. "And at the same time they were pulling the hard-core ghetto!"

White girls attended concerts in droves and leaped onstage to re-move their clothing. Many of their boyfriends viewed rap as synony-mous with disco or dance music, which they disliked (they preferred rock bands like Rush, Metallica, and Def Leppard), but agreed to ac-company their girlfriends to Together Forever shows. They ended up liking what they saw and heard onstage. "So the female audience came out in droves and drew the guys that were with them into it, along with the hard-core rap fans, mainly black males," Shocklee re-called. "It all mixed together: white and black kids all going crazy, and white girls losing their minds, and taking off their clothes."

Some nights, Run and D had the Beasties join them for an encore. Newspaper articles kept presenting both groups as symbols of racial unity and brotherhood, but backstage, Run was tired of the white trio's practical jokes and food fights. Run was also coping with mild depression, worrying that their upcoming movie or delays in releasing their next album would cost them their audience. Nevertheless, Run made it onstage every night. D meanwhile continued to drink heavily and to join the Beastie Boys—during Run-D.M.C.'s encores—in spraying beer at the crowd, and dodging beer cans thrown by overzealous audience members. During one show, the Beasties had so much beer onstage that MCA slipped. "He came down hard, and it got real quiet," said D. "We thought he was dead. Then he gets up with his head busted open, laughing."

On the surface, the Together Forever tour was like one long party, Beastie Boy member Ad Rock remembered. "We were just getting fucked up the whole time, and having fun," he said. "We'd go do interviews with these radio stations and all pile into a van or limo. It'd be all of us hanging out. It was amazing. Like summer camp where you could smoke weed and drink beer." But when Run-D.M.C. and the Beastie Boys were offstage both groups wondered whether Rush Management was handling their careers properly and whether they both shouldn't leave their respective record labels.

During the tour, D.M.C. kept playing Public Enemy's debut album, *Yo! Bum Rush the Show* despite sales of 150,000 copies making it what Rick Rubin called "the least successful Def Jam record at the time." Though rap radio DJs had been playing only instrumental versions of rapper Chuck D's songs since the album's release in March 1987—"They felt the beats were good, but he wasn't," Rubin said—D.M.C. saw Chuck as the future of rap.

Public Enemy had decided to sign to Def Jam in June 1986. The deciding factor for Chuck D was hearing Run-D.M.C.'s *Raising Hell* album. "The *Raising Hell* record told me this rap thing is growing up," Chuck explained. For Chuck and his producer, Hank Shocklee, *Raising* was the greatest hip-hop record ever recorded: the first concept album and, Hank quipped, "a greatest hits record." Hearing the album and its variety of styles and themes inspired Chuck to say that he and his group would accept Rick's offer of a recording contract with Def Jam. "There wouldn't be a P.E.," Hank added, "if it weren't for that album!"

Photographer Glen Friedman, well versed in punk rock music, remembered telling Rick Rubin, "You know there is already a skinhead group in England called Public Enemy." According to Friedman, someone answered, "Well, we never heard of them so it doesn't matter."

Russell Simmons predicted that no one would like Public Enemy's political lyrics, Hank Shocklee recalled. "Matter of fact, if it was left up to him P.E. would not have been signed. Because he 'disapproved.' " Rick pushed for the group, but Chuck remembered Russell kept saying, "I don't know, I don't know, I don't know about that." In recording rooms in the studios Chung King and INS, rapper Chuck D looked to Run-D.M.C. and L.L. for inspiration. If his girlfriend, an R & B fan, heard a song and said, "Turn if off," Chuck felt he was on the right track. Then Chuck D told Def Jam employee (and executive producer) Bill Stephney that, for a song called "Sophisticated Bitch," he wanted a rock version of a bass line on Heat Wave's disco classic "Groove Line." Stephney invited Vernon Reid of the metal band Living Color to play the riff over the beat first heard on Whodini's hit "Friends." After spending $17,000 on recording, Public Enemy submitted *Yo! Bum Rush the Show* to Def Jam, and Rick Rubin excitedly played the LP for Russell, but Russell said, "Rick, I don't know why you're wasting your time with this garbage. No one's ever going to like this. This is like black punk rock."

When Def Jam released Public Enemy's debut in March 1987, it turned out Russell was right. Influential radio DJ Mr. Magic told his WBLS audience he objected to P.E.'s song title "Mi Uzi Weighs a

Ton." Magic also smashed a copy of their single "Public Enemy No. 1" on the air, and promised, "No more music by these suckers."

But D.M.C.'s support was unwavering. "I would bang all their records twenty-four-seven," D recalled. "Everything Chuck and them made." He'd also memorized every word on the album. "That shit was mean. And it wasn't 'social' to me. That was dope-ass rapping. One rhyme went: 'Run in the room hang it on the wall in remembrance that I rocked them all! Suckers! Punks!' He knew slang! And he was the educated college motherfucker—dope. I thought he was better than me and Run. Way better than Run-D.M.C."

Jam Master Jay also loved Chuck's music, and kept telling everyone "P.E. No. 1" was his "number one favorite joint," Hank Shocklee recalled. And after DJ Doctor Dre dubbed them a copy, the Beasties played it too.

The few music critics that reviewed the album described it as political and "controversial," but D.M.C. and Jam Master Jay appreciated it first as hip-hop music: "The beats, Chuck's flow, Flavor Flav," said D.M.C. "Actually, Chuck D and them made me step up my game. Made me get a little better."

Everywhere he went D.M.C. played songs like "Too Much Posse," which had sidekick Flavor Flav describing his gang over ear-splitting drums, or "You're Going to Get Yours," where Chuck described fleeing from police in his Oldsmobile. "I thought it was so cool," D continued. "You don't understand. There were the records I heard on radio but then I heard 'Sophisticated Bitch' on the album. I was like 'Oh shit! This motherfucker—! Oh my God, what's this? Damn, I have to step up my game, man. This shit is like killing me.' "

The Together Forever tour continued into summer 1987, and Run-D.M.C. couldn't help but notice that relations between the Beastie Boys and Def Jam, to which Run-D.M.C. hoped to sign, were deteriorating because of the proposed Beastie Boys movie

Scared Stupid. And when the tour reached Hollywood, things got even worse. Executives at Universal Pictures met with the Beasties and said they'd be willing to film their proposed haunted-house movie for $4 million, a budget large enough to pay for decent special effects. "Rick Rubin was like, 'If you make a movie without me, then you can't have any of the music,'" Adam Dubin recalled. "Almost like what Profile was pulling on Run-D.M.C. with *Tougher Than Leather*. And Universal came back and said, 'Well if we can't make a Beastie Boy movie with music then we don't want to make a Beastie Boy movie.' It killed the deal right there."

Already, L.L. Cool J was suing Rick and Russell. In court, L.L.'s lawyer battled to have a judge void L.L.'s contracts with Def Jam and Rush Management, and order Rick and Russell to pay $1.5 million the lawyer claimed both companies owed L.L. for his first two albums *Radio* and *Bigger and Deffer*. "They put out the first L.L. record without a contract," L.L.'s attorney at the time, Joseph Giaimo, told a reporter.

The court decided in L.L.'s favor, author Jory Farr reported in his book *Moguls and Madmen: The Pursuit of Power in Popular Music*. L.L.'s attorney, Farr wrote, had the contract shelved, and Def Jam paid L.L. $1.5 million. Inspired by L.L.'s triumph over Def Jam, the Beasties hired their own attorney, Ken Anderson.

In June 1987, two months after Rick Rubin finally pronounced *Yo! Bum Rush the Show* a flop, Run, D, and Jay were about to board a flight at New York's Kennedy Airport. They were going to join the Beastie Boys—whose relationship with Rick and Russell was growing increasingly strained—in Europe for a few dates on the Together Forever tour. Michael Jackson wanted to record with Run-D.M.C., but D recalled, "we went on tour and said 'Fuck Michael' like it wasn't ignorant of us. We were just having fun. Break up the tour to do the record? Nah, that's all right. And it wasn't an ego thing. It's like 'We'd rather go to London to do the show, man.'"

However, the tour wasn't as carefree and fun-loving as earlier tours had been. While reporters from various newspapers described the tour and the Beasties and Run-D.M.C. sharing stages as promoting an image of racial unity, both groups concealed their disappointment with where their careers had gone. The Beasties—angered over what Rick and Russell offered for *Scared Stupid*—now had an attorney looking into ways to get the white trio off Def Jam Records. Run-D.M.C. were having their own share of difficulties with their own record label, Profile Records. Profile and Def Jam continued to battle over whether the songs Run-D.M.C. recorded for inclusion in the movie *Tougher Than Leather* would appear on a new Run-D.M.C. album for Profile, or on a *Tougher Than Leather* movie sound track released by Def Jam. Run meanwhile struggled with depression and doubts about the new material. To Run's ears, it had begun to sound dated, since editing *Tougher Than Leather* continued months after Rick Rubin completed filming, and new rap acts were emerging every day to take the rap genre into new directions and attract Run-D.M.C. fans to these new acts' own albums, singles, and music videos.

Before they boarded their flight at the Pan Am terminal, Chuck D and Hank Shocklee arrived to see them off and play them P.E.'s newest song, "Rebel Without a Pause." Chuck and Hank loved Run-D.M.C.'s music and came to the airport to ask their favorite group for their opinion of P.E.'s new direction.

Run-D.M.C. were blown away. Like Eric B and Rakim's hit "I Know You Got Soul," Chuck's new lyric was set to a fusion of two James Brown–produced beats: in this case, "Funky Drummer" and a clarinet on J.B.'s "The Grunt" that evoked a siren. During a bridge, Chuck's DJ, Terminator X, blurred a noisy guitar chord and mixed a little-known Chubb Rock single ("Rock and Roll"). "Oh my God," D remembered thinking. "You thought his first shit bugged us out? Yo, we heard that shit and got nervous. That was like the best record we ever heard."

Jay was just as impressed. The number of bass drums P.E. piled on "Funky Drummer" astounded him. "Too many, man," Jay later said. "They were trying to outdo us, that's what it was."

Instead of trying to be Run-D.M.C. or L.L., Chuck's lyrics were as smooth as those by literate newcomers Rakim and KRS-One. " 'Yes! The rhythm the rebel! Without a pause!' " D.M.C. quoted. "That shit was terrifying! Evil! Fucking Armageddon; the end of the world."

Chuck told them he wanted Def Jam to release "Rebel" immediately, as the B-side to their single "You're Going to Get Yours," but Russell opposed the idea. Since Rick Rubin was working with rock bands, creating a sound track for the motion picture *Less Than Zero*, Russell had more say in what happened at Def Jam Records. "Russell wanted the songs off of *Yo! Bum Rush the Show* to sell the album," Chuck recalled. Chuck disagreed; he felt *Yo! Bum Rush the Show* would not sell any more copies and that it was time for P.E. to present rap fans with an exciting new sound.

Run, D.M.C., and Jam Master Jay agreed with Chuck's decision to try something new. "We said, "Yo, y'all motherfuckers got to put that out now,' " said D.M.C. Chuck agreed, but didn't know how to persuade Russell to change his mind. Chuck and Hank followed Run-D.M.C. to the door of the plane. "And then Run turned around and said, 'Yo, man, just do it,' " Chuck remembered. Chuck and Hank ignored Russell's decision to not release "Rebel Without a Pause" immediately and went over his head, to executives at Def Jam's parent company, CBS. CBS executives heard the song, Chuck continued, and decided Russell was wrong. Without consulting Russell, Chuck claimed, CBS worked on including "Rebel Without a Pause" on the B-side of P.E.'s next Def Jam single, "You're Going to Get Yours." Fourteen days later, Public Enemy saw "Rebel Without a Pause" arrive in record stores and change the direction and sound of rap music. Russell, Chuck claimed, did not even know the song was in record stores until radio stations began to play it on the radio.

The Together Forever tour arrived in Europe, to English reporters who wrote stories describing the Beasties as the most unruly pack since the punk band the Sex Pistols. It was the first major tour that the Beasties had played in Europe, and Russell, along for the ride, worked to keep the group in the headlines by manufacturing publicity stunts. "Run-D.M.C. was huge," Ad explained. "And we were all at some weird Swiss rock festival and were like, 'Well how can we [purposely] fuck this up?' " Russell told MCA to cross the crowded party and punch Jam Master Jay in the face. MCA did as told, and Jay—who had agreed to participate in the publicity stunt—swung back. "That was Russell being a manager trying to create some excitement," said D.M.C. "Because [reporters] were mad we were there, Russell was like, 'All right, we're gonna give them what they want.' " But they really had to hit each other, D noted. "It was some stupid high drunk shit, too."

When in Europe, Run-D.M.C. inspired the Beasties to improve their stage show. "We showed them how to put their shit in order, because they were wild, all over the place," said D. "We showed them how to rap to the crowd and not worry about dancing and being corny and to use the whole stage. They learned, 'Okay, I see on certain records D will stand there and fold his arms. So we'll throw the beer on this record and bring the bitches out on that one,' as opposed to just being unorganized."

Run-D.M.C.'s approach, said Ad Rock, was better than Russell's. "Russell tried to make some suggestions about what we should do onstage and we didn't really listen." He couldn't remember specifics but "everything he said was nuts. He wanted to be as berserk as possible."

Between shows in Europe, Russell kept manufacturing publicity stunts to keep the group in the headlines. If Russell wasn't staging a fake fistfight, Ad recalled, then every group member joined a crowd turning a parked automobile onto its side. The Beasties, already unhappy with Rick over the aborted *Scared Stupid*

deal with Universal Pictures, became even unhappier about being perceived as a pop group (anathema to punk rockers) and with how Rick and Russell were controlling their image and encouraging them to act rowdy. But Russell, delighted with newspaper headlines, continued to include the white trio in outrageous publicity stunts. "We got on the cover of every paper all over the world," Russell later said of his campaign of publicity stunts. "The Beasties did it 'cause it was fun. I did it because it would make us money."

These antics drew rowdy fans to concerts. During one show in Liverpool, audience members spit on the heads of two bald security guards near the front of the stage, then started throwing beer cans at the group. The Beasties said, "Cool out" and "Don't throw shit," but the crowd started hurling cans. To avoid being hit, Ad Rock swung a baseball bat, knocking the cans aside.

After the show, deranged fans demolished everything onstage. Back in their hotel in London, Liverpool police arrived to arrest Ad Rock, since a woman in the Liverpool audience claimed one of the beer cans he had knocked aside struck her in the face. "It was total bullshit," said photographer Ricky Powell, who joined the Beasties on tour. "She was eighty feet back!" Regardless, Ad Rock spent a night or two in jail. After Ad Rock's release, the Beasties were accosted by a female autograph seeker when they were leaving their hotel. Beastie Boy MCA said, "I'm sorry, we have to go." The woman replied, "If you don't give me an autograph right now, I'm going to stitch you up in the press."

MCA told her, "Fuck you," before getting into the waiting car and leaving.

The next morning's *Daily Mirror* headline claimed, "Pop Idols Sneer at Dying Kids." Because of the scornful woman's fictitious claim, England's Parliament wanted the Beastie Boys expelled from the country.

The Beasties finished the tour, returned to America, and took umbrage at Def Jam asking them to enter the studio to record something new for an album called *Kick It: Def Jam Sampler*. The

Beasties wanted to take a break and relax with big royalty checks for their historic 4-million-selling debut *Licensed to Ill.* "So, October hit, time to get paid, no check," Beastie Boy Mike D remembered. The group called Def Jam to ask why, and were told, "We're not paying you till you go back in the studio and make a new record."

"We're going to make another record," Mike remembered telling Def Jam, "but we sold *these* records. You know, you *got to pay.* That's just the way it works."

"Well, we're not paying you," a Def Jam executive (Mike D never specified who) told them. "We think the group's breaking up; that's it."

The Beasties and their attorney, Ken Anderson, assured Def Jam that the Beasties were not disbanding and were not trying to renege on the terms of their contract with Def Jam, but the record label didn't believe the group and refused to pay royalties for *Licensed to Ill.*

The Beasties refused to record. Def Jam's parent company, CBS, complained about the delay in getting a follow-up to the best-selling rap album of all time out to fans. Rick Rubin claimed CBS withheld royalties for the Beasties and every Def Jam artist because, by failing to provide a second Beasties album, Def Jam had breached its own contract with CBS. "That's why I couldn't pay them," Rick claimed, and why CBS told Rick, "You don't get paid on anything because you lost the Beastie Boys record."

The Beasties wanted to talk things over with Def Jam, but, Ad claimed, Rick and Russell didn't want to hear it. When the Beasties met with each other to discuss Def Jam, Ad claimed, they learned that Rick and Russell "were trying to play us against each other. They were like, 'Aw, you know, he's crazy, he's making all these demands, MCA is this. Mike doesn't do this.' They would get us alone and talk shit. I don't know if that's a plan Rick and Russell had ahead of time, but that's what happened."

As Def Jam delayed in paying royalties, and as Universal backed out of producing *Scared Stupid,* "We were like, 'Fuck these guys,'" Ad remembered of Def Jam. Until now, Anderson seemed to have been trying to negotiate a deal with Universal for *Scared Stupid;* then the lawyer gave the group advice on how to respond to Rick Rubin's offer of a certain percentage of profits for a movie with Def Pictures; then October arrived and Anderson told the group Def Jam was delaying in paying royalties. Anderson then tried to inform Def Jam that the Beastie Boys were not disbanding. Now Anderson finally told Def Jam that the Beastie Boys were leaving the label. Def Jam's lawyers maintained that the Beasties had breached their contract by not recording a second album. Russell was to blame, Ad Rock claimed, since he had kept them touring for almost eleven months. "If your manager is the owner of your record label and puts you on tour, you can't physically go into the studio."

The Beasties were not the only artists questioning their deals with Def Jam and Rush Management. Rapper Slick Rick, who signed to both companies as a solo rapper in 1986, said it "seemed like a conflict of interest. First you're signed to a record label, that's Def Jam; then your manager happens to be Russell Simmons, who is also involved with Def Jam. So now, you're forced to give up all of these different percentages for every little thing you do."

The Beasties grew tired of debating with Rick and Russell and in October had Ken Anderson file a multimillion-dollar lawsuit that alleged "breach of contract," "breach of fiduciary duty," and—like L.L. Cool J, whose victory inspired the group's decision to sue— nonpayment of millions of dollars in royalties. "We alleged they did a lot of other things in addition to not paying royalties," Anderson told the media, including structuring deals to "benefit themselves rather than the Beastie Boys."

One of the Beasties soon told their DJ, Hurricane, "We didn't get our fucking money, and we just sold a couple of million records." Hurricane then visited Russell's apartment at 111 Barrow Street, a block away from Def Jam, and in the same building where Jam Master Jay also rented a loft, to talk about the situation. Hurricane remembered the beleaguered Russell telling him, "Yo, if we go to court, Hurricane, remember that MCA was in my house walking around talking about he wasn't going to make a record again, just in case I need you."

Hurricane thought, "Man, I ain't going to court."

"No one really knew what was going to happen next," Hurricane explained.

"Ultimately, the Beastie Boys got everything they wanted and then some," Ken Anderson later told writer Jory Farr: Def Jam let them go, paid them money they were owed (after Def Jam executives had claimed they couldn't, since CBS had delayed in paying it to the label), gave the Beasties their master recordings, and returned publishing rights.

CHAPTER 22

Suing Profile

The Beasties' battle against Russell Simmons and Rick Rubin slowed Run-D.M.C.'s momentum. "Whatever was happening was happening," Run said coldly. As it was, "everything got confusing" in their own career because though the movie was being edited, Profile opposed the idea of Run-D.M.C. on a Def Jam sound track, and management hinted that Run-D.M.C. should sue their own label. Run waited, thinking, "When is the next time I can do something incredible?"

In November 1987, Run-D.M.C. sued Profile Records. Run-D.M.C. was supposed to deliver *Tougher Than Leather* to Profile by then, but Rush Management started arguing with Profile over the extension of Run-D.M.C.'s contract, Doctor Dre remembered. "Basically they wanted to get out of their contract, and Cory said, and I quote, 'Run-D.M.C. will never record a record for Def Jam.' And he was right."

Russell had had no idea back in 1983 that he would be able to form his own record label or that he would sign a distribution deal with market leader CBS Records. There weren't as many rap labels and majors telling people, "Yeah, I'll let *you* make a rap label and be part of this big industry," Dre explained. At the same time, the major labels he contacted had all rejected "It's Like That." Only Profile wanted Run-D.M.C. "It wasn't a bad deal based on what it was—Cory and them were getting the records out where they needed to be. It was a bad deal based on what the future held for Run-D.M.C. And they locked them into a seven-album deal and couldn't get out."

However, Russell continued to dream of having Run-D.M.C. signed to Def Jam, and of running an empire that would accurately reflect rap music in all its creativity, exuberance, and rebelliousness. When Profile wouldn't let Run-D.M.C., the genre's biggest draw, go, Russell had the band sue the label. " 'Cause that *Tougher Than Leather* album was supposed to be on Def Jam," said Dre. "That was the problem. *Raising Hell* was their swan song for Profile."

Profile president Cory Robbins knew it bothered Russell that Run-D.M.C., which included his younger brother, weren't on his label. And Cory heard that the group had been "entertaining offers from other labels or at least having discussions with other labels besides Def Jam." And it was to be expected, really, since Run-D.M.C. was coming off a triple platinum album, *Raising Hell*. "Had they been free agents and had they been able to break their contract they would have been able to get an enormous advance payment to sign with a new label," Cory explained.

But Profile wasn't battling just any major label trying to lure an act off an independent once the act sold millions of albums. "It was the major label that Run's brother was involved with, so it became very personal," said publicist Tracy Miller. "At the time Russell

probably thought he could do a better job, now that he had the resources, to steer his brother's career," she continued. "But when he
first started out with his brother, he didn't have those resources."

Because Profile and Rush had been so close in the past, and the
rap business hadn't yet been overrun by accountants, Miller continued, "people took it very personally and were offended, and from
that point on Russell Simmons and the two guys from Profile never
ever had the same relationship."

During the winter of 1987, the holiday season, Run, D, and Jay
stopped by Def Pictures' film-editing studio in downtown Manhattan to see how *Tougher Than Leather* was coming along, and learned
that personnel problems had delayed editing. The first editors
worked too slowly, so producers—either Rick Rubin, Russell Simmons, or their experienced coproducer, Vincent Giordano—fired
them, said screenwriter Ric Menello, who helped with the editing.

Then one of Rick's friends at MTV suggested a replacement
who would remove scenes from the film without the approval or
consent of his employers, Menello added. Rick returned to the studio after a week's absence, saw the new editor had recut the whole
film (putting scenes in different order), and demanded that the editor undo the changes.

Run, D.M.C., and Jam Master Jay watched the movie in
progress and were shocked to see how everyone's behavior on the
set affected the final product. Since the film had gone over budget,
two additional scenes with the Beastie Boys were not filmed, so the
Beastie Boys, who were introduced early in the film, suddenly van-
ished from the movie. The same happened with Russell's character:
he disappeared halfway through the film but reappeared for a few
seconds at the end.

Without these scenes, *Tougher Than Leather* felt incoherent.
Then new editors complained that Rick's cameras hadn't provided
enough coverage to make for interesting or articulate scenes. Sometimes it seemed he just set up a camera and had people parade in
front of it, they felt.

The film managed to include a few explosions, but its look changed from scene to scene: one minute everything was well lit; the next, it was crude and low budget. And Rick Rubin, busy producing albums, didn't attend many editing sessions. "He'd come and go," said Menello. "He had other work to do. That's the other problem."

But that was the least of it. Since Run and D didn't always follow the script, they left out pivotal information that drove many scenes. Without certain lines of dialogue, parts of the movie didn't make much sense. That it was taking so long to edit (Rick Rubin had finished filming in December 1986) meant Run-D.M.C. had to dig into their pockets to pay their part of production costs, which rose from $200,000 to $500,000 and then, "close to a million because of the postproduction," said Menello.

When they saw their concert footage, however, Run was ready to spend a little more. He watched the footage and shook his head. "Yo, these rhymes are old," he said.

Menello replied, "No they aren't. They're great. They're still fly. Maybe you've seen it a lot."

"No, no, these rhymes are old," Run insisted. "This stuff is old. We got to do new songs."

Run started developing ideas for new songs to include in the film. "Public Enemy used 'Funky Drummer' [for the single 'Rebel Without a Pause']," Run said, and he wanted to use the same sample on a new Run-D.M.C. work. In his basement, Run mixed the by then overwrought break-beat "Funky Drummer"—ubiquitous, since most rappers were using "Funky Drummer" on their own songs that imitated Public Enemy's energetic sample-driven sound—with Michael Jackson's ballad "I Just Can't Stop Loving You," and felt that a rhyme to the same melody Jackson sang would make for an interesting song. D loved the idea, as did Jay, who filled gaps in lyrics with a variety of scratches (including one in which ir-reverent comedian Sam Kinison yelled, "Dick in your mouth all day"). But instead of using "Funky Drummer," in the studio Jay fashioned a track from the similar-sounding break beat "Amen Brother," a few dreamlike bells from Bob James's "Nautilus," and a vinyl test pressing of Run and D's vocals for this new work, "Beats to the Rhyme."

Run then created another new song for the film, called "Mary Mary," by mixing the Monkees' break beat with Run's beloved "I Can't Stop." D and Jay loved its rugged sound. Then D suggested, "Let's get Rick. He knows this rock shit."

Rick Rubin visited Run's house to hear the idea. "I'm scratching 'Mary Mary' with 'I Can't Stop' and it's crazy," Run told Rick. "We should make a record called 'Mary Mary Where You Going?' "

"No," Rick said. "Why don't you say 'Why are you bugging?' "

It was another great idea, so Run ran down to his turntables and created the sound track. Rick joined them in the studio to make "Mary Mary" as enjoyable and commercial as *Raising Hell*'s break-out hit "Walk This Way." Run-D.M.C. had initially resisted record-ing with Aerosmith, but in the almost two years since the crossover hit's release in 1986, they had accepted that a white audience wanted this sound from them; other, newer acts like P.E. had usurped their position as kings of rap; and they really needed a surefire hit to bring in money. "It was short as hell," D said of the recording ses-sion. "That shit was easy. I came in and wrote my rhyme in a sec-ond." They had no way of knowing "Mary Mary" would be the final Run-D.M.C. release produced by Rick Rubin.

While they created more songs for *Tougher Than Leather*, D noticed Run changing his distinctive style, rapping faster and cramming too many words into each sentence. "He's fucking bug-ging out," he told himself, but he also figured Run wanted to compete with rappers KRS-One, Rakim, and Big Daddy Kane, and let them know "I could do it better than you." Still, D felt it wouldn't go over well with the audience. "Regardless of what was going on, people wanted to hear us as we were," he said.

After recording a few new songs, Run told D, "Yo, D, you're incredible, 'cause your shit is like simple"—the same thing he claimed the Beasties said during the *Raising Hell* tour. D.M.C. was hurt. "Run was competitive with other rappers and I was just doing what I was doing in my bedroom when I was twelve."

Run and Russell then pressured D.M.C. to adopt Run's new style, said Runny Ray. "Russell was stressing them, screaming, telling D, 'Come on, you got to rhyme like this!' D was saying, 'I don't want to do that shit, man. That's not the way I rap.' But Russell kept forcing him and he had to do it."

To cope, D.M.C. looked to Public Enemy's Chuck D for inspiration, reciting crowded, Chuck-like lyrics on "Beats to the Rhyme" (their take on P.E.'s "Rebel Without a Pause"), "Radio Station" (informed by a lyric from "Rebel"), "I'm Not Going Out Like That" (which, like "Rebel," opened with a sampled speech), and "Soul to Rock and Roll" (which included the same Chubb Rock sample as "Rebel").

It bugged Chuck D out a little, but the influential Public Enemy star understood what was happening. If a few Run-D.M.C. tracks evoked the music on recent Public Enemy songs, Chuck said, "That was Jay and [new coproducer] Davy D getting together" and only right since "they influence you and they're influenced by you, no different from Motown and Stax."

Public Enemy producer Hank Shocklee, however, felt Run-D.M.C.'s decision to imitate P.E. records was "the recipe for disaster. Your record is your voice, your way of communicating. If you're looking at everyone else, trying to emulate what you see out there, you've lost your voice."

His bandmates had D.M.C. confused about how he should rhyme. He'd listen to cassette tapes and personal copies of songs from *Tougher Than Leather,* and question whether songs that featured his original, simpler style were any good. So before *Tougher Than Leather* was released he asked Jay: "Yo, how are my rhymes on this album? Because it is really starting to mess with me."

Jay said, "Are you stupid? Eric B and Rakim were flipping over everything you said. D, everybody loves you. Your fans can say all your rhymes."

After a nod, D asked, "Yo, Jay, you really like this album?"

Jay wasn't sure but said they needn't worry. "He was like, 'Yo, the shit is dope because *Eric B* said it was dope," D remembered.

Rick Rubin handled reshoots for *Tougher Than Leather* in January 1988. "Rick reshot at least three songs," Menello remembered. Since Profile eventually let Def Pictures have the sync rights—how this came to occur has never been revealed and sources interviewed for this work did not discuss the subject in detail—Run and D could be shown performing the new songs in the movie.

"They wanted 'Mary Mary,' " said Ric Menello. "They had 'Tougher Than Leather,' 'Beats to the Rhyme.' " And they were excited about "Run's House," another new song set to a "Funky Drummer"–style beat. "They said, 'This has to be the song at the end; we can't have that other song. We got to have "Run's House," ' " Menello added.

But not as many people attended the reshoot at the Manhattan rock club the Ritz, so filmmakers faked the audience by editing scenes of crowds from earlier sequences. And though the Beasties were still suing Def Jam in 1988, trying to officially leave, and had no intention of recording for Rick and Russell again, Run-D.M.C. wore Beastie Boys T-shirts for a scene in which they performed "Mary Mary" at an outdoor jam. "It was love!" D said.

Then Rick and Russell decided they needed to show more of Runny Ray, and had a second-unit film crew create a montage of scenes—Ray walking the streets, helping fellow citizens, looking very nonthreatening and sympathetic—that would play while Run-D.M.C. performed "Mary Mary" on tour and more fully introduce the character to viewers. Costs spiraled even more. "Oh hell yeah," D snapped. "There were a couple of things we had to reshoot, like the very end. In the beginning, I'm heavy and at the end, I lost about ten pounds since I had started working out. We lost a lot of money on that, too. We took about $250,000 of our money, reshot it, and the movie flopped." But they were to blame, Menello recalled: "Run-D.M.C. wanted to reshoot the songs."

Things got even worse. During the final days of postproduction, for whatever reason, the film editor cut the ending (Run-D.M.C. backstage considering D's proverb: Every man is every child's father). "Put that scene back in!" Rick demanded. The editor said he would, then shipped the film without it. With the film behind them, Run felt depressed. They'd be following their 4-million-selling *Raising Hell* with an album that featured a new P.E.-inspired sound he lacked confidence in, and a movie that had sucked up $250,000 of their earnings. "We didn't really think about it till the end and said we'll never do it again," D.M.C. sighed.

Run-D.M.C. had an album finished but couldn't release it, since they didn't know which label they'd be signed to. Profile would have put it out, but for six agonizing months, Russell and Rush Management insisted on feuding with the label over contractual terms. Russell also wanted to see how the lawsuit he encouraged Run-D.M.C. to file would turn out. He and other Def Jam executives hoped Profile would finally allow Run-D.M.C. to leave the label, sign to Def Jam, and fill the void left by the best-selling Beastie Boys, who had now moved to California to sign a new deal with major label Capitol Records, and record their follow-up, *Paul's Boutique*.

When the Beasties left Def Jam, Rick Rubin started working with rock bands, and Russell began to sign more R & B groups to the label. Once Russell saw his signing Oran "Juice" Jones score a number one hit with "The Rain," Russell began to seek out other R & B singers and to devote his attention to creating the sort of romantic ballads he had enjoyed during his childhood in Hollis. (He even convinced his hard-core artist L.L. Cool J to record a love rap to an actual ballad for L.L.'s chart-topping pop hit "I Need Love.") But none of Def Jam's other acts could match the Beastie Boys' historic sales of *Licensed to Ill* (which remained the best-selling rap album of all time).

"Let's face it, Def Jam was technically over with," said P.E. producer Hank Shocklee. "The Beastie Boys were the crossover act for the entire label. They were the ones getting white kids into hip-hop while maintaining the credibility of the streets. With the Beastie Boys gone, no one could fill that role, so Rick started making rock records, and Russell started trying to make rap records, which wasn't the formula. The formula was Rick makes the records, Russell promotes the records, and the Beastie Boys gave Rick credibility to produce hip-hop."

Both partners were creating music, and heading in different directions (Rick signed metal band Slayer and comedian Andrew Dice Clay, and Russell recruited R & B acts Oran "Juice" Jones and the Black Flames). They were also divided on the issue of Rush employee Lyor Cohen, who had risen through the ranks to act as Russell's right-hand man at the management company. Russell kept involving Lyor, who had helped with Run-D.M.C.'s Adidas endorsement deal, in creative decisions that affected Def Jam. "Lyor was trying to tell Rick what to do with Def Jam," said Doctor Dre, "and Rick was like, 'You just take care of . . . get Run-D.M.C. off of Profile!' "

The more Lyor was involved, the less Rick reported into Def Jam's offices. "He just wasn't there," Adam Dubin remembered. Run-D.M.C. also wasn't dropping by Def Jam as much. "Russell was at Rush Management sometimes but he got Lyor in and Lyor was running that," said Dubin. "Then all these people showed up that were not there in the beginning and it became a 'record company.' It became like business."

To earn money, Run-D.M.C. turned to touring, performing hits from their first three albums in various arenas. Otherwise, the still-respected trio would have been at home, angry and embittered about their career coming to a halt. The irony was that they were battling to sign to Def Jam after seeing the Beasties emerge triumphant from their lawsuit against the label. When the Beastie Boys broke free of Russell and Rick Rubin, D.M.C. revealed, "I was jealous. And I was like that was a good thing and we should have done it but we were trying to show too much loyalty to Russell and Profile, and not getting enough money. I was fucking jealous," he repeated, " 'cause they were taking control of their own careers. When a band does that, they move on to bigger and better things. We just stayed under the wing of Russell and everything."

Run-D.M.C.'s lawsuit against Profile was getting them nowhere. The lawsuit also delayed the release of their fourth album so long that even their new songs were beginning to sound old-fashioned. In his apartment at 111 Barrow Street, right under Russell's place, Jam Master Jay regularly played every song from Public Enemy's upcoming second album, *It Takes a Nation of Millions to Hold Us Back.*

Everyone was excited about Public Enemy's new album, said Def Jam promotions man Bill Stephney. "I remember playing Rick most of the stuff we finished and him basically saying he was retiring from producing because he can't top Public Enemy."

Jay was just as amazed by its sound, which was created in various studios, where producers the Bomb Squad—Chuck D, Hank Shocklee, Hank's brother Keith, Eric Sadler, William "Flavor Flav" Drayton, and sometimes Bill Stephney—had sifted through huge record collections, sampled break beats, and then added their own personal touches. Each producer had different approaches. The result was an album with beats as energetic as those by new producers Eric B and Scott La Rock, songs as powerful as those made by Run-D.M.C. and Larry Smith, and a sound as funky as singles by WBLS radio DJ and producer Marley Marl. Once the Bomb Squad created a beat, Chuck tried various lyrics on it; then they piled on horn blasts, guitar riffs, recorded speeches, and two-part scratch solos (blurred guitars and prominent vocal chants from other rap singles). And on songs like "Don't Believe the Hype," they mixed the break-beat "Substitution" on two turntables before piling on dozens of samples from other records.

Jay, who received a copy of P.E.'s finished album from one of its producers, kept playing and enjoying it. "Just heavy, heavy rotation," said Bill Stephney. "Wouldn't even play any of the stuff they were working on."

D.M.C. also played borrowed tapes of songs from the P.E. album, and felt the collection was a work of genius. Once Hank Shocklee supplied D.M.C. with an advance copy of the entire album, D.M.C. kept playing it on his truck's sound system. "You could hear the shit from fifty blocks away," D bragged, and he kept blasting "Don't Believe the Hype" even though Public Enemy felt they should leave this song off the album because its tempo was too slow and Chuck's lyrics about radio and the media were too cerebral.

However, D.M.C.'s and Jam Master Jay's opinions soon changed that intention. One evening, after midnight, D drove Jay to 125th Street in Harlem, where they'd hang out with friends like heavyweight boxing champion and rap fan Mike Tyson in front of Dapper Dan's clothing store. Since Jay wanted to hear P.E.'s new song "Don't Believe the Hype," D.M.C. said, "I pulled up in front of Dapper Dan's with the shit blazing: 'Don't believe the hype, hoo-ah!'"

Chuck D and Hank Shocklee had just left a recording session and were driving by. They saw D.M.C. and Jam Master Jay playing the song for a crowd that had just left the Apollo Theater. "Me and Chuck didn't go up to the truck, because we couldn't get through the crowd," said Hank. "But when we heard that, we said, 'Let's pull 'Don't Believe the Hype' out the "don't do" pile.' "

In the spring of 1988, six months after filing it, Run-D.M.C.'s law-suit against Profile Records had got them nowhere: Def Jam still wanted Run-D.M.C.'s new songs on the Def Jam sound track to the upcoming movie *Tougher Than Leather,* and Profile wouldn't budge. Jam Master Jay wanted this to end and hoped that no matter where Rush Management led Run-D.M.C., he would be able to sign a contract that would give him an equal share of profits from the group. The delay was killing them, he knew, and would only hurt the *Tougher Than Leather* album. It was good, but new rappers were changing rap's sound every day, and their new work might sound old when it was finally released. The worst thing about this lawsuit, Jay felt, was that Rush Management had started it, and all Run-D.M.C. could do was wait it out.

Rush sent someone to Profile (many people said Lyor Cohen) to finally resolve the dispute. Rush employees felt the group had the upper hand, and that Run-D.M.C. would join the Def Jam family. But by the close of business that day, word spread that Run-D.M.C. had instead signed to Profile for a few more years. They'd receive money, an insider noted, but the long battle resulted in them "rene-gotiating *for a long contract* rather than going to Def Jam." They wouldn't win the case. They wouldn't sign a new deal with another label. There would be no huge up-front payment.

Rush and Profile still hadn't finished negotiations, but Jam Mas-ter Jay headed to Profile's office with a shopping bag in each hand, and without an appointment. In Cory Robbins's office, Jay handed him the two bags.

Cory asked, "What's this?"

Jay said, "There are the masters."

The issue of the lawsuit had been that Run-D.M.C. supposedly didn't want to release its next album on Profile. As the lawsuit continued in court, Run-D.M.C. had held on to the master tapes—enormous reel tapes that contained the actual music they had spent the last two years recording. Without these tapes, Profile would not be able to release the new works. Cory was touched, since the lawsuit hadn't been settled yet, and both sides were supposed to be in a big fight. Softly, he asked, "Why are you giving this to me?"

Jay wouldn't take them back. He just wanted the battle over with, and for Run-D.M.C. to get back to releasing hit albums.

While heading toward a locked closet that held tapes, Cory said, "All right. Well I'm gonna put them in the vault. I'm just gonna put them there. Thank you. That's a good sign."

As part of the settlement with Profile, Jay finally became an official member of Run-D.M.C. by also signing to Profile. Since he wasn't originally signed to the label, he had appeared in photos only on the back of the first two album covers. Now he'd appear with Run and D in every official group photo, and receive an equal share of the monies Profile Records paid the group for new albums and royalties. Cory Robbins felt it was about time. "He always contributed equally anyway," Robbins noted.

Jay was ecstatic, his cousin Doc recalled. " 'Finally. Finally, I'm an official part of the group. Now to get my "official" funds.' " According to Doc, up until that point Jay never felt he was getting his fair share.

After six heavy months, both sides behaved as if nothing had happened. "It was really like a big cloud had been lifted and everybody was nice again," Robbins said. But the battle hurt Run-D.M.C.'s fourth album, *Tougher Than Leather*. Profile scheduled release for April 1988, but Cory Robbins felt "they should have had an album out sooner after *Raising Hell*. It was two years, a long time in the world of rap, and the longest they had taken between albums. When they handed *Tougher Than Leather* in, we thought it was great and expected it to be an enormous success, bigger than *Raising Hell*, but it wasn't."

Run-D.M.C. forgot about signing to Def Jam, which was probably best, since Rick Rubin had told Russell he was unhappy with how things were changing at the label. Rick said to Russell their partnership had to end, and that one of them should leave the company. "Do you want to leave?" Rick asked.

Russell said, "No."

Rick nodded. "Okay, fine, I'll go."

When he learned Rick was leaving, Chuck D of Public Enemy got Rick an advance copy of the just-completed *Nation* album as a parting gift. On an airplane headed to his new home in Los Angeles, where he'd start producing rock bands, Rick listened to every groundbreaking track, and felt no one had ever done anything like this. Instead of Rick's slow and low Def Jam sound, rapping to one beat, P.E. sped the tempo, piled hundreds of samples on, and kept changing beats every few bars. "And that was the album where Chuck really started getting political," Rick recalled.

After hearing a few songs, Rick felt tears stream from his eyes. "I was so proud," he said. "Because to me it just took it to a whole new level and I remember crying, thinking that this is just such a beautiful thing that's evolving and growing." But he also felt something had ended. The era of albums like *Raising Hell* and *Licensed to Ill*, and the innocent early Def Jam sound that had helped Run-D.M.C. carry rap to the mainstream, was over. "It was really sad," Rick said, "really sad."

Profile released *Tougher Than Leather* in April 1988. Despite the delay, fans and radio stations reacted positively to both songs on its first single, "Run's House" and "Beats to the Rhyme." But to

Cory Robbins, the single was "not like the hits from *Raising Hell* that were bigger."

Profile remained optimistic, shipping advance orders of 1.25 million copies, but reviewers described Run-D.M.C.'s new lyrics as timid compared to "Hard Times," "It's Like That," and "Proud to Be Black."

Some reviewers rejected the funk guitar on "Miss Elaine," dubbed "Mary Mary" a failed attempt at another "Walk This Way," and unfavorably compared "Soul to Rock and Roll," "I'm Not Going Out Like That," and "Run's House" to Public Enemy's critically acclaimed *It Takes a Nation of Millions to Hold Us Back* (released during the same month). "While the members of Run-D.M.C. aren't yet in danger of losing their self-applied titles as the kings of rock," *Rolling Stone* felt, "the future is far less certain than it was two years ago."

In June, Rush Management told them they had to tour. Run didn't want to. He'd coped with his depression for months by keeping busy, devoting himself to writing new songs. But he didn't want to face an audience and perform songs he had mixed feelings about. But Rush Management said deals were signed, and they had to honor commitments. "I had to!" Run said. "They pushed me! They knew something was the matter with me and they pushed me out there." Run's resentment showed in a few performances, and in some of his interactions with opening acts Public Enemy, Jazzy Jeff & the Fresh Prince, EPMD, and other groups Russell managed. "He was mad at everyone," D.M.C. said. "He thought niggas was stealing from him and everything." Run felt they deserved more.

Jay didn't like seeing Run like this. "Because that's his man," said Jay's cousin Doc. " 'Damn, my man ain't feeling right. Things are not going right for my man right now.' " But Jay understood why Run was angry. Jay was facing just as many money problems because of financing their upcoming movie and the unsuccessful two-year battle against Profile. And in some ways, Jay had it even worse. Though the group had toured a little, Jay had reportedly neglected to pay income tax on some of his *Raising Hell* earnings, and the IRS was charging him interest and penalties that brought his debt to the IRS above the six-figure mark. And with Run falling into a depression that could potentially ruin a much-needed money-earning tour, Jay stepped forward to assume a position of leadership, keep the tour going, and keep money coming in.

When the Run's House tour (in support of *Tougher Than Leather,* which had sat in stores since April 1988) reached Philadelphia, Jam Master Jay learned that Chuck D planned to hang a Ku Klux Klansman doll in effigy onstage. Jay and towering road-crew employee Big D Jordan combed the halls of the Spectrum Arena, seeking the defiant rapper. They found Chuck backstage, and Jay calmly told Chuck he couldn't do it. "So me and Jay got into a discussion where Jay was being nice about it, I was being kind of aggressive, and Jay had to pretty much put me in check by saying, 'This is a Run-D.M.C. tour, this is the Run's House tour, and when Public Enemy headlines a tour, then you guys will do what you want,' " Chuck recalled.

Jay then explained that it was a matter of safety, Chuck said. The Run's House tour would play all kinds of venues. "You know, you got nonunion crews," Chuck remembered Jay explaining. "Some places down south, you got straight crackers. 'Yo, they could put a stanchion up wrong and have a light fall on somebody's head.' When he explained that, I was, like, 'Cool.' "

By July 1988 *Tougher* had sold over a million copies, but some critics still described it as a flop. "They were comparing it to *Raising Hell,*" said publicist Tracy Miller. Others harped about the dearth of rock-rap songs. "They got the hard-core that Run-D.M.C. started with," said Hurricane. Lower sales by at least a million didn't bother D as much as the fact that they wouldn't be able to rush-release a better, new album. "Actually I was jealous of people on Def Jam," D said. "Profile would never let us put albums out when we wanted. I had so much material in me and in my book and Chuck and L.L. were able to make albums every year. It seemed they had freedom and we would have to wait three years and 'wait to see the success of the single.' I was like, 'Put *Tougher Than Leather* out, and six months later put the next album out.' And that shit was frustrating."

Meanwhile, Run was growing despondent. Onstage in twenty-thousand-seat arenas, Run noticed eight thousand seats were empty. And since *Tougher* was nowhere near matching *Raising Hell*'s sales, Run worried that peers, reporters, and fans would say they had fallen off. He was competitive to the point "where his biggest enemy is himself, as with many great cats," Chuck D said.

Obsessing over low sales figures depressed Run even more. "I didn't know any better," said Run. "You kind of go nuts when you're Michael Jackson in your mind. You sell 4 million and then. . . It was too much, too much pressure to worry about." He was also angry with Rush Management for pushing him to tour. "They were like, 'The show must go on,' I guess."

On tour, Run would withdraw to his hotel room to brood about falling off and to wonder why everyone seemed to be ignoring his displeasure. "If you study up on depression you'll see what I went through. Study up on deep depression. That's where Run was at: clinical depression."

Onstage, Run performed with his usual energy, but offstage, "He'd just stand there," said Ray. "People trying to talk to him but he ain't saying shit." When it became apparent that *Tougher Than Leather* would sell only 1.5 million copies, Run believed he was right: people *were* gossiping about how Run-D.M.C. was over. He didn't even want to go onstage. "They just pushed me out there and said, go. I would get pushed onstage every night."

His tourmates—Public Enemy, Jazzy Jeff & the Fresh Prince, and EPMD, all inspired to begin rapping because of Run-D.M.C's early albums—noticed Run's shift in mood, and sympathized with his situation. "Run had success for a long time," said P.E. producer Hank Shocklee. "When you're out there on the road, in the public, and your record is 'number one,' 'blowing up,' and 'doing all kinds of great things' and everyone admires you, adores you, and that happens for years, well, when that stops, there has to be something inside you that dies. And everybody deals with that differently."

D.M.C. partied with road-crew members and crates of Olde English 800. He tried to bond with Chuck D over forties, but learned Chuck didn't drink or smoke. Humbled, he retreated to his dressing room to continue drinking with his pals.

Midway through the tour, they reached Houston. Run continued to regret making the movie *Tougher Than Leather* with their money. As he now understood, film studios financed production if executives liked a script. Quincy Jones and New Line had both wanted to foot the bill, but Rick and Russell had insisted they do it on their own. Run worried that the movie would flop like the album and cost Run-D.M.C. what little remained of its audience. Run also felt his managers—Russell Simmons; Russell's right-hand man at Rush, Lyor Cohen; and their various subordinates—didn't care about his feelings. They just wanted him to keep making money for them. Nothing could cheer Run up. He didn't even want to smoke weed anymore, and wondered if he should even be alive.

"I was beyond depressed," Run explained. "Not because records weren't selling but because depression is an illness."

D.M.C., however, felt *Tougher*'s sales were somewhat responsible. "Once it wasn't as big as *Raising Hell* he got depressed." D urged him to lighten up, and reminded him that Run-D.M.C. had made history with *Raising Hell* and many other achievements. "We just sold 3 million *Raising Hell*s!" he added.

At a truck stop between shows, Run bought some sort of product that could prove fatal if ingested. No group member ever revealed what it was, but Run poured some of it into a can of cola in his hotel room, set the can on a table, and stared it down. I may be crazy, he thought, I may be depressed, but I'm not drinking it. Another time, he stepped onto a balcony outside of a hotel room, and considered the fifty-story drop. I may be depressed, I may be crazy, but I'm not jumping, he thought.

Russell somehow learned about Run's suicidal mind-set—perhaps from Rush employees, road-crew members who had grown up in Hollis with Russell, or even other members of Run-D.M.C.—and tried to help, D recalled, by asking, "Yo, Run, what the fuck are you buggin' out for? Motherfucker, you're stupid! You sold a half million records and bands wish they could do that." Then: "Do you know how many people would want to sell a million and a half records? Do you know what you're throwing away?"

"He *tried* to talk to me but it was going in one ear and out the other 'cause I was nuts," said Run.

Chuck D also tried to cheer him up. "I would counsel, and sit with Run," Chuck recalled. "It's very hard to know you made the greatest rap album of all time. You think you're supposed to be better than that but the fact that he wasn't kind of threw Run into a little spin." Run was as impervious to Chuck's pep talk as he'd been to Russell's.

After a concert in Phoenix, Arizona, road-crew employee Runny Ray stopped by Run's hotel room to see how Run was doing, and saw Run had turned the heat in his room up to maximum. "We in Phoenix, Arizona!" Ray said. "What you doing with the heat on? What is wrong with you, man?" The tough-love approach didn't work, so Ray sat and listened to Run say, "Yo, man, I'm depressed." Ray became so sad he said, "Yo, Joe, you fucking me up, man." Ray added: "I used to go sit in his room and cry with this nigga."

Ray tried to cheer Run up on the tour bus by playing him Michael Jackson's inspiring song "The Man in the Mirror." "I would always play that in my bunk. Him and me were right across from each other. I would open his curtain and play it."

The tour ended but Run was still sad when Run-D.M.C. traveled to MTV's midtown studios in August 1988 to be the first guests on a new show called *Yo! MTV Raps*. On the colorful set, cohost Doctor Dre, who had also left Def Jam, stood behind the turntables. "They were still pretty huge," Dre recalled. After taping the segment, Dre told Run that fans still loved Run-D.M.C.

"It's hard," Run replied. "I don't know. I can't believe this. We were doing 4 million. Dre, you remember. . . ."

"Nah, dude," Dre said. "Everything grows and moves on."

Before they left, Jam Master Jay asked Dre, privately, what he thought about Jay creating his own record label. Jay realized Run-D.M.C. was in decline, sales had dipped, and that Run was suffering from severe depression. Jay asked Dre if he thought starting a new record label without his bandmates would be disloyal to Run-D.M.C. Dre told him absolutely not: "Try to take a vacation so you guys can just enjoy your lives a little and the fruits of your labor," Dre added. "And then start thinking about something else."

At home during the autumn of 1988, Run's depression persisted. "It affected everything around me," he said. "I couldn't think straight. I really should have been on medication." He was also reclusive, said Jay's cousin Doc. "He would stay in the house. If he needed something from the store he would send someone like Runny Ray because he couldn't handle that much attention." Run also neglected his personal hygiene, and began to balloon in weight, Ray recalled. "He'd get a cheeseburger, order of fries, order of onion rings, a chocolate shake, and have the big apple pie à la mode. He'd always get that. He was also a sloppy eater. He had ketchup all over his face." If people rode with Run in his impressive 735 BMW, they might see moldering slices of pizza tucked in the door pockets, Ray said.

Russell's big plan for a book, a movie, and an album to arrive in stores and theaters at the same time had failed. Their authorized biography was released first to critical acclaim. Thankfully, *Tougher Than Leather* was described in the *L.A. Times*

"Calendar" section, the *New York Times* entertainment section, and many national magazines as a major production, not a low-budget action film. "People were comparing it to *Beverly Hills Cop*, so audiences were expecting this big slick film," screenwriter and costar Ric Menello recalled.

Before the movie's release, and before his departure, Rick Rubin and Menello created a TV ad that included action-packed scenes, and Public Enemy's Flavor Flav saying, "Yo, it's the brother man versus the other man!" But New Line, the studio that had wanted to distribute the film since seeing its screenplay and also the company that paid Def Pictures for the right to distribute the film, "didn't care," Menello felt, and didn't pay TV stations to air the commercial, since the distributor felt the low-budget film would earn more money as a videocassette sold exclusively in stores.

Tougher Than Leather arrived in theaters in September 1988. Many hip-hop acts came to the premiere to show support, but in the darkened theater, Run-D.M.C. watched the film, and felt it should have been more realistic.

Some film critics considered *Tougher Than Leather*'s mix of gunplay and slapstick comedy uneven. They liked seeing Run and Jay help D.M.C.'s character regain his footing when he left prison, and seeing all three members interact with their outspoken manager, Russell, but reviled Rick's acting, the Beastie Boys' subplot, and a few rambling monologues. Other critics felt the film promoted "reverse racism" toward whites, screenwriter Ric Menello recalled.

But Run-D.M.C. fans were excited. For them, *Tougher* had all the best stars in it: Run-D.M.C., Slick Rick, the Beasties, even Flavor Flav providing a voice-over before the opening scene (added quickly during postproduction). The film opened in fifty theaters, mostly around New York, and when they couldn't get in, fans grumbled and complained. Those who did buy a ticket didn't want anyone ruining the experience for them. In Long Island, one kid stabbed another. In Detroit "one guy stood up at one point during the showing and was shot in the back," Menello remembered. "I think he must've been blocking someone's view of the screen."

There were few violent incidents, but some newspaper reporters immediately claimed the film was causing riots. Run and D had to go on television to defend themselves, as they had in the Long Beach incident. They pointed out that the movie wasn't terribly violent and that violence had existed since the dawn of man—Run-D.M.C. didn't create it.

The first weekend brought in tremendous profit, but New Line continued to feel the movie would do better as a video, Menello recalled, and "didn't release it nationally, like they would an urban film now." Many people on the West Coast wanted tickets, but limited showings were sold out.

Tougher Than Leather quickly recouped its production costs, but everyone around Run-D.M.C. felt that if it had been released a year earlier—if sync rights and the lawsuit against Profile hadn't caused delays in its release—the movie would have been a hit. The experience of seeing *Tougher Than Leather*'s mediocre success further embittered the group. "It was just some cold bullshit," D.M.C. said.

CHAPTER 23

It's Called Survival

After the release of *Tougher Than Leather,* Run-D.M.C. asked Cory Robbins for permission to do a song for a movie sound track. Cory said, "No you can't do the *Ghostbusters* song cause it's a stupid idea and it's not cool for Run-D.M.C."

"But it's *Ghostbusters,*" Run said. "You got to let us do it!"

For a week, Run and D.M.C. visited Cory's office to sit on his couch and complain.

Cory kept saying no. "It was stupid," he felt. "It was like give me a break! They were just desperate to have a hit and be associated with some kind of movie, a mainstream thing like that."

He told Run, "You guys are much cooler than this. Why would you want to do *Ghostbusters?*" It wasn't even *Ghostbusters,* he thought. "It's *Ghostbusters 2.* And it was a stupid song."

"But they're gonna give you a lot of money," Run replied.

"I don't care," he said. "It's not about the money. This is the wrong thing for you to do."

The movie company started calling Profile every ten minutes to offer big bucks. "I don't care," Cory said into his telephone. "This is no. It's not good. It's a bad idea."

Run and D were upset, so Cory heaved a sigh and gave in. "All right, fine," he said. "You really want to do this? Go ahead. But this isn't cool. Its not a good idea for Run-D.M.C. to be doing the *Ghostbusters* theme."

Run and D were struggling now, trying to hold on to the last of their fame. They were also struggling financially. And since his nervous breakdown, "Joe was constantly eating and getting really heavy," Tracy Miller remembered. "There were jokes that he was gonna be one of the Fat Boys. And Darryl was drinking excessively, to the point where he almost died. Jason was the only one that could ever really handle anything. And Jay was just probably going crazy dealing with the two of them because they were so neurotic. So I think Jason decided to do some experimenting on that record, and it didn't do as well."

Jam Master Jay now felt that Run-D.M.C. wouldn't last forever. He told Runny Ray, "They're fucking driving me bananas. I'm gonna move on and get another group in case they break up." He was working with his old friends Hurricane, Cool T, and DJ Kippy-O, who planned to rap as the Untouchables. But one day while watching Robert Townsend's *Hollywood Shuffle*—a movie about young blacks trying to make it in white-run Hollywood—they were inspired by a scene in which white film producers pressure aspiring young actors to wear big Afro wigs. When Hurricane started mimicking one character's high-pitched voice, Jay said, "Yo, man, why don't we just do the Afros?"

"All right, cool," Hurricane answered. "Fuck it, let's go get some Afro wigs."

Jay decided to include his group the Afros on a new Run-

D.M.C. song called "Pause," which would appear on the B-side of their commercial "Ghostbusters Rap" single.

In the studio, they worked without a producer. "After *Raising Hell*, it wasn't as tight of a production life with Russell and them," said Run. "We took over our own life after a while." Sales were slipping, fewer promoters booked them, and their asking price was nowhere near the $150,000 a night they commanded during the *Raising Hell* era, so Jay consciously set out to imitate the R & B rap then popular on daytime radio, and Run supported Jay's decision to change Run-D.M.C.'s sound.

Jay programmed a thumping beat with the "Catch a Groove" drum sound, and played a horn blast like a bass line. He then invited twenty-one-year-old black keyboardist Stanley Brown to play riffs that evoked Bobby Brown's dance hit "My Prerogative."

Jay then had the Afros pile into the recording booth. "Afros . . . ," Hurricane whined into the mike.

The others chanted, "Yeah . . . ?"

"Afros!"

"Yeah . . . ?"

"Brothers be out there doing crack. . . ."

"No. . . ."

"They be doing dope. . . ."

"No . . ."

"They be gangbanging!"

"No . . ."

"All them brothers need to just . . . pause. . . ."

Jay's new R & B track started, and Run and D ad-libbed: "Here come the Afros, and the forty-ounce crew."

When it was time to shoot a video for "Pause," Run and D didn't wear their trademark hats. D wore an Apple Jack model with the brim turned back. They also abandoned their leather blazers and matching pants. Jay wore colorful baggy shirts and jeans that evoked De La Soul, a popular new Long Island trio with a flower-power image, and instead of a hat, Jay showed fans the embryonic dreadlocks he'd been growing since working with the similarly coiffed Jersey-based group the Fam-Lee. Then he called Hurricane on the phone to say, "Get the guys together. We're gonna do a scene in the beginning of the video with the Afros."

On the set, Run and D watched Cane, Kippy, and Kool—attired in wigs, dashiki shirts, and sunglasses—perform their intro for the camera. Jay then performed his rap while doing a dance he hoped to popularize—basically the preexisting "running man" with a few dramatic pauses. And during one of the song's lengthy keyboard solos, Jay said, "This beat is dope, D. I'm telling you, this beat is dope, just slamming, it's dope." Then: "Ah yeah, I like this R & B shit. Pause, pause, one more time!"

CHAPTER 24

Leaving Hell

arly in 1990, money problems were really getting Jam Master Jay down. He owed the Internal Revenue Service over $100,000 and the federal tax-collecting agency informed him that unless he remitted payment, the agency would place a lien on all of his earnings. Jay hoped to catch up on his bills, and ensure a place in the industry, by starting his own label, JMJ Records. This way, if Russell or Rush Management started feuding with Profile again, or if Run and D disbanded the group, Jay would have a way to support his family, his then-girlfriend Lee and their two-and-half-year-old son, Jason junior.

After inventing the Afros, Jay pitched Russell on his idea of JMJ Records. Russell agreed that the new company—with Jay, producer of Run-D.M.C. hits like "Peter Piper" and "My Adidas" at the helm—would contribute greatly to Russell's huge Rush Associated Labels project. RAL was part of a deal Russell had renegotiated with Def Jam's parent company, CBS, now owned by Sony, after Rick Rubin left in 1988. In exchange for bigger advances, more royalties, and money to hire new employees, Russell gave Sony 50 percent of Def Jam, but he bristled under the terms of the deal. It wasn't as 50-50 as it looked on paper since they split profits *after* Sony took 30 percent off the top, Russell claimed in his autobiography, *Life and Def*, and kept charging Def Jam fees for administration, distribution, marketing, manufacturing, and Sony overhead. So, in trying to "figure out how to create new profits to share with Lyor," Russell pitched Sony on RAL, "a bunch of labels under Def Jam." Sony felt that Def Jam acting as parent company to small new labels was a good idea, so Russell created six other imprints, said Hank Shocklee, the P.E. producer, who also worked in Def Jam's offices as a publicist. But instead of creating trends, RAL labels followed them, and glutted the market with poor imitations of other labels' top draws. RAL signed deals with female rapper Nikki D, producers LA Posse, R & B group Blue Magic, Orange Krush singer Allyson Williams, and De La Soul producer Prince Paul. "Then they felt the 'De La Soul vibration,' and Lyor started getting in and brought in Resident Alien and producer Sam Sever," said Shocklee. But these acts, and hardcore white rappers 3rd Bass, singer Don Newkirk, and female gangsta rapper the Boss, failed to match the Beasties' success with *Licensed to Ill*.

However, JMJ was one of the more successful RAL labels. The Afros' wigs, dashiki shirts, and comical raps attracted fans of NWA, Slick Rick, and 2 Live Crew, while their song "Federal Offense" offered Public Enemy–style politics. While Jay recorded the Afros' debut, Run and D stopped by to watch them record, party a little, and try on their wigs.

Jay worked around the clock to finish the Afros project and soon released a single called "Feel It," and its video, which had Flavor Flav—in a white tuxedo and top hat with shades—making a cameo. Then Jay released the Afros' album, *Kicking Afrolistics*, to good reviews and respectable sales. Since fans had reacted positively to the Afros, Jay felt his company had a chance to make it in an industry crowded with new labels and rappers competing for the same audience. Though he wanted to work with new discovery the Fam-Lee, and despite his physical exhaustion (brought on by all-night recording sessions for the Afros' debut), Jay immediately began work on Run-D.M.C.'s fifth album. "Russell was completely out of the picture," said D. "We didn't even give a fuck if he liked the record. And actually *he* wasn't caring either."

Russell was busy with a movie development deal, a syndicated show (*New Music Report*), a move into pop diva Cher's old apartment on nearby Fourth Street, and a change in lifestyle (giving up drugs, wearing preppy clothing, working out, eating healthier, and hanging with models). He was also overseeing the many Rush Associated Labels. When he did try to offer suggestions for new songs, the group ignored him. " 'Pause' was big," said Run. "We were doing our thing."

Jay and Run controlled the sessions, and kept session players busy adding keyboards to their beats. One night Jay invited singer Aaron Hall of the R & B group Guy onto a song. "Jay would fucking have a polka dancer on a record," D laughed. "I wouldn't have had the keyboard shit. I wouldn't have had any R & B on the damn record. It would have been just rock and rap, hard shit."

After Hall crooned on "Don't Stop," Run recorded a lyric to denounce his rivals, and D's rap evoked Chuck D: "D.M.C. the king is me and I be the voice of black community." They abandoned another trademark, sharing sentences, and seemed to be heading in opposite directions (Run dissing like on "Sucker MCs" and D revisiting messages from "It's Like That"). They recorded "Faces," another confused number filled with Run's wordy rants and D stammering: "Yo, yo, yo: they don't understand me . . . when they always try to ban me."

"Bob Your Head" and "Not Just Another Groove" presented more of the same, with Jay repeatedly referring to the Afros. At first, Run—whose depression was no longer as pronounced as it had been during the Run's House tour—was enthusiastic about the new sound. "Anybody who doesn't like what me and my crew is doing, fuck you," he yelled on one song. "Punk motherfuckers! I'll break your fucking neck!"

But his opinion changed for some reason when they recorded "Party Time." This song had female singers doing a chorus that would have been at home on an old Kurtis Blow single: "It's party time, and we came here to party. So get up and move your body, 'cause it's party time." After recording a lighthearted verse for this song, Run surprised everyone by snapping, "All right, turn that bullshit off." Jay kept taping, and instead of removing the comment during the mix, Jay sent it to Russell. "Actually, Jay wanted Russell to hear how stupid his brother was acting," Jay's cousin Doc recalled.

The group was beginning to splinter, and Jay made matters worse by saying, "Yo, we gonna have Glen Friedman do a beat."

D was taken aback. "Glen Friedman? He's the photographer!"

"Yeah, but it's gonna be dope," Jay promised.

The thin, wiry photographer had helped nine other people shout "Run's house" on *Tougher Than Leather*. Now Friedman suggested they call the album *Back from Hell* and rap to the groove on the Stone Roses' recent single "Fool's Gold." The group loved the idea, Friedman claimed, so "I stayed in the studio and tried to help them 'cause it was *my* song, or I was working with them on it." Friedman wanted it to be as political as punk rock bands he used to manage, so Run rapped about gunfights and ambulances in the ghetto and D yelled, "The Ku Klux Klan is fucked up! And every good man will understand." Then Jay mixed the song and, Friedman felt, "kind of fucked it up." Friedman received a producer's credit but was unhappy with the result, "What's It All About."

D meanwhile watched Run cram even more words into every sentence of his new lyrics. He figured it might just be another symptom of the erratic thinking Run had been exhibiting since the onset of his depression circa 1987. "I just got mad when they told me, 'D, you got to write like Run,'" said D.M.C. "I was like, 'Okay,' but I should've just been me." D would try to sneak simpler rhymes into songs, but Jay would stop the tape and say, "It needs to rhyme more," meaning add more words like Run.

Jay and Run also alienated D by discussing grandiose marketing strategies. Instead of letting ideas come naturally, as with *Raising Hell*, Run and Jay wanted to imitate the latest groups and sounds. While they discussed ideas, D sat nearby, thinking, "Just put the damn record on, let me say my rhyme, master it, and let's give the people what made us the group they like." But he didn't speak up. He listened to people say things like "Oh, we need to be like Rakim," and shook his head. "No," he thought. "We need to be like the motherfuckers from Hollis that the world loved since 1983." After recording his part for a song, D would tell the others, "Call me when you want me." He now made a habit of leaving the studio, heading for a lounge, and staring at a television screen, alone. "D really wasn't feeling it," said Ray.

Then they had songs in which they tried to sound as hard as chart-topping gangsta rappers NWA. For D, NWA's style—expletives, descriptions of violent acts, odes to their crew—reminded him of stuff he'd written in his basement back in 1980, about shooting people and leaving them in alleys. Now D wrote about getting drunk with his new "40 Ounce Crew" and smacking people with a gun. Run and D.M.C. rapped about crackheads on "The Ave," convicts on "Back from Hell," and an armed-robbery gang on "Naughty." D's solo moment, "Livin' in the City," promoted education, but most new songs strayed from their simple, heartfelt lyrics, tag-team vocals, and hard, empty beats.

Their hangers-on said the new songs sounded great, but behind Run-D.M.C.'s backs, gossip was poisonous.

Unhappy with the new material, but unwilling to speak out, D.M.C. drowned his sorrows in Olde English 800 malt liquor. During shows he got onstage while "stinking drunk," forgot his rhymes, slurred them, spoke through Run's part, and tried to keep from falling while rushing across the stage to high-five a fan. His boys would warn him of how he was pissy the night before, but he'd still drink before shows and interrupt Run's self-congratulatory on-stage banter.

When Run and D attended a concert by Heavy D & the Boyz— a group led by an affable tall, overweight rapper who wore dapper suits and occasionally rapped for the ladies—Heavy, a loyal Run-D.M.C. fan, told his audience, "D.M.C. in the house." D got on-stage and asked for the mike. Someone said no, but D.M.C. wouldn't leave the stage. Heavy's audience witnessed D.M.C.'s complaining. He didn't stop until Run appeared in front of D.M.C. and said, "Yo, D, get off the stage. You're making a fool of yourself. D, you're drunk, people can't understand what the fuck you're saying."

Other times, in nightclubs, Runny Ray would have to stop his friend D from embarrassing himself by yelling lyrics at some kid who wanted to battle him.

"Jay put his foot down with D more than with Run because D was out in the street driving around drunk with a case of forties in his trunk," said Jay's cousin Doc. "The normal person goes to the store to buy one beer. D would wake up and get a case of forties. And that whole day was definitely for forties in the back of the trunk."

Jay told D.M.C., "D, you got to stop this drinking, man, going to the store early in the morning, drinking all day." But D ignored him. He'd have friends load cases of frozen beer into the trunk of his black Chevy Blazer. "And then when that ran out he'd go back and get another case of frozen forty ounces," said Ray. "D was *crazy*, man."

In the studio, D.M.C. soon rapped about his drinking on the reggae song "P upon a Tree." "I got to take a piss, man," he said; then, over reggae music, "I got to pee I got to pee upon a tree, right?"

ne night in the studio, after smoking marijuana together, Run and Jam Master Jay decided to include Chuck D of Public Enemy and popular gangsta rapper Ice Cube (formerly of NWA) on a remix of "Back from Hell" that would appear on the flip side of their single "Faces." They told D.M.C. that including them as guests would guarantee its success on rap radio, but D objected to the very idea of a remix. It was another step down for the group, he felt; their singles and album were supposed to be hot, not new versions of old songs. Chuck D should join them on a real song, not a remix. But Jay said, "Come on, D, this is how things are now. This is how they do it today."

Jay told D.M.C. to be at the studio at a certain time. D left his home in Long Island (where he'd moved in 1987) but instead of going to the studio, he went and got drunk. He finally arrived at midnight, hours late, and reluctantly recorded his verse. Whether D saw Chuck D or Ice Cube at this session is not known.

Run's new lyrics offered more descriptions of life in jail: Ice Cube rapped that he was "raising hell with Run." Chuck D offered a rare profanity. D quoted a recent NWA lyric: "Word to the '90s, rebels still rebelling. Cube, Run, and Chuck! Yo, what the fuck are they yelling?"

During the playback, however, Jay shook his head. "Yo, D, you could have did it better!" he yelled. "You sound pissy drunk on it. Yo, you're trying to fuck shit up!"

D yelled back, "I didn't want to do it! You made me come out here and do this remix!"

"Yo, I'm'a punch you in your face, man."

Run shouted, "No you ain't! You ain't doing nothing!"

With *Back from Hell* completed, Profile and Rush discussed releasing "Don't Stop," with Aaron Hall, as the first single. "And here's Run talking about, 'Oh, I ain't trying to revive nobody's career,'" Doc recalled.

Profile instead released "What's It All About," and shipped *Back from Hell* to stores, but knew something was wrong. "It didn't have the same kind of excitement as the previous albums," said Cory Robbins. When Profile employees called record stores and distributors to see what reorders were like, they learned that "they weren't good."

Rolling Stone's review panned the album. In November 1990, sales stalled below the 500,000 mark. "I was like, 'Cool, can we make another record?'" D.M.C. said. Profile said no. "We had to wait."

Cory Robbins felt these sales figures were horrendous. "*Back from Hell*, that album really didn't even go Gold." Then the star-studded remix flopped, and in fury Jay told Run, "You made me waste my money on that fake-ass remix!"

"You were with the idea too!" Run answered.

CHAPTER 25

Ohio

In late 1990, with hip-hop records streaming forth from so many companies, including Russell's grandiose but low-selling RAL imprints, Run also decided to start a label. He had discovered a rapper named Smooth Ice, who was as melodious as Rakim, wore an Applejack Kangol hat, hailed from Queens, and inspired MCA Records to back Run's new label.

Run was working with Jam Master Jay on music for Smooth Ice, D.M.C. recalled, when he said, "D, you ain't doing nothing now. You want to get down?"

D agreed, paid $10,000 for a share in the new label, JDK Records, then created a track for Smooth's lyric, "Smooth but Def."

D also worked with Jam Master Jay on Smooth's song "Do It Again."

Smooth's music, however, imitated the Bomb Squad sound on Public Enemy albums. And with so many other rappers already using "Funky Drummer" and "The Grunt," the samples didn't sound as fresh on Smooth's "I'm Coming" or "Without a Pause."

Yet JDK's distributor, MCA, saw the value of having Run-D.M.C.'s brand name in production credits, and felt "Smooth but Def," was commercial enough to appear on Smooth Ice's first single, so Run-D.M.C. optimistically chatted about the label in *Billboard* magazine. "Run and I had been thinking about this for some time," D, then twenty-seven years old, told *Billboard* in January 1991. "People kept asking us to produce them, and we saw the success of companies like Profile. We decided to do it now while we're young."

But Smooth Ice's two singles flopped, and MCA dropped the JDK label deal. Even worse, according to D.M.C., Rush Management was leading Run-D.M.C. into another round of disputes with Profile Records.

Run-D.M.C. had wanted to follow *Back from Hell* with another, hopefully better, album, and could desperately use the cash advance another album would bring. But when Russell asked Profile to revise a few undisclosed terms in their contract, Profile refused to renegotiate the contract, and Russell advised Run-D.M.C. to withhold their services until he worked this out. "In all honesty there were always these maneuvers going on to try to get them onto Russell's label," Tracy Miller said with a laugh. But these episodes affected their career. "I always thought, 'This is stupid. If management would stop playing games, if everybody would just knock it off and let these guys knock out their albums, they could have been off the damn label by now.' "

Their original commitment had been for seven albums. "So you could have knocked one out every year and been off by 1990," Miller continued. "But they were always dragging it out, lawsuits that cost *the group* money. Management would file a lawsuit, and D.M.C. says the group would have to pay those fees. It wasn't like management was paying out of their pocket; it came out of the guys' money. So at the end of the day the band got screwed."

D wanted to record again. "I basically had a good relationship with them cats," D said of Profile. "It wasn't *me*: the relationship between *Russell and Profile* was volatile. It wasn't necessarily us."

Run was at the end of his rope. He told the others, "We don't need Russell for our management. We can find somebody else." People thought he was venting, but he was serious. "He got vexed at his own brother and said, 'I don't want Russell to manage me no more,'" said Doc. "I heard him say that personally. He was fed up with Russell." Jay paid little heed to this latest contract dispute and focused on working with groups at JMJ Records. Then Profile planned to release a greatest hits collection instead of a sixth original Run-D.M.C. album. Since a greatest hits album would bring no advance, Run-D.M.C. booked a few concerts to earn much-needed cash. "There was no *Back from Hell* tour," Run explained. "We were in a van. We did shows for five, six, seven grand, ten grand here, five grand there, ten grand, oh, snap a twelve-grand gig; just doing it. A little van . . . It didn't matter. I would drive anywhere, do anything. I'd play for free. I loved winning. Even if I didn't have a big album when I got onstage, if I was overweight, anything: 'I'm gonna win tonight.'"

D wasn't as content. Though *Back from Hell* had been in stores for about eight months, he said, "The biggest crowd we had might be five hundred people." More R & B on the album translated into fewer white audiences and much smaller venues. Now D—like Run during the Run's House tour for *Tougher Than Leather*—was half-hearted about performing with the group in concert. Run meanwhile was still a little depressed but determined to earn money to support his family. "I wanted to do a solo record but out of loyalty I didn't," D added. "There was so much other shit out there I liked and we weren't doing it. We were bugging out."

Russell suggested they record solo albums. By doing so, they could possibly sign to labels other than Profile—since they would officially be soloists and not Run-D.M.C., and since a new deal would bring them money. Run was open to calling himself "Fat Joe." D was reluctant until he learned Jay would produce. But nothing came of this idea, either, so D started living on his savings and what little he earned from shows that paid the group less and less. "And because Russell had to protect his brother, I was just in the middle of the bullshit."

Run's eighteen-month depression was lightening, Ray said, but Run kept "smoking his weed, blazing as usual." After a show one night in Amsterdam, Run barged onstage during a concert by C + C Music Factory, a chart-topping dance rap group with a ponytailed shirtless rapper, house music beats ("house" being a faster, stripped-down form of disco), and fat ladies singing "Come on, let's work." Inebriated, Run kept running onstage to dance with them. "And everyone was looking at him," D remarked. "But he was having a good time. Didn't think about whether it went over well or not." Though the plan for solo albums was shelved, for reasons unknown, D kept wondering if he shouldn't strike out on his own. Run-D.M.C. was going downhill. He realized his situation. Run would continue to act like he was "leader of the group." Jay would blindly do his bidding. Their manager, Russell, was Run's brother. D had no say in any decisions. But then he remembered how tight he and Run had been before their first record, and decided to stay. "Okay, you can't beat them, join them," he explained. "That's what happened when I stayed with Run."

Their friends were sad to see once-mighty Run-D.M.C. reduced to playing small venues. One of Jay's friends in the Hollis Crew, Big D Jordan, was acting as their road manager, and they couldn't get anything better. *Nigga, we doing a damn club that only hold about fifty people!"* Ray remembered one group member saying (Ray didn't specify who). Some observers began to agree with Run, and felt Run-D.M.C. needed new management. "At that point of their career, they should have gotten away from Russell, and hooked up with a better, bigger, more established manager that does rock venues," said producer Hank Shocklee. But they never did change management.

In early August 1991, Run-D.M.C. and Jam Master Jay traveled to Ohio to perform another small show. Loyal fans were still nostalgic enough, and willing to pay to see them perform "Peter Piper," "Walk This Way," and other old hits.

After the show they returned to their hotel. In the hallways, groupies waited, hoping the group would pick them from the crowd. "Run met the girl the usual way," D later wrote in his auto-biography, *King of Rock*. She was a woman who had attended their show, stood in the front row, learned where they were staying, then arrived at the hotel with friends. By this point, a member of L.L. Cool J's entourage was already serving a ten-year prison sentence after partying with a supposedly willing groupie following a con-cert. D went straight to his hotel room, thinking he'd see Run back home, since "Run was flying home the next day." D did not see Run for the rest of the evening.

That night at 2:00 a.m., someone—possibly road manager Big D Jordan—barged into Runny Ray's room and woke Ray up. "Yo, we going!"

Ray suspected something had gone wrong, but didn't want to know anything about whatever it was. Instead of "Why?" or "What's going on?" he said he asked, "When are we leaving?"

This person, Ray recalled, blurted out, "Some girl just came out the room and said Run raped her!"

They told D.M.C. they were leaving. Bewildered, D went downstairs, got in the van alongside Jam Master Jay, and settled in for the ride back to New York. While describing this evening in *King of Rock,* D's official position was that he did not know about the unidentified woman's accusation about being raped. D also did not detail whether he asked anyone in the van why they had to leave town that night. Runny Ray meanwhile stayed behind in the hotel. "I didn't do a damn thing," he said.

The next day, D.M.C. wrote in his book, he was driving in Hollis when his car phone rang. It was Big D Jordan: "Yo, D. What's up with this girl in Cleveland that said Run raped her?"

D's hands jerked on the wheel and he nearly drove off the road. *"What?"* A woman said Run had taken her to his room and forced her to perform oral sex. D was stunned. He had known Run since kindergarten, and Run was no rapist. Still, would a jury in Cleveland believe this? Suddenly he felt very afraid for Run. "What if he's got to do years?" he thought.

When D.M.C. reached Run by telephone a day later, his bandmate was at Taco Bell with his children. This was so crazy, Run told him: unbelievable. He complained about having to find a lawyer, having to fly back to Cleveland and surrender to the police. And Run told Runny Ray, in a weepy tone, "Yo, man, I'm telling you, man. I didn't rape this girl."

Tracy Miller "thought it was insane, that it was crazy, there's no way that it's true." Still, reporters wanted to speak with Run.

As Run's book, *It's Like That: A Spiritual Memoir,* told it, after the show he returned to the hotel, and saw groupies crowding the hallway. "Like we did after every show if we didn't have to perform the next day, we went home," he claimed. So he went home that very night, he wrote. Then while he was sitting down to dinner in his home in Queens, Big D called his cell phone: "Yo, some girl in Cleveland said you raped her." His appetite was ruined. Next, he learned cops in Ohio had found condoms, weed, and rolling papers in the hotel room. "It just didn't look good," Run wrote.

Russell helped Run find a good lawyer. Run's wife, Valerie, was upset. She believed he had slept with groupies and cheated on her. He said he didn't know his accuser; he'd never seen her before. "She wasn't in my room." *Ebony* and *Jet* wrote about it, and Tracy Miller told Russell: "We've got to get a statement out there because it needs to be met head-on."

People in the entourage gossiped. Run asked Runny Ray to accompany him to Ohio for moral support. They arrived and met with Run's lawyer before going to the courthouse. The lawyer, Ray recalled, assured Run he'd be fine. "We got there, he got locked up," Ray continued. "They locked him up when he went in front of the judge." Police handcuffed Run and led him out of the room. His lawyer got him released on $10,000 bond that very day, but in the first-class section of the flight back home, Run saw his face on a huge television screen: part of a news report telling fellow passengers he'd been arrested and charged with rape.

While Run awaited his court date, Run-D.M.C. returned to performing small shows here and there, for money. The group was still withholding services from Profile Records, as Russell had suggested, so Run's mood darkened, D drank more, and Jay watched Russell beef with Sony over the RAL deal; Russell was having trouble getting RAL albums out on time.

For these small shows, instead of Big D Jordan, D.M.C.'s friend Erik Blamoville served as road manager. In previous years, Erik had accompanied D.M.C. on tour and to other shows, just as a friend. He always made sure D showed up on time and "had everything I'd need waiting in the dressing room," D explained. He was reliable, so Run and Jay sat Erik down and told him, "Erik, we want you to be the group's manager." Erik agreed and became responsible for setting up shows.

Instead of huge arenas and large fees, they played oldies like "Rock Box" and "King of Rock" in tiny clubs for $2,500 to $3,000,

and backstage, Run told entourage and road-crew members, "No girls in the dressing room or near it." Said D.M.C.: "He said he ain't fucking nothing 'cause he don't want to get in trouble," and that the accusation "scared the shit out of him." But the crew ignored him.

When home, Run could see that Valerie continued to believe he'd slept with other women, so a marriage already made rocky by an eighteen-month depression deteriorated even more. "He came home off the road one day," said Ray. "She was gone. The kids were gone. All their clothes were gone." When she left, Ray added, "It seemed like he just gave everything up. He wasn't doing shit." His life seemed to stop.

"I don't want to get into all that," Run said coldly.

Valerie would bring the kids over every so often, Ray said. "And I used to watch them. 'Cause he used to go out and see if he could get her back, but it wasn't happening."

Friends sympathized with Run's plight. "She was his high school sweetheart," Larry Smith said of Valerie, and "out of all of them, Joe was the best father. Joe was one of the best fathers a child could ever have. Joe was home for that dinner. If he felt he'd be gone too long, he'd pack the family up and 'here they go around Europe!'"

Run himself had loved being a family man. He never hung out with the others. He'd go home. He liked to watch his kids sleep, to wake up early and help Val with the chores, to take out the trash and wash the car. "It's a real *organized* life," he once told biographer Bill Adler.

But Valerie's friends encouraged her belief that he had been with another woman. She kept asking whether he had cheated on her, and according to Ray, Run said he "didn't do anything," even though "there were condoms on the floor and shit like that."

They had been so happy. "I was at his first wedding," Glen Friedman said wistfully. "I remember Val, and the two girls when they were little, the old house in Queens."

hile Run's life was falling apart, D.M.C. was facing his own personal problems. One day in summer 1991 he woke up with an acute pain in his side. He'd dealt with this intermittently for six months, and decided it was caused by jumping around onstage. But on this particular morning, it really hurt. He tried to ignore the pain, as usual, thinking it would subside. He showered, dressed, and went out to get his morning beer. He hung with a road-crew employee, known as "Garfield," then early in the afternoon went home to put some food in his stomach. He ate rice, steak, and vegetables, but felt the pain return, worse than ever. He was staying with his parents—whether he lived with them is unclear (he's never mentioned it)—and when his mother, Bannah, arrived from her nursing job at 4:00 D.M.C. met her at the door, doubled over in pain. "Mom, don't come in," he said. "Turn around. I got to go to the hospital."

In a nearby emergency room, she filled out forms. After twenty minutes, he told his mother, "Ma. They have to take me now. They got to." But the clerk at the desk told her D had to wait his turn. Twenty minutes later, a nurse led them to a bed behind a curtain, and after another fifteen minutes, a doctor arrived. "Lie back," the doctor instructed.

D.M.C. couldn't do it. He also didn't let the doctor probe his abdomen.

"Do you drink?" the doctor asked.

"Yeah. Beer, malt liquor."

"How much do you drink a day?"

"Twelve forties."

The wide-eyed doctor told D.M.C.'s mother, "He's not going home." He then told a nurse: "Put him on an IV."

In bed, D.M.C. suffered more. They wouldn't give him painkillers until they learned what ailed him. Nurses kept taking his blood. The next morning at 11:00, the doctor diagnosed him with pancreatitis, an inflamed pancreas. "Thank God it wasn't your liver," the doctor added. "This is treatable."

D.M.C. again asked for a painkiller.

The doctor said no, but he'd receive vitamins through an IV.

D spent three weeks in a hospital bed, trying to ignore the pain that returned whenever he inhaled. At night, he couldn't sleep; he'd watch *Leave It to Beaver* at 4:00 a.m. and reflect on his years with Run-D.M.C.—boozing, fast food, big plans, stress, and being broke. Before he finally left the hospital, the doctor said if he drank again, the pain would return, and the illness might even prove fatal.

After his release, D.M.C. traveled to Germany to join Run and Jay for a show. On the tour bus, he watched Run, Jay, and the road crew drink, smoke weed, and eat junk food. Now D watched and thought, "Dag. How can they do that?" Run tried to bond with him by offering a glass of wine. "Here, D," he said. "Take a sip. It ain't gonna hurt you." D did, only to bolt from the bus and into a nearby Burger King to use the restroom. He returned, and decided he would never drink again. "He definitely changed his life," Hurricane remembered. "He was quiet after that. He didn't really hang around too much."

Run was going through his own changes. One night in late autumn 1991, in his darkened hotel room after a show, he couldn't sleep. Bathed in the flickering glow of a television he had on for company more than anything else, he sat and watched white televangelist Robert Tilton tell an audience that if they turned their backs on God, things would surely go wrong. Tilton asked his crowd, and viewers, to bow their heads and pray. Run did, and felt at peace. After praying, he considered the room—empty save for fancy furnishings—and felt he could change his life.

He kept watching Tilton's program at night and donated huge sums of money to the televangelist. D said he donated everything he owned; Run said, "I gave a lot. I was doing it weekly, monthly, $1,000, $2,000, $10,000, $2,000, $5,000."

The turn in Run's life didn't surprise D. "Even when we were little, and used to walk around Jamaica Avenue or Forty-second Street, he would stop to listen to the street preachers." He would say, "D, I'll be right here." D would say, "Okay, I'm gonna get a forty." When D returned with his brown-bagged bottle he'd ask Run, "You ready?" Run would answer, "No, let me sit."

During the winter of 1991, a bodyguard told the twenty-eight-year-old Run that he should come by his church, Zoë Ministries. Run, who had seen its Bishop E. Bernard Jordan on television, agreed to visit the church (on 103rd Street and Riverside Drive, on Manhattan's Upper West Side), but did so one morning while high on marijuana.

The bishop put his hands on Run's shoulders and said, "I see success coming toward you in the air. I see prosperity. I see things turning around for you." Run was confused, Bishop Jordan added, trying to find his way; but Jordan assured Run that he hadn't come there by mistake; God had led him there, and God was saying, even now, he'd be back on his feet in no time. "Things shall turn for you," Jordan continued. "You were on the right track once you walked through this door, young man." And the bishop knew all about positive changes. He had quit his job at the post office, started his church with five people, preached that God helped those who donated gifts to His prophets and trusted in God to watch over contributors. Jordan's ministry thrived and he became a millionaire. "Get ready for a new life now!" the bishop told Run, who started crying.

Run continued to attend services at Zoë Ministries, and felt he was healing: becoming obedient, humble, and dedicated to the church. But Tracy Miller recalled, "People were turned off by that." Run ignored their disapproval and made an honest effort to stop smoking marijuana. He relapsed but kept trying. Soon he could be seen carrying a Bible.

By February 1992, about three months after he had begun attending Zoë Ministries, Run had a new girlfriend, and he would marry her days before his trial began. Her name was Justine, and he'd known her in high school. A mutual friend had reconnected them, and they'd become inseparable. "She's just one of the sweetest people you'll ever meet," said photographer and friend Glen Friedman.

They married in Zoë Ministries on Valentine's Day. "My reception was at the bishop's house and then we went to Hawaii," Run said. And Tracy Miller remembered, "I think I actually put something in *Billboard*."

With his trial about to start, Run's lawyer told him that neither D.M.C., Jam Master Jay, nor any of the road crew should be present in the courtroom during the trial. They should only have his mother, Evelyn; his father, Daniel; Russell; and any witnesses they'd call.

In mid-February, Run flew back to Cleveland and sat in court listening to his accuser allege she was forced to perform oral sex. "The girl made a convincing witness as she laid out her tale against Run," D opined in *King of Rock*, though he may not actually have been present when the woman testified.

On February 21, 1992, a friend of the alleged victim took the stand to say the accuser had once bragged about making up a similar story about another man, and to imply that her accusation against Run was just as false. "I think her friend said she made up a story and asked her to collaborate and then her whole story fell apart and the judge threw [the case against Run] out," said Tracy Miller. The judge dismissed it with prejudice so the charges could never be brought up again. "I beat it," Run explained. "It was a lie. Bottom line, it was crap."

Everyone congratulated Run on his victory and called his accuser an opportunist. But D.M.C. said, "I don't know. I don't know. All I can say is this. We were fucking everything. And I say 'we.' We were fucking, we were taking drugs, we were sniffing coke; we were bugging. Sex, drugs, and rock'n' roll to the fullest. It was a way of life for everybody involved in all our tours. And you can't be ashamed of it. I'm glad we came out of it. I'm glad Run ain't in jail."

With the accusation behind Run, and D no longer drinking, they still had to find ways to earn money: management's latest dispute with Profile still wore on. Run and D decided to appear in television commercials for a service called "1-800-Yes-Credit." When someone at *Rolling Stone* told publicist Tracy Miller about the low-budget ad, which did not include Jay, she was appalled. "Oh, I thought it was horrible," she said, but when she actually saw the commercial, she felt compassion for the once-proud group. Run, she figured, had asked D to do it, and D had submissively gone along with the idea. Runny Ray meanwhile suspected "Russell had something to do with that," and he was just as incredulous. Watching the commercial in his home, Ray shouted, "These niggas! Get the fuck out of here!" The commercial was yet another odd and disquieting career development that had some rap fans predicting Run-D.M.C. were over. But it was also, Jay's cousin Doc explained, "another venture to bring income."

During 1992, Jay continued to enjoy success with JMJ Records but worried a few close friends by hiring his old pal Randy Allen to act as the label's bookkeeper. Randy had just been released from prison, Doc recalled. Jay ignored questions from other friends about his decision; hiring Randy was a way to help an old friend land and keep a legitimate job.

Doc had known Randy since junior high school in Brooklyn, and remembered when Randy's family moved to the same Hollis neighborhood as the Mizell family. Randy was also reportedly a member of the burglary crew that in 1980 had burglarized a home in Jamaica Estates, Queens; Jay's accidental companionship with one member that night got him arrested. "He would do things that certain people didn't appreciate," Doc said of Randy. "Jason's father, my uncle Jesse, God bless his soul, never liked Randy." Whenever Jesse caught Randy in his house visiting Jay, Doc claimed, "Randy would flee from the neighborhood."

While Jay's star began to rise, along with Run-D.M.C.'s, Randy Allen experienced a number of setbacks. His older brother Frankie—also reportedly a member of the burglary crew—died of a drug overdose. Randy was then imprisoned for a reported felony (the details of which remain murky). But Jam Master Jay remembered the old Randy, the friend who accompanied him to Disco Fever to see how the Bronx nightclub did things when Jay wanted to start promoting parties. Jay wanted to be loyal to Randy, Doc recalled, so he mailed Randy food and clothing, and regularly visited him, while Randy was in prison. "After he was released, he went straight to live with Jason," Doc said, and felt offended if anyone tried to get close to Jay. "He didn't want anybody in Jason's ear but him, basically." Jay was soon separated from the Hollis Crew and the Afros, he added.

By late 1992, Jay was working with a new JMJ signing, a group called Onyx. The bald and menacing trio of rappers—who yelled lyrics about firing guns—had released a single on Profile in 1989 called "Aw, We Do It Like This" but were then working in a barbershop called New Tribe in South Side Jamaica, Queens. "Cutting hair," said Doc.

Jay enjoyed their demo tape, signed them to JMJ, and saw their 1993 debut, *BacDaFucup*, quickly sell a million copies. "What Run-D.M.C. was going through was a little setback, but he was still making money," said Doc.

At the same time, Jay teamed with talented designer April Walker for the clothing line Walker Wear—the very first by a rap artist—and asked Public Enemy's entrepreneurial leader Chuck D—who was a master at coining catchy phrases, including his description of rap as "the black CNN"—for marketing advice. Chuck, then planning his own label P.R.O. Division and a fashion line called Rappstyle, was honored. "Damn," he thought. "Jay asking me."

Like Onyx's debut, Walker Wear was another success: "Jason

was the first one, before all these other lines," his cousin Doc stressed. "Every celebrity was wearing Walker Wear," and Russell soon wanted to buy in, he recalled. "Jason and April Walker were like, 'Nah.' April was telling me, 'Russell wants to try to buy up the whole clothing line.' I said, 'April, you worked too hard to do this. You don't sell out like that.' I don't care, Russell, whoever." Russell Simmons soon unveiled his own clothing line, Phat Farm.

By late 1992, Run, down to his last $1,000, wondered if he'd have enough money for Christmas presents and a tree. Then two days before Christmas, Bishop Jordan and another preacher asked the congregation of Zoë Ministries for money. For months, the bishop had read Run Bible stories about people giving priests all their food and had asked, "Do you believe the Bible? I'm the prophet. You guys are broke. Give me your last and you will eat for the rest of your days."

Run used to think, "This guy is gonna jerk me."

That day, December 23, 1992, Run thought: "I've got no other choice. I've got to believe in something."

Sitting with Justine and the kids, he wondered if he should really donate the last of his money. "I owe all this stuff," he thought. "I'm getting myself together and I have a little bit of money in my pocket but I'm basically just surviving from week to week. I've got money, but I don't even have enough for a 'real Christmas.' "

Still, he had faith in God. He rose to his feet, walked to the front of the church, and donated all the money he had on him: "I still had no idea how my family was gonna make it through the holidays," he recalled, "but somehow I knew we would prevail." A few days later, he learned that his accountant had a royalty check for Run-D.M.C.; but Run still continued to endure hard times.

As 1993 began, the dispute with Profile Records hadn't yet been resolved. Run-D.M.C.'s managers—Russell, and employees like Lyor Cohen of Rush Management—wanted more royalty points and for the group to have more publishing rights. While their last two albums hadn't attracted as many consumers, "Walk This Way" remained one of the most-aired videos on MTV. Since the owner of a song's publishing was paid whenever the song was performed live or broadcast on television or radio, "Walk This Way" alone had the potential to earn them a fortune.

But Profile was supposedly adamant about retaining rights, so Run hoped God would bless him with money. D meanwhile lived off dwindling savings, and Jay saw the IRS place a lien on all of his earnings for nonpayment of back taxes and penalties. Run-D.M.C. were not enjoying success. And the little money Jay received for performing a few small shows here and there was not enough to settle his tax problems.

By August 1993, Run had filed for bankruptcy. "I can't talk about that," Run said when asked during an interview for this work, but the filing delayed the renegotiation with Profile. Then D filed as well. In court, both Run and D maintained they were broke. And Profile publicist Tracy Miller said that people at Profile speculated, "There was a lot of talk that the only reason Russell was having them file for bankruptcy was so they could get out of their legal obligations, including their recording contract, that it was just another ploy to get them off the label."

Reporters called Profile to ask about the filing. Profile and Rush executives were threatening lawsuits and she couldn't divulge much information, but Tracy Miller did try to defend Run-D.M.C.'s image; she didn't want the general public "to view them as, you know, losers. It's like, 'Oh, if you're that successful and that talented, then why are you broke?' I thought it was a bad reflection on them and it really wasn't their fault."

With Profile battling their filings in bankruptcy court, D finally decided to take Run's advice and visit Run's church. Run was now a deacon. For two years he had been telling D.M.C.: "You need to come, you need to come." D.M.C. decided to try it. Sitting in the church on 103rd and Riverside in 1993, D watched the bishop say, "Whoever wants to give their life to God, come up to the front." D.M.C. thought, "All right, I'll go up there and say the words because that's part of everyday churchgoing." He walked to the altar and the preacher prayed over him. "D.M.C. was going to church and he was happy," said Larry Smith, who also somehow made his way to Zoë Ministries and regularly attended services. And Run was happy to see D.M.C. there. He was "getting more spiritual," Run recalled, and they were working together. "I was a deacon. So was D."

But people close to Run questioned what they perceived as Zoë Ministries' emphasis on money. Russell had told Run: "What does God have to do with money and prosperity?" Run had answered, "What does God have to do with poverty and ill health? I'm here for prosperity, I'm here for health, and I'm here for joy and happiness."

Run's dad had also said, "Now you sound like that Reverend Ike."

In spring of 1993, Russell called to say they could start recording again. "I guess we fixed the contract or they gave us some money," Run said of Profile Records.

They entered the studio to create an album they wanted to call *Still Standing*, but Jam Master Jay was "pretty much tired," his cousin Doc remembered, and didn't want to produce. Jay had tax bills piling up and complained that Run's and D's personal problems were driving him bananas. Their last two albums hadn't done well, and Run wanted to fill this one with guest stars and outside producers. "We kind of just said, 'Let's go under the tutelage of younger producers,'" said Run.

Run and Jay invited storyteller Slick Rick, Naughty by Nature (whose string of hits satisfied both pop and hard-core audiences), producer Jermaine Dupri, and Q-Tip of A Tribe Called Quest to produce new songs. "Run and D were very excited because so many people wanted to be involved," said their old friend Doctor Dre, who was then enjoying success as a radio DJ on Hot 97's morning radio show *Ed Lover and Dr. Dre* (and starring alongside Ed Lover in the movie *Who's the Man*).

EPMD—tourmates from 1988—also provided music and lyrics. D didn't mind saying their words—EPMD's approach evoked their own—but he bristled when Jay led Onyx in and told him, "Let Fredro write your rhyme." D objected. On their records, Onyx bragged about being bald-headed bad guys. D told Jay, "I'm bald but I'm nice." Jay let D do what he wanted, but kept trying to mold Run-D.M.C.'s look and sound in the image of his million-selling group Onyx.

Jay and D did agree that a track producer Pete Rock created around a melody from "Where Do I Go," a song from the musical *Hair,* could be a hit. Run freestyled; and Pete Rock and his rapper, C. L. Smooth—with whom he recorded albums for Elektra— rhymed, crediting Run-D.M.C. with bringing rap to the mainstream. D.M.C. had yet to record his verse when Russell heard the song and said he didn't think it was a good idea, D recalled. The group kept working on the song, titled "Down with the King," and D recorded a stanza that found him, after years, finally moving from the Chuck D style. "After we put out *Back from Hell,* all the bullshit, I came back with the real: 'taking a tour (tour), wrecking the land (land),' " D reminisced.

They interrupted recording to do a few quick shows, but got into it with Profile again; D claimed the label withheld money while they were on the road and needed to cover expenses.

Back from touring, D and Jay headed to Russell's apartment on Fourth Street to discuss the happy resolution of the minor misunderstanding with Profile (which was resolved to everyone's satisfaction, since the group continued recording a new album). Run was supposed to meet them there, but he was late, so they walked over to Broadway to buy carrot juice. On the way, D saw a woman on the street, walking with her friend. He was instantly drawn to her. The friend noticed D and Jay and cried, "Oh, you know who that is? That's Run! That's Run!"

D was nervous but walked up to the woman anyway. He asked her name and she said Zuri. Zuri was from Hartford, Connecticut, and had previously thought Run-D.M.C. was white—since they rapped over metal guitars. She preferred the music of L.L. Cool J (who had been including hit love raps on every album since Russell first encouraged L.L. to rap over ballad-styled music for his 1987 pop hit "I Need Love") and the R & B group New Edition. All this made D like Zuri even more. He asked her, "Are you married?" She wasn't, so D asked for her phone number. Five days later, the twenty-nine-year-old rapper took her to City Island for seafood.

Zuri was ten years D's junior and had danced on the short-lived TV series *Club MTV*. They got close, and D found himself wanting to marry her. Jay said, "Yo, D, you gonna have problems." Jay had by now separated from his son Jason junior's mother, Lee, the reasons for which he never discussed. Since then, Jay had remarried, to a woman named Terri, six years his junior. "You definitely gonna have a problem because your wife's younger than you," Jay went on. "So you got to be ready for that."

In the studio, D rapped about Zuri on "What's Next," and sure enough, they were engaged and soon after married.

When they finished recording songs for *Still Standing*, D played every new song and told himself, "My rhyme about 'G-O-D' on 'Down with the King' saved this album." The new songs were enjoyable, a notable improvement over *Back from Hell* that found them sharing sentences, eschewing R & B, discussing familiar subject matter, and steering clear of cursing; but it was still a far cry from their milestone *Raising Hell.* "We could have had five or six more hits but Jay tried to put a lot of that Onyx influence on it," said D.M.C. "Like that song 'one little, two little, three little Indians.'" They had also adopted an Onyx-like image: all-black outfits and bald heads.

They ended *Still Standing* by recording D, without any music, saying, "For the past decade, the last ten years . . . many reps were made . . . many debts were paid! Some crews, paid dues; others refuse to lose, and that's all the news!" They called this piece "For 10 Years."

The final step was officially naming the album. After hearing D's verse on "Down with the King" (where he yelled, "And the G-O-D be in me 'cause the king I be"), Russell said, "We're gonna talk about y'all being 'born again'!" Run-D.M.C. saw the album title change from *Still Standing* to *Down with the King.*

At Profile and Rush, some executives were reluctant to release the gentle "Down with the King" as lead single, but "Jay fought hard to get that record made and for it to be the single," said D.M.C. Jay knew that rap fans loved producer Pete Rock's sound—heavy on beats and echoing horns—and that "Down with the King" would attract Pete Rock's loyal following to their own album.

After Profile agreed to release "Down with the King" as the first single from the new album, Run-D.M.C. then met with Profile's publicist to discuss how to market the album and the group. Tracy Miller then learned about Russell and Run's plan for a new "born again" image—mentioning God a lot and claiming that D's lyric about "G-O-D" was gospel-inspired, and not just D letting people know he felt Chuck D was "God on the mike," but also felt he was just as talented as Chuck. Miller didn't believe Run was sincere about the spiritual image, though she did consider D's belief heartfelt. "He got caught up in [the religious image] and believed it. Almost like he was, I wouldn't say duped, but D's the kind of person that never would think anyone had an ulterior motive." Still, *Down with the King* wasn't bad, and the new look (solid black) "was kind of cool," she added. "It had a hard-core edge to it."

Label president Cory Robbins did not think the new spiritual image would have any effect on sales. "I mean the previous album had sold so poorly that I don't know that I was really worried about it," he said. "I don't know what our expectations were for *Down with the King* because *Back from Hell* was such a failure. But *Down with the King* did turn out to be fairly successful. Not like their previous days in the eighties, but at least it was a respected album and it had a Gold single."

In March 1993, "Down with the King" landed in the Top 40 and topped the hot rap singles chart for two weeks. Then in May the album arrived in stores, topped the R & B album chart for a week, and earned Run-D.M.C. their kindest reviews in years. And with better sales, all three group members looked forward to receiving royalties that would help settle a few debts and allow them to rest easier.

Rolling Stone felt *Down with the King* had "the same infectious enthusiasm and the same in-your-face attitude as Run-D.M.C.'s raw earlier classics," while *Entertainment Weekly* wrote that they managed "to sound young, lean, and hungry after 10 years in the rap game." *The Source* loved its sound, and *Musician* announced, "When it comes to hardcore rhyming, they still run rings around the competition." And their gospel image landed Run-D.M.C. a story in the *New York Times,* in which Run was quoted saying that once the "Down with the King" single became a hit, "That's when I knew for sure that God was with me, because he let that be our comeback."

Some of their friends, however, shook their heads in disbelief. "They were full of shit to me," Runny Ray felt. "When [Run] got born again he was still drinking, he was still smoking weed."

Many rap fans had mixed feelings about the group including guest stars on nearly every song. They felt Run-D.M.C. had borrowed the style of whatever big-selling star had produced the particular song. "It's weird because they were the trendsetters and when they started trying to follow trends that was their downfall," said the Beastie Boys' Ad Rock.

Though *Down with the King* sold a million copies, D.M.C. felt people didn't like anything but the single with the *Hair* sample—"Where Do I Go"—and told the others their next album should continue in this vein. But Run and Jay ignored him and, during an interview on a morning radio show in England (after the host asked where they saw themselves being in the year 2000), Run said, "Darryl's gonna be naked on some mountaintop with an acoustic guitar somewhere."

Everyone laughed at D. "Including myself," said Tracy Miller, "because everyone knew the direction D was going in. He was just so ahead of his time." D wanted to include acoustic guitars on Run-D.M.C. songs. "After that, people started incorporating acoustic sounds into hip-hop. If D had put out the record he envisioned and was playing around with during the early nineties, he would have been at the forefront again with a new sound."

CHAPTER 26

You Talk Too Much

In 1994, the name Run-D.M.C. still drew crowds. Fans forgave them for marginal works, and knew that if they were left alone, and inspired, they could easily deliver more classic works. In the industry—a handful of major labels, a few independents, and a couple of rap magazines—everyone had fond memories of when they first heard Run-D.M.C.'s music, and if a project involved Run-D.M.C., some executives were more than willing to take meetings. Even without hit records, Run was able to interest record companies in compilation album projects, and when it was time for meet-and-greet sessions in corporate offices in midtown Manhattan, more often than not he'd reach for the telephone and call D.M.C. But now that D was married, the dynamic between them was changing, D said.

They were both attending Zoë Ministries—Run had in 1994 been declared a reverend by Bishop

Jordan, and D was still a deacon—but D was also enjoying married life with Zuri, which his oldest friends noticed made him happier, "calmer, more relaxed," said Hurricane. But with Zuri in the picture, D felt a tension develop between him and Run. It was no longer acceptable for Run to call every two minutes to say, "Hey, D, be here" or "You going to be there [at a meeting]? You have to be there, man. You know, you going to mess everything up for me." But Run kept calling despite the inconvenience to involve D.M.C. in discussions with labels about compilation albums that could monetarily benefit them all. "I had a girl so it was different," D said.

At the same time, D was concerned with his voice. During the occasional shows they performed (they weren't touring), it would crack. He asked the bishop for advice about whether to stop performing (since he feared he'd reached the end of his career), and the bishop advised D to "go out there and continue doing the shows. It's not that they just want to hear you do your record perfect. They want to see that that's really D.M.C., who they heard on these records and tapes all these years."

The pep talk worked. Thirty-year-old D now viewed Run-D.M.C.'s audience in a new light. He had worried that going on-stage with a failing voice would be akin to cheating the audience, which he did not want to do. But now he realized that the group's fans just wanted to see him, bond with him, relive the past, and let Run-D.M.C. know how much their old hits had meant to them. He was feeling this way when Russell called Run-D.M.C. in late 1994 to invite the group into the all-star cast he'd assembled for his documentary *The Show*.

The Show featured many of rap's trendiest acts in 1994—the Notorious B.I.G. (also known as "Biggie Smalls"), the Staten Island collective Wu-Tang Clan, energetic crowd-pleaser Craig Mack, and numerous profanity-spewing gangsta rappers—but presented imprisoned storyteller Slick Rick and Run-D.M.C. as examples of what rap music used to be, could still be, and should be.

Modern rappers heaped praise on Run-D.M.C. Chart-topping hard-core hero the Notorious B.I.G. said during his interview, "I grew up to that shit," and Treach of Naughty by Nature opined, "If you're dissing Run and them, you're dissing hip-hop." Run-D.M.C. was then filmed sitting in the backseat of a car rolling through Hollis. It had become a more violent, drug-infested neighborhood over the past decade, but Jay, who had moved back since marrying Terri, the mother of his second and third sons, Jesse and T.J., was staying put. He was a neighborhood staple, helping friends pay their rent, playing basketball or chess in the park, discovering young Hollis rappers, working with artists in his second-floor studio loft on Merrick Boulevard, throwing Christmas parties, marching in local parades, and hiring old friends at his JMJ label, his studio, or as part of Run-D.M.C.'s ever-growing road crew.

In the car, for the camera, Jay described his early days. "Like the first few years of our career? We were just big, we were just—"

Run interrupted. "God's plan."

"God's plan," Jay resumed. "We didn't even see it. We were dazing. Just coming back to Hollis—"

Run interrupted again. Raising his arms, he said, "The blessing overtook us. We didn't overtake it."

Jay looked frustrated. "Yeah, yeah, right," he unhappily agreed.

"It just came and like over-engulfed us."

For another of the few scenes that would feature Run-D.M.C., the group arrived at a concert venue, a huge auditorium with a stage as large as those during the Fresh Fest and *Raising Hell* days. After technicians set up lights, a large crowd entered, and Jay and his assistants checked to see that his turntables worked properly. Run-D.M.C. then began their concert for the cameras.

Run was stocky, confident, shrill, and imposing. The youthful cockiness had been replaced with mature self-assuredness. Records and films may have tanked, but he knew, as did the audience, that no one could compete with Run-D.M.C. onstage. Run wore a black denim jacket, matching jeans, and his trademark hat. D, broad-shouldered, gaunt, without glasses, and swaggering confidently across the stage, wore his hat with a baggy black T-shirt and track pants, and looked like someone the crowd wouldn't want to mess with. Jay and his turntables were on the drum riser. Behind Jay, a huge tapestry displayed a silhouette of their group pose on the *Down with the King* cover.

Holding a mike during this late 1994 concert for *The Show,* Run yelled, "I'm a slow it down on a real ill b-boy catch-your-heart-from-back-in-the-day jam and bug your whole life out, make you go home and slap yourself in the back of the head. Put your hands up like this. We're gonna go side to side. Everybody that's with old-school hip-hop and know about Run-D.M.C. from way back and know what we gonna do . . ." He paused. "You don't even know what we gonna do next. We got so many hits." He raised his left hand. "Put your hands in the air, everybody, like this . . ."

D added, "Reach for the sky."

Run faced him with annoyance, then added, "We gonna do it like this." Jay scratched his name: "Run."

"What's my name?" Run walked toward the turntables. "What's my name what's my name?"

Jay kept cutting his name.

Leaning in toward the turntables, hand cupping his left ear, "What did you say? That's cool." Then at the front of the stage: "Now put your hands back in the air. Come on! Don't front on a nigga!"

"Together Forever" played and the entire crowd swung their hands and cheered. D swaggered across the stage. Run stood at its center, in profile, bending and extending his knees, yelling, "Louder, louder, louder." But throughout the song, D's voice kept cracking. Before another number, Run crossed the stage. "Now check this out," he snapped. "I'm ready to go to the next level. You all ready to go to the next level? We gonna do it like this." He grabbed D's T-shirt, pulled it toward him. "D, what's this right here?"

"Yo, this my black shirt. You mess around, you get hurt."

Run lifted the bottom of his shirt. "What's this under here?"

"Yo, this my black belt. I whip MCs and I give them welts."

Run leaned over. "What's this on your leg?"

"Yo, these my black pants. I'll beat you *down* if I get the chance."

Run nodded. "Do me a favor."

"What?"

At full volume: "What the *fuck* are these, man?"

D yelled, "My—"

"Uh . . ."

"Didas!" Both leaped in place to thunderous applause.

During another segment for *The Show*, however, Run—self-appointed leader of Run-D.M.C.—and Jay engaged in a conversation that hinted at tensions in the group. First, Jay was filmed in a black tank top and shorts, entering an outdoor basketball court. Joining a group of black teenagers, he said, "What's up, nigga, what's going on?" to one. Then, "What's up, man?" Shaking another kid's hand in introduction: "Jay."

Someone said, "He's gonna play with us. He's good."

After the game, Jay sat next to Run, who had been watching the game in the crowded park. Run wore a black Adidas jacket. His eyebrows were raised, his face purposefully soft while crooning Def Jam artist Warren G's lyric to Jay: " 'Its kind of easy when you listen to the G-dub sound.' " He sat up. "Why would he even say the word 'easy'? You know what I'm saying? When you say 'easy,' you think of easy listening." He shook his head. "This music is ill." Tapping his knee. "But what makes it the most interesting to me about the whole thing is he's [best-selling West Coast producer] Dr. Dre's little brother."

Jay quickly answered, "It's like you and your brother."

Run looked toward his own lap. "Yeah, but that's . . ."

"That's how people were seeing it," Jay said, refusing at his age to placate Run with the answer. "*How* you gonna have Russell Simmons managing all these people and *Run* being down as the main rapper?"

Run tried to back out of it. "Yeah, I ain't worrying about how Dre—"

Jay kept talking. "Dre—"

Run now tried to leave behind the subject of nepotism. "Dre is Warren G's older brother—"

"Yeah," Jay said expectantly.

"And I got Russell doing what he do," Run said, showing Jay and the film crew that he too had matured, and was more than willing to let bandmates express differing opinions.

"There you go," Jay said happily.

D.M.C. meanwhile conducted his interviews for the film not with his overbearing bandmate Run around, but at home, near a sun-filled window. As he spoke, D.M.C. struggled to maintain Run-D.M.C.'s image of unity and brotherhood. D.M.C. told the film crew, "To this day if we weren't making records we'd still have to get together and go in Hollis Park and throw a party. You know, I'd still be writing rhymes." But he hinted that the group might not last forever. "If I were working at the post office," D continued, "I'd have a book of rhymes."

Much of *The Show* was also devoted to Russell Simmons, Run-D.M.C. noticed. The media had already spent a decade describing Russell as the "mogul of rap." The media credited Russell for the band's look, for the beat on "Sucker MCs," for the 1986 endorsement deal, for creating Def Jam Records.

Now, *The Show* presented Russell at fashion shows, hanging with models, exercising on the treadmill in his office while berating a Def Jam employee via speakerphone, and adding a few L.L. songs to a greatest hits compilation. He was also filmed telling fashion models about his friend, label owner Sean "Puffy" Combs, and in a chauffeur-driven car, going to visit rapper Slick Rick in Rikers Island prison.

Jam Master Jay was distressed, and looked it throughout the filming of *The Show*, partly because his project with Russell—his label JMJ—was in trouble and partly because tax bills and other debts were getting him down. Over the past five years, Russell's RAL labels had continued to churn out single after single, but Doctor Dre said, "There wasn't anything there. They were trying to put out quantity rather than quality."

JMJ Records meanwhile had done well with the Afros. "Then Onyx came, went platinum, and brought in some money for Def Jam," said Jay's cousin Doc. But Onyx's second album in 1995 had sold poorly, and JMJ's relationship with RAL (parent company Def Jam) deteriorated, Doc claimed, because of an unnamed employee. "He did some sheistiness that Def Jam didn't approve of and they told him not to come back, and Jay caught feelings. Russell and Lyor felt, 'Well if you're rolling with that kind of guy, we don't want it.' " Def Jam believed someone at JMJ had pocketed moneys earmarked for the promotion of Onyx. Onyx then left Def Jam Records. "It wasn't so much about Jay," said Doc.

Jay worked to iron out the relationship with Def Jam, but the RAL labels were on hold, as Russell and Def Jam were on the outs with their parent company, Sony. Sony told Russell he owed them $17 million as compensation for the poor sales of products by RAL. While discussing this matter in his autobiography, *Life and Def*, Russell never explained why Def Jam would owe Sony money for a failed venture; Russell never explained if the $17 million was repayment of an advance, fees Sony charged Def Jam for manufacturing RAL albums, an amount Sony believed someone at Def Jam had embezzled, or something else. What is known is that Russell objected, telling Sony that if it didn't charge Def Jam so many fees, it would see that Def Jam actually earned money. Russell also accused Sony of attempting to get L.L. Cool J and Public Enemy to leave Def Jam and sign directly to them. "Sony was preparing to rape me of my company, which is what happens to almost every independent record company," Russell claimed in *Life and Def*. As the acrimony between Def Jam and Sony increased, no one knew whether "Def Jam would survive or fall," said Doctor Dre of the years 1993 to 1995. "Def Jam couldn't put out one album."

Jam Master Jay had discovered acts, sold millions of albums, and delivered projects on time. But JMJ Records was over. "He couldn't do nothing about it," said Doc. "It was a business decision."

In 1995, Sony wanted to buy Russell out or fire him. Russell convinced multinational Polygram to sign a $35 million joint venture deal with Def Jam. After signing the deal, Russell handed Sony $17 million, took various works in progress (albums by Warren G, L.L. Cool J, and P.E.) with him, and folded most of the RAL labels. "It was a good time to scrap some of their losses and come up with new ideas," said rapper Chuck D of Public Enemy. But before he could leave, Russell had to battle for his catalog upon hearing one Sony executive say, "We aren't giving you your catalog."

"If you're selling me the company," he replied, "you're selling me the catalog."

Sony wanted the master rights to the Beastie Boys' *Licensed to Ill*, but eventually let Russell have the album, and the right to continue to press up new copies. "Lucky for us," Russell later wrote. "It is the most popular album in our catalogue, and one of the most important catalogue albums in the record business." Until 1995, *Licensed to Ill* continued to sell 600,000 copies without promotion. And when the Beasties released new albums on Capitol Records, *Licensed* sold even more.

While JMJ Records folded, Run started his second label (after the short-lived 1990 venture JDK), Rev Run Records. After noticing many performers in the audience at Zoë Ministries, Run told fellow parishioner Wes Farrell (CEO of a company called Music Entertainment Group) that these individual talents could be pooled to create a compilation album. Farrell, whose company distributed records by Nashville-based Christian label Benson Music Group, negotiated a deal with Run and looked forward to releasing a gospel album that included Run and other church talents.

D wasn't part of the deal. Originally, he had enjoyed services at Zoë Ministries, serving as a deacon and an usher, and worshipping alongside old friends like producer Larry Smith and Tony Rome, who wrote "You're Blind" and was now a pastor at the church. But D.M.C. tired of their new ecclesiastic image once rap fans began asking, "So you're doing gospel now?" Then after Bishop Jordan declared Run a reverend in 1994, Run started wearing a black suit and clerical collar, and preaching to reporters who really wanted to ask Run-D.M.C. about their rap music. And at Zoë, worshippers kept hinting that D.M.C. should become a minister as well. According to Runny Ray, Run also hinted that they should change their group name. "Run even tried to get D.M.C. down with that," Ray added. "'Reverend Run and Deacon D.M.C.' D didn't like that." D.M.C. eventually stopped attending church. At home, he continued to read books about theology—really, other people's opinions about how God wanted to be served—but people from Zoë kept calling to ask why he wasn't coming: I am not coming because I am not coming! he thought.

Said Run: "I looked up and he wasn't there!" He didn't know why D had stopped coming, and had no idea D's religious convictions were changing. "Didn't know or care. I was too focused on God." Run was also busy working on the compilation album for his own new label, with Larry Smith coproducing songs for the Zoë Brothers, who sang like Def Jam's soul singer D'Angelo; the Sin Assassins, a Bronx group that was "talking about how hard it is in their hood"; and Soul Tempo, who recorded Boyz II Men–style a cappella renditions of standards like "The Lord's Prayer." But Larry was not happy with Run's delay—for reasons neither Run nor Larry described—in releasing the music. "If I'm doing music for the church, put the music out," Larry said. "I walked away."

Run and his wife, Justine, kept working. She helped manage the Rev Run label and sang on the Sin Assassins' song "Things Ain't What They Used to Be." The plan was for each group to have three songs on the first compilation, *Rev Run Records Presents,* for Russell to help with advice, and for Run and his wife to follow the compilation with individual debut albums by the Sin Assassins, the Zoë Brothers, and Soul Tempo.

In early September 1995, Run told *Billboard,* "If you want to know what the album will sound like, think of 'Down with the King.' That was a gospel record," he claimed. "With lyrics like 'only G-O-D be a king to me and if the G-O-D be in me then the king I'll be.' " Run also talked up the God-fearing compilation in a 1996 interview in *People.* But when *Rev Run Records Presents* was released on September 20, 1996, and sold only 330 copies, Run rushed back to Run-D.M.C.

By summer 1996, three years after the release of *Down with the King,* Run-D.M.C. had adopted a new vision for their career: that they were like the Rolling Stones, and could tour without a new album.

In all-black clothing and trademark hats, they played about twenty-five concerts a month. They hadn't had a hit in three years, but Run kept talking as if they were the biggest things in rap. "The people in the rap community look at us, and they're like, 'Wow—Run-D.M.C.', " he told one reporter. But in reality, Run-D.M.C. had gone from playing for billions at Live Aid to being happy if eight hundred people bought tickets to a show.

"It was good for Jay cause he would DJ at the after-parties," said his cousin Doc, and these gigs brought in much-needed cash to support Terri and their three sons. "D.M.C. would do it because he needed the money. Run's words were, 'Oh, I'm doing it to help my boys out.' He started to ego-trip. He's 'Russell Simmons's brother.' He 'don't really have to do shows.' "

During these pickup gigs, Run still kept trying to speed-rap, a style from recent albums that fans rejected. He also wore his black suit and clerical collar in public and continued to talk about his religion though only 330 people had bought *Rev Run Records Presents*. He appeared with Bones-Thugs-n-Harmony in that group's gangsta-rap-style "World So Cruel," and tried to sell the Special Olympics on a project called *Reverend Run's Christmas All-Stars* that would amass Yuletide greetings by more successful acts such as the Fugees, Foxy Brown, Redman, and Snoop Dogg, among others.

D.M.C. meanwhile received a phone call from Bad Boy Entertainment. Their charismatic overweight star Biggie Smalls wanted to use an old D.M.C. lyric as the chorus for a new song. D was happy to oblige and reported to the recording studio. While he liked Biggie personally—Biggie had praised Run-D.M.C. in *The Show*, and he and D.M.C. got along great in the studio—D also felt Biggie and his rival, the late Tupac Shakur, were somewhat overrated. Rap magazines like *Vibe* and *The Source* continued to claim Biggie was the "greatest of all time." D thought he was talented, and enjoyed many of his raps, but felt neither Biggie nor "co-greatest" Tupac Shakur could really match Chuck D of Public Enemy for delivery, voice, and lyrics. "I felt Chuck was God on the mike and I still think that," D said.

But in the studio, tape rolled, and D.M.C. shouted his old lyric for Biggie's new chorus: "But that's not all, MCs have the gall. They pray and pray for my downfall." Despite experiencing a few voice troubles at one or two shows, D.M.C. said, "I did that live. I was going through the thing with the voice, but there were things I could still do."

Run, D, and Jay then got back to waiting for the newest situation at Profile to settle. This time Run-D.M.C. had not instigated the situation. Cory Robbins, who had already sold his part of Profile to Profile cofounder Steve Plotnicki in 1994, also wasn't involved. While Run-D.M.C. had hoped to have an album in stores by October 1996, Plotnicki was trying to sell Profile Records to a major label. "So I don't know what's happening there," Run told a reporter at the time. "If it gets sold to another company and changes its name and all that, I don't know what we'll do. I don't understand any of it."

In the interim, Run-D.M.C. kept performing small shows booked by their de facto manager, Erik Blam. (Russell, though not as involved with Run-D.M.C.'s career, still helped the group if they needed advice or needed him to represent their interests in a meeting with Profile.) On both a personal and professional level, it was a good stretch for Run and D. They weren't arguing, still sounded good together, and eschewed material from their last two albums *Back from Hell* and *Down with the King.* Said D.M.C., "We didn't have no Russell, no record company, no producers controlling: it was us being who we were when we were kids." And if drunks in the crowd started fighting, Jay grabbed his own mike to yell, "Yo! We ain't gonna have none of that shit here!"

But at his turntables onstage, Jay noticed that D's voice cracked when D performed certain lyrics. And when they recorded a few demos for a seventh album, Jay, Run, and D noticed it even more. D told Run and Jay not to worry, so they didn't. This had been happening since they first started out, doing two shows a day; after almost forty-five minutes of banter, D's voice usually began to tail off and Run would call the next day to say, "D, you was losing your voice last night." Since the next show was usually better, no one thought twice about it.

On these new demos in autumn 1996, however, D emitted a harsh rasp, and lyrics sounded forced. "I didn't know what the fuck was going on," D said, but they kept touring, since he and Run shared most lyrics anyway. Jay also backed D up on his own mike, and if D's voice cracked, fans wouldn't notice a thing. Privately, however, D worried. He hadn't told them how serious he felt this was. Every night he worried about having to perform parts of "It's Like That" without accompaniment. "I couldn't do that shit," D said. "I was up in a high register, which I think was wrong since the early days. Because if you listen to 'Hard Times' and 'It's Like That' I'm like high: 'Just like the flu.' " He'd adopted this tone in 1983 because Russell didn't like D's voice and D didn't want to be left off their first single. And it had worked. People had loved his high-volume rhythmic style, and he'd proudly dubbed himself the "new wave yeller." "But then it got worse as it went on," D said. "I was doing that shit night in, night out my entire life."

He entered the studio to try recording more songs, but his voice waned even more. Run-D.M.C. didn't deliver any new music to Profile in 1996; then D heard scuttlebutt about Run telling one or two people, "Me and D ain't gonna rap no more." Hurricane remembered, "There were definitely some disagreements. D wanted to do the record. And I don't think Run thought D could."

D.M.C. didn't know what to do. By now, he and Zuri had a child. He had a family to support, a career as a rapper, and a voice giving him trouble. In bed all day, he lost himself in documentaries about the Beatles' acrimonious split or in the pages of biographies about the Fab Four, or in the ups, downs, and collapses of newer bands on VH1's high-rated series *Behind the Music*. He would lie in bed, asking himself, "Should I keep rapping?"

D felt even more anxious because, he claimed, Profile's owner, Steve Plotnicki, wanted to be able to tell potential buyers of the label that a new Run-D.M.C. album was on the way. A new album would add value to Profile and allow Profile's owner to command a higher asking price, D felt; but months passed, D's voice kept cracking, and Run-D.M.C. still couldn't submit any new music to Profile.

At home in 1996, away from recording albums, D.M.C. kept busy with a newfound hobby, reading books about the careers of legendary rock groups. D had changed since the days when he told Jay and coproducer Davy DMX that he didn't want to record any rock-rap for *Tougher Than Leather*. Back then, in 1988, he'd been listening to and enjoying the Beatles' landmark *Sgt. Pepper's Lonely Hearts Club Band,* but felt that including rock music would cause rap fans to view them as sellouts in the age of rappers topping the charts with singles set to break beats and pro-black political singles like Public Enemy's "Rebel Without a Pause." Eight years later, he had time on his hands, since Run-D.M.C. was not recording a seventh album. "I was reading about rock-and-roll dudes 'cause I'm a big rock head," D said. "And I was reading about how a singer with a problem goes to the throat specialist." So D decided to visit specialists who worked with opera singers. "And the funny shit is they would all just say it was vocal strain: 'Don't sing for a couple of days.' "

Jay was worried and soon told his old friend Hurricane on the telephone, "Yo, my man D's voice is fucked up."

Hurricane—in Los Angeles working on a solo album—asked, "What's wrong with it?"

"I don't know, man. He can't really yell and stuff like that."

Cane was worried. "Shit, he needs to go to the doctor."

"He *went* to the doctor, and the doctor said there ain't nothing *wrong* with his voice!"

While visiting a doctor who examined well-known pop singers like Mariah Carey, D sat in a waiting room, lost in his thoughts and worries.

In the examining room, the doctor told D, "Your vocal cords aren't red. They aren't bruised. There are no abrasions. It's something else."

He referred D.M.C. to Mount Sinai Hospital in Manhattan. After a month of visits, the doctor there finally called D at his home with a diagnosis. "We don't know how you're going to take this," the doctor began, "but you have an incurable neurological disorder. It's called spasmodic dystonia."

D was puzzled. "What's that?"

"Have you ever seen people that twitch and have to keep moving their arms? They move their head and eyes all the time?"

D said, "Yeah."

"Well you have that, and your brain is sending involuntary electric signals to your vocal cords," the doctor continued.

D had to sit down.

"You're a unique case," the doctor pointed out. "There are two types: abductor and adductor. You have both."

After the doctor hung up, D kept sitting there. Throughout his entire life the odds had always been against him, he felt, but he had always made it through. Now, he sat back and faced the ceiling. "God, not only did You give me this, but You gave me both!" Everyone always thought he had it good, he told himself. No one knew how much he actually had to struggle: "Football, even rapping. Russell hated my— Russell didn't want me to do it and I did it and became the king. I never thought I would, but I loved it so much!

"And the doctors were saying, 'There's no cure for this,' " D continued. "They gave me Botox injections. What people use for cosmetic surgery: they put that in my throat. And they'd put needles in my neck and numb my shit up. They put this foot-long needle down my throat right into my vocal cords and squeezed the Botox into it. So much pressure in my head it knocked me out."

Despite the diagnosis, D wanted to keep performing, to not give up, so he visited a woman who coached singers in Broadway musicals. "She said it could come from abuse of the vocal cords because my brain must have said 'He's forcing us to yell "people in the world" every night.' So my body's fighting to make that happen all day now."

Hearing tapes of his live concerts, the vocal coach added, "D, you hear this part where you try to yell this lyric in a higher key? Don't do that anymore." She suggested he rap at a lower register. "As long as you can talk you can make a record and you can make people understand: okay, so what? You have *this*, you can't do *that*, but you can *still* make a good record." D was grateful for her kind words of encouragement. "While everybody was saying 'You can't, you can't, you can't,' " he said, "she focused on what I *could* do. I believed I could still make records."

When he called Profile in late 1996 to issue a progress report, a Profile exec casually mentioned that Run had a new solo deal. D was shocked. "He's making records with Slick Rick!" the executive added. "Hey, when you come up here tomorrow we'll let you hear it!"

The exec was surprised to learn D knew nothing about Run's deal. Then, D claimed, he learned Run's solo deal called for him to work on music, receive payment for each submitted track, and allow Profile to tell potential buyers the songs were for a Run-D.M.C. group album. When asked about D's claim, Run only said, "They didn't ask me anything. They didn't have an obligation to ask me. It's their label."

But D continued to believe Run was working on a solo album and allowing Profile to tell potential buyers of the label that it was a Run-D.M.C. work. "On one hand, I was like, 'Cool,' " D remembered thinking. "On the other, I took it like Run was thinking, 'Everything's good with me so fuck D.' He could have thought instead, 'Let me see how I can bring my man up,' you know? So I was fucking hurt."

Upon hearing about Run's deal, a friend (D never said who) asked, "What would make Run play you like that?"

D answered, "He thought I'd be jealous they were giving him money."

D.M.C. called Jay to ask if he knew about Run's solo deal and to inquire if Jay was working on the new songs. Jay told him, "D, if you never rap again, you're gonna write for me. You're gonna produce, you're gonna be fucking CEO of my company."

D didn't feel any better. He'd been worrying about how his voice was affecting Run-D.M.C. while Run was signing a solo deal without telling him and Jay was helping Run create new songs. "Profile wanted to sell the label," D repeated. "They couldn't sell the label without D.M.C. there." To give the impression that the new songs were by Run-D.M.C., and not simply Run, D claimed, Run and Jay "went back to early-eighties albums to get all the vocals that we never used. They tried to throw them on new songs so they could tell people this is a Run-D.M.C. album."

D also contended with doctors who didn't know what exactly had caused his voice troubles. The doctors heard recordings of his concerts, D performing "It's Like That," but could say only, "If you were doing that all night it could have attributed to the condition." He felt lost, confused, angry, and frustrated until July 1997, when he heard a new song by Sarah McLachlan, an introspective singer-songwriter with a lilting voice. MTV was playing her "Building a Mystery" video nonstop, but McLachlan had also written an album cut called "Angel" in three hours, after reading a *Rolling Stone* article about heroin use in the rock music industry. "Fly away from here, from this dark cold hotel room," she sang at one point. "There's vultures and thieves at your back and the storm keeps on twisting," she sang at another.

In her words, D.M.C. saw his own situation: smaller shows and cheap hotels; managers he claimed never invited him to meetings; bandmates who seemed indifferent to his voice troubles. The song so affected him that after hearing "Angel," D changed the direction of his music. Like McLachlan, he wrote about his personal life: "Up in the morning, hit the treadmill. Read the morning paper. Get the head fill." While Run and Jay worked on Run's "solo" album, D invited Davy DMX, Run-D.M.C.'s first DJ and coproducer of

Tougher Than Leather, and other musicians into a studio to help fill his new song, "Cadillac Cars," with drums, bass, guitar, and harmonica. Some people felt it sounded like Everlast's sleeper hit "What It's Like," but D didn't mind. Everlast had also made the transition from aggressive rap, appearing as a member of early-nineties ensemble House of Pain on hits like "Jump Around," to meditative lyrics and laid-back acoustic rock.

During a meeting at Profile in early 1998, an executive told Run-D.M.C. that the company had decided to purchase and release a remix of "It's Like That"—vocals set to insistent house music—created by an ambitious young New York DJ named Jason Nevins. Run-D.M.C. had never recorded any house music, and this music would definitely alienate rap fans, but they were in no position to argue. "I didn't care," Run said of hearing the remix. "Wow," he remembered saying flatly. "This sounds good. Okay, whatever."

D was just as unperturbed. "All right, cool."

Jay was angry that they hadn't been consulted. "He didn't make a deal with us when he made the record," Jay said of Nevins. "He made a deal with Profile." Jay also didn't like that Nevins didn't invite them into his video, which featured break-dancers and happy teens and was all over MTV. But they stopped grumbling once they heard promoters in Europe wanted them to come over and perform the song in concert.

"Nobody knew how big this thing was gonna be," said Run.

The remix was number one in Australia, rising quickly in the UK, and popular enough to inspire venue owners to send private jets to come pick them up. Jay told Run and D.M.C. they'd add the Nevins song to their set list. " 'Cause it was a hit," D said. "That record took the Spice Girls off the number one rating in the UK." It also sold a staggering 10 million copies. "We made a ton of money," Run said. "We had a smash! It was as big as MC Hammer's

'U Can't Touch This.' It knocked 'Candle in the Wind' off the chart." They played Germany for a month, gallivanted across Europe, and raked in millions. Back in America, they were asking for and receiving $12,000, then $20,000, then $50,000 per show. And one promoter even agreed to pay $70,000. MTV meanwhile kept playing the video, and fans looked forward to Nevins's remix of "It's Tricky."

After years of playing colleges, small rock clubs, and radio station festivals, in February 1998 Jay and Run invited Rick Rubin to produce a song for their new album. Since leaving Def Jam, Rubin had become one of rock's most respected producers. He had changed a bit—he was heavier, spiritual, and more mellow—but still wore shades and had a long beard and still knew how to create hard rap tracks. In the studio, he created a beat based on Kraftwerk's classic "Numbers." Run-D.M.C. recited a lyric with the same title, but Run explained, "D didn't have a voice that day, either." Even so, D was excited enough to tell a reporter in Vegas, where they played a fashion show at the Hard Rock Café, "It's an extension of what Jason Nevins did" and that "it should be coming out soon."

However, the song went unreleased because, D said, Kraftwerk refused to "clear," let them use, the sample on the record. "We love Run-D.M.C. and we would love for them to do it but it would be wrong because we didn't let anyone else use our music and we don't want to play favorites," D remembered the avant-garde German duo saying.

Despite this setback, things were still going the group's way. The Gap called in March to invite Run-D.M.C. into a thirty-second television ad, and on the set, with cameras rolling, they did their rap live: "Now Peter Piper wore khakis but Jay rocked jeans and D.M.C. bought a pair from a Gap out in Queens." They did more shows in Europe for higher fees and learned that, in America, fans treated the Gap ad like a new record.

They met Nevins for the first time at Manhattan nightclub

Tramps before going onstage one night, but didn't hit it off with him. "It was unbelievable," Nevins said. "They didn't have that much to say to me, which I thought was kind of weird but all in all I guess they were cool."

Jay felt Nevins had insulted them during an interview in a European magazine. "I think that Nevins was complaining in the press that he wasn't compensated," Tracy Miller explained. "The group made a lot of money off of that record since they got royalties from the use of 'It's Like That.'" In response, Jay told a reporter his interpretation of events. "Somebody asked him if he thought the group was appreciative and he said that he didn't think we were." Jay said Nevins had done nothing but "a remix of a record that we do every night, something we already know is a hit." Jay said using the same tempo and adding a kick drum "wasn't the hardest thing for him to do," and that it wasn't hard for "radio stations over there to make it the biggest thing in the world," since Europeans already loved house music.

If Run-D.M.C. was big, Jay continued, it wasn't only because of Nevins's remix. "It was because of the history of Run-D.M.C. It was because of the Gap commercial. It was because we were on television shows and the fact that we toured before that without a hit record and we ripped shit up."

By May 1998 the remix had sold 100,000 copies in America, and they kept playing shows for higher fees. But the issue of Run's solo deal meant they weren't speaking much when offstage. D's voice not being what it used to be was also a problem. Yet fans kept paying to see them do what they viewed as their new hit, the Nevins remix, and their old classics, so Run and D stayed on the road. And if D's voice faltered at a crucial moment during a show, Run explained, "I'd jump over him, trying to make nobody notice his voice."

During this time, some fans turned to Run-D.M.C. for a reminder of what the music used to be. Their show began with Jay—wearing an Adidas running suit, gold chain, and hat—coming out to lead the crowd in chants that praised old-school values and sounds. He was no longer the silent third member. On his turntables, he'd scratch "Peter Piper" and call D to the stage. D, his tracksuit jacket open to display the Phat Farm logo on his T-shirt, adopted a folded-arms b-boy stance at center stage. Run then joined him for parts of "King of Rock," "Rock Box," "Sucker MCs," "Here We Go," "Together Forever (Krush Groove 4)," "My Adidas," and the Nevins remix. Some fans shouted for "30 Days," "Dumb Girl," "Hard Times," "It's Tricky," "You Be Illin'," "You Talk Too Much," and "Walk This Way," but instead, Run would test-market new speed raps, and Jay human beat-boxed. Before leaving the stage, they performed "Piper" again, and "Down with the King." Shows ended with either Jay or Run mixing Cheryl Lynn's break beat "Got to Be Real," and when Run did it, he'd scratch it so it evoked L.L.'s oldie "Going Back to Cali," one review noted. Once he was finished, he'd let the record play, yell "I love you" into a mike, and run offstage.

But fans would see Run minutes later, at a table with D, selling autographed T-shirts. D would nod along as fans told him how their next album should sound. Jay, standing nearby, chatted with fans about fast food, DJ Premier's obvious talent, and their own next album. Run wouldn't say much aside from "Here" after signing a shirt and shoving it at a fan, one witness remembered. He'd sign another, say, "Here," and throw that one. Then another, "Here," until the shirts were all sold and they each had about a thousand extra bucks in their pockets. One night a fan told Jay that Run seemed to have an attitude. "That's the Russell in him coming out," Jay quipped. "Sometimes he gets a little uptight. He does all the worrying for the group; I just like to do the music."

As summer 1998 continued, Profile wanted the group—hotter than ever because of the Nevins hit—back in the studio. "Profile had to get involved 'cause they were trying to sell the label and needed D.M.C.," D.M.C. said. "They sent me to a psychiatrist because they thought I was going through depression and it was affecting my vocal cords and thought pattern. And I went to the psychiatrist and it was real good for me too." During their session, the psychiatrist learned all about the projects Run, Jay, and Russell were doing, and said to D, "Run is doing his solo album, Jay has JMJ Records, Russell has Def Jam and Phat Farm; what do you want to do?"

D sulked. "I want to make my album."

"Then why aren't you doing it?" she asked.

He kept recording new songs, but didn't release them because he wanted to be a team player.

"So it's selfish to do what's good for you?" she asked.

"Yeah."

The psychiatrist led D to understand that his bandmates seemed to be out for themselves, and that his waiting around for others to consider his feelings explained why he was now in her office. When the psychiatrist rebuked D, it sank in. He'd spent years trying to be a team player when, the psychiatrist noted, there didn't seem to be much of a team. D had been torn between self-preservation and loyalty, and was relieved to hear he not only could, but should, consider what was best for him. "I just walked out," he laughed. "I was like taken; I've never had to go back to the psychiatrist again. She made me think, 'Why are you going through all the bullshit? Do what's in your heart.' "

He visited Profile to say, "Thank you for sending me! I feel better now!"

D forgot about Run's solo deal. So did Run. With young fans clamoring for a new Run-D.M.C. album, D told a reporter they would start working on it in October 1998. "And it's gonna be older than old school," he vowed. "It's gonna be super classic Run-D.M.C. Another *Raising Hell*."

CHAPTER 27

Run Ruins Everything

BMG-backed Arista Records bought Profile ("for many millions of dollars, based on the expectation of a Run-D.M.C. record," D said) in November 1998. "Everybody was real excited," said Tracy Miller. "They thought, 'Okay, here's the major-label opportunity we kept thinking we needed all these years.'"

Run and D.M.C. weren't as friendly anymore, but professionally things were looking up. They signed a contract (with a clause, Run claimed, that barred them from disparaging Profile), received an advance, and began a new phase of their career. "Me and Clive were off to a great start," Run said of industry legend and Arista head Clive Davis. Davis, who had worked with everyone from Santana to Whitney Houston, had many exciting ideas about how to reintroduce Run-D.M.C., after a five-year absence, to the modern hip-hop audience (younger listeners buying their very first rap records, and older fans devoted to newer artists and styles). Davis wanted to release an album called *Greatest Hits 1983–1998* and then rerelease their catalog. Davis, age sixty-six, was open to Run's ideas, including a cover of "My Funny Valentine" he wanted to do with his second wife, Justine, for Europe. Run was so pleased with the deal and the promise it held that he soon told Will Smith—by now a big movie star—that he wanted to create a follow-up to *Krush Groove* that showed Run-D.M.C. leaving a small "go-nowhere" imprint and signing with a supportive Davis-like executive. "I feel like I went from the pit to the palace," Run told *Billboard*. "From the very bottom to the very top."

With a budget in place, Run-D.M.C. stopped recording demos and focused on getting a new song on a sound track or single by early 1999. And, Tracy Miller said, D was excited about recording again. "I definitely wanted it to just be raw and not caring about what we're doing," D explained. Run, however, didn't know about D's claims of creating another *Raising Hell*. "If something was coming out his mouth about it, he was just talking promotional," Run said of the new album.

While D felt the best course of action for this new album would be to record for three months away from distraction, in Jamaica or Hawaii, and then "pick the best records" created during this time, Run didn't agree.

"Darryl really thought people were gonna listen to his ideas and it would be a group effort," Tracy Miller said. Once D saw Run and Jay wouldn't, the old familiar frost settled over Run and D's relationship. They toured but didn't speak unless they were onstage, and drifted further apart. D also stopped coming by the studio, and Run figured, "He's unhappy 'cause his voice is gone." He claimed, "D didn't care about *Crown Royal*, man."

In early 1999, Run-D.M.C. traveled to San Diego for a BMG distributors' convention, to get everyone feeling enthusiastic about their upcoming album. After glad-handing distributors, posing for photographs, and performing on a stage, D and Run found themselves alone in a room for the first time in months. Run said to D, "Yo, this is wild, everything that's happening."

In response, D finally told him his voice problem was untreatable.

Run didn't believe him.

D said it was true.

"It was gone," thought Run. "What could I do? Wow." Looking at his bandmate, Run said, "D, I hear that. But just go along for the ride. Let's get our money."

D then complained to Run about the direction of their new album: another with numerous guest stars and producers and the R & B sound rampant on radio and most other rappers' hit songs. "I'm not doing this shit," D added. "It's bullshit. If y'all want me there, why can't I put some of my music in?"

"After I told Run that, Run took it as 'Oh shit, D's buggin','" D remembered. "He went and told on me. It was like the little kid. He's not getting his way so he's gonna go tell [Russell]."

At home in New Jersey, D moved to separate himself from Run-D.M.C. He had Tracy Miller—by then promoting the group from her own company—getting his paperwork and accounting straight. "He wanted to set himself up," she said. "I don't want to say separate himself from Run-D.M.C, but he felt it was time for him to be his own person. I don't know if he thought he was being taken advantage of all those years, but a lot of times he would let other people handle stuff, then find out later it wasn't handled in the best way. He took the initiative and said, 'Okay, I got to do this myself.'"

Since D's young son played with Miller's daughter, their families grew close. Soon, the McDaniels and the Miller families were dining in each other's homes. D began to open up to Tracy Miller about how Run and Jay were excluding him from new songs. "He had some great tracks and great ideas," she continued. "Unfortunately, Run wasn't open to them." Run was also frustrated, she added. "Here he's used to always being in control of the situation and now Darryl's changed. Now D's telling him, 'No, I don't want it this way, I want it this way.' He's not used to D creating any friction. Then D had problems with his voice, so I know Joe was concerned about that."

In Jay's recording studio on Merrick Boulevard in Queens, Run and Jay worked with Jay's business partner Randy Allen, also a music producer, on new tracks. After the BMG convention, Run had told D, "Let me handle this. I'll get this album made. We'll be all right." Now, every waking hour was spent in Jay and Randy's studio, an intimate, relatively private place with a b-boy feel. People sometimes distracted Run by walking in and out, but for the most part Run could work in peace. Still, without D around, the mood was strange. "Even if Jay didn't like that I wasn't involving D—maybe Jay did have a problem with it—there wasn't anything we could do," said Run. "His voice was gone. We had this big opportunity here. Clive Davis was involved. I was good at what I did. I had Jay. I had money backing me. We're making an album. I figured I could pull it off with or without D but with a little bit of D if he wanted to come around."

There were moments when Jay's face showed he missed D's presence. "It felt like a missing link," Jay's cousin Doc said, but Jay would get over the sadness and find a way to keep working; he would tell himself they were merely preparing tracks, getting them ready for when D finally arrived in the studio. "That was an awkward situation for them," said Hurricane. "I still think D.M.C. was capable of making a record. He just had a little voice change. He couldn't do a lot of yelling, but if he was calm, they could work with it."

Instead, Jay found unused verses from "Rock Box," "King of Rock," and "Jam Master Jay" and sampled them onto new songs, but the old vocals clashed and sounded dated.

Run and Jay soon reached out to Rick Rubin, the Beastie Boys, DJ Premier, and the Dust Brothers (who'd produced the Beasties sample-heavy second album, *Paul's Boutique*), and reportedly invited Russell to become more involved even though he hadn't overseen production of a rap group's album since the Flatlinerz's 1994 debut *USA*. By reuniting Rick with Russell, they hoped to recapture the magic of their best-known album, *Raising Hell,* the 1986 classic executive-produced by the former Def Jam partners.

Run wanted *Crown Royal,* as the album was titled (after a brand of liquor), to position Run-D.M.C. as relevant in the age of players and "ballers" like best-selling Jay-Z, a performer whose upscale suits, cigars, and habit of imbibing bubbly in videos evoked the late Biggie Smalls (murdered in March 1997). "Jay-Z's amazing!" Run felt. "Jay-Z's incredible!"

D, however, felt Run was following trends again. "Maybe," Run said. "Perhaps. Maybe I was. I don't know. I was trying to make new rhyme styles."

D felt that if Jay-Z worked with a certain producer, Run would immediately try to enlist that same producer for the new album. He felt Run and Jam Master Jay were both thinking, "Let me get ten producers, have them dress me a certain way, let them write for us, and we'll get famous and get $20 million to be on *Lifestyles of the Rich and Famous*." They weren't greedy, D stressed, just overly concerned with getting rich and living well.

When people close to Run-D.M.C. heard the gossip about Jay and Run recording without D, they were shocked. "I felt like it wasn't a Run-D.M.C. record," said Hurricane. At the time, Hurricane called Jam Master Jay on the carpet, shouting, "Yo! Why y'all doing a record and call it Run-D.M.C.? Just call it Run!" Jay understood but had mixed feelings; if Run weren't spearheading the project, Run-D.M.C. would cease to exist; and besides, Run and Jay planned to compensate D, who could use this money, especially now that his voice might be permanently damaged and he had a family to support. But to Run, it was no different from what happened during the Run's House tour in 1988. People were forgetting, he felt, that "when I went nuts for a while they had to do stuff without me."

To help in the production of *Crown Royal* Run enlisted Wu-Tang's Ol' Dirty Bastard, whose session in the studio was nothing if not memorable. "Yeah, he laid on the fucking floor," Jay recalled. Ol' Dirty Bastard also stood in the booth, facing a wall, while he rapped. Then Prodigy, half of the rap duo Mobb Deep, and acclaimed lyricist Nas also joined Run in the studio on the song "Queen's Day."

Other contributors were Fat Joe and Wu-Tang Clan's charismatic Method Man. After everyone rapped, Jay reached for the group's master tapes, searching for old lyrics by D.M.C. "A whole lot of money was given to us," Jay said. "So we were just giving him a part of it."

While making the album, Run continued to join D for quick shows. At the March 5, 1999, House of Blues show in Los Angeles, Run asked the large crowd, "How many of you here are from the old school?" They did "Rock Box," with Run and Jay ready to back D up during D's solo verses, and both rappers trod carefully across the stage, since fervent fans pressed up against its edge, rapping along and trying to touch Run's and D's Adidas.

After Run-D.M.C. performed "My Adidas" and "Sucker MCs," the crowd went crazy. Unbeknownst to Run and D, Steve Tyler and Joe Perry had walked onstage. Run and D were momentarily confused, but Jay didn't miss a beat; he immediately threw on "Walk This Way," and for the first time Run-D.M.C. and Aerosmith performed their popular duet, still one of the most played videos on MTV, onstage. Afterward, a dazed Run told the crowd, "I don't know what we're gonna do after that."

C irca May 1999, Run and Jay had finished *Crown Royal*. Each felt they'd created a surefire hit with back-to-back hip-hop cuts and the genre's hottest talents. But Arista head Clive Davis listened to it, D recalled, and said, "Take this album back. I'm not putting it out. Where is the Run-D.M.C. rock?"

In response, Run and Jay approached members of the pop rock band Sugar Ray at an MTV *Campus Invasion* promotional concert and invited them onto a song. The band agreed to record with them during a two-day break. On a private jet after the concert, Run wondered what he and Sugar Ray should collaborate on, and then remembered "Here We Go," on which Jay cut "Big Beat." An update would do, he decided. Sugar Ray stopped by the Hit Factory studio in Manhattan one day in May. Run had them play a rock track. "It was really cool, and hopefully it turned out really, really well," one member of Sugar Ray soon told a reporter. "We never got to hear the finished product, but I think it's gonna be great." Run finished the song, and called it "Here We Go Again."

One day in early July 1999, Run-D.M.C. and Jam Master Jay traveled to Beastie Boy Ad Rock's apartment in New York City to work on a cut for the album. They'd recently performed with the Beasties at the June 13, 1999, Tibetan Freedom Concert. On the day of the concert, Ad Rock saw for himself how Run-D.M.C. had changed. D was with Run and Jay, despite his objections, because he wanted to catch up on old times with his old friend Ad Rock. "They'd been doing it for a long time," Ad said. "It was different times and they weren't selling records. They weren't having the recognition. They were trying to find themselves." Ad continued: "Jay seemed fine. D seemed like himself. Run was a mess. He was even that way day to day when they were the biggest things in the world." And the day of the Tibetan Freedom Concert, Run acted like "the world is gonna end today," Ad said.

In Ad's apartment, the Beasties worked on music with Run-D.M.C. At the end of the informal session the Beasties handed Run a cassette tape of what they'd done. When Run finally called to invite the Beasties into the studio to record, Ad Rock was the only Beastie Boy in town; his bandmates were in Tibet "or trekking in the mountains or doing some crazy thing."

Ad Rock arrived at Jay's studio with his drum machine and sampler, and played a few beats he'd been working on. "I guess they liked one of my instrumentals, so I recorded all the elements down on tape and hung out for a couple of days," Ad recalled.

D watched Ad play guitar, and wondered what could have been if Run-D.M.C. had done like the Beasties and severed their ties to Russell and their label. He wondered if, like the Beasties, Run-D.M.C. could have gone on to bigger and better things. As the session wore on, Run and Jay described to Ad Rock a few of their plans for future projects: a *Krush Groove* sequel with Will Smith producing was one of them. "And we're gonna get in touch with Aerosmith and do 'Walk This Way Part Two.'"

Ad's face drooped.

Jay saw Ad's expression and asked his opinion. "What? I really want to know what you're thinking. What's going on with you?"

Ad grinned. "I got to be honest. I think that's corny."

"And they were like, 'You're right,' " said Ad.

They needed a second day to finish recording, but D.M.C. didn't show up this time. Ad hooked up the track while Run described his plan to fill the new album with guests and producers. Ad thought, "Run-D.M.C. doesn't need 'guests' on their album. Run-D.M.C. doesn't need the 'five hottest producers in the world.' They're Run-D.M.C." Ad wondered if Arista was behind this. "But it didn't feel like it. It felt like it was a Run thing. That he wanted to be 'hip with the kids' or something," Ad continued.

D felt the same way and traveled to the Arista offices in Manhattan during late summer 1999 with his new attorney to meet with Clive Davis. Until now Davis had dealt mainly with Run, Russell, and Jam Master Jay. At the outset of the meeting, Clive complimented D.M.C., saying, "You're the king of rock, D. You should be doing rock." D was flattered but had things he wanted to say. Then they got down to business. D voiced the same complaints about guest stars that he'd told Run at the BMG distributors' convention in early 1999. "I can't be part of this project," D began.

Clive replied: "I hear what you're saying. But your timing could have been a little better. I just spent a million dollars related to your record." D remembered Clive then adding that as a member of the group, D was a shareholder, and now wasn't the time for this, especially when D could make some money.

D's lawyer silently listened as Davis explained that he merely wanted *Crown Royal* to be as successful as Santana's recent chart-topper *Supernatural*. "I spent a million on him, brought all these other artists in," Davis explained. "His album is number one on the charts!"

After the meeting, D told his lawyer that Davis didn't understand him either. At home, D's phone rang. It was Run, having heard about the meeting, calling to confirm that he and Jay could use D's name and likeness on the new album. In response, D again told Run that this album wasn't going to work. D claimed Run then said, "You are messing my money up."

Both got a little heated until D suggested, "Let's just talk about people in general and life and what's the right thing to do." He told Run that when he was going through the voice problems, he felt Run, Jay, and Russell didn't show enough concern; that they seemed to talk only about what his voice troubles meant for the new album; they didn't seem to acknowledge that even when this album—this career of theirs—was forgotten, he'd still be suffering from this condition. "How would you feel if this was happening to you?" D continued. "And every time you go to somebody looking for the right answer they're telling you, 'Think about the money, think about the money'?"

Days after the conversation, Russell wanted to meet with Run and D.M.C. D agreed. While Run sat quietly, D recalled Russell saying, "D, I know you don't want to be on this album, but here's a chance. If you just walk away now it's gonna be hard for you. Think about the money. They'll give you a nice advance. You can go on the road."

"Russell, it's not about the money. I don't want the fucking money."

"Think about your kid."

"I am thinking about my kid because my kid is able to look at me and say, 'Daddy made a fucking decision that everybody thought was insane but it was the right way to go. He wasn't selling his soul and he wasn't fucking buying in. He didn't do it just for the money and materialistic or earthly gain.' If everybody loves the fucking record and Run is so fucking good, why don't y'all just put the damn fucking Run album out and stop dragging me through the fucking mud!"

Russell responded calmly, "Okay." Then, according to D, Russell pulled out a Rolex watch. "You see this watch here, D? You see that name on that watch? The reason why this watch sells is because it's Rolex and it says 'Rolex.' You take that name away, it ain't gonna sell. That's why we need you . . . we need this. . . . We got to promote this record as Run-D.M.C."

"I don't care about that."

"What do you want?"

Run then surprised D by saying, "D, do whatever you want to do. If you want to walk away tomorrow, I'll support you."

But they really wouldn't take no for an answer, D claimed. They kept calling, he said, to pressure him into letting them use his name and likeness to promote *Crown Royal* as a Run-D.M.C. work, and not Run, Jam Master Jay, and some old samples of D.M.C. along with numerous guest stars. "I went through that negotiation back and forth with Russell and Run, and it came down to them saying, 'Yo, let us just do this last album,'" D said. "Sort of like, 'D, let's just do the last album; let us use your name. Do the last album; come out on the road; let's just go on tour to have fun.'"

Soon D.M.C. had Jay telling him, "D, just do the shit!"

"Okay, I'm gonna do this," D said finally, "but not because I'm being nice." He hoped that vowing not to announce his departure would end the confrontation and advance his solo career. "And I got tired of these motherfuckers calling me," he joked. "I got to the point where I said, 'All right! Put the damn album out and leave me the fuck alone!'"

"Then Run called me out of nowhere," D continued. "I guess he probably thought, 'Damn, D's doing this shit. He'll probably never rap again and I got Russell, I got solo album possibilities, I got Profile giving me advances for my solo shit, we on Arista, I'm getting ready to make moves, so whatever I do I'm gonna be all right.'"

D listened to Run say, "D, I'm gonna give you publishing on the songs that you weren't even involved in," but D felt Run was only offering the rights out of self-interest. "It was Run trying to keep himself paid and get what he wanted, what they wanted. He wanted to last, so he called and said, 'All right, I'll give you publishing on all the records because at least that shows you support us by allowing us to use your name on a cover.'"

"Run basically had to," D went on. "He couldn't just be a sucker. Because if the story came out later, 'Y'all used D's name, ain't give him nothing and sampled the lyrics?' it would make him look very bad. I guess him and Russell had to cover their asses."

But D.M.C. didn't want to make a big deal out of it, so he told Run, "Okay, thank you. That's very thoughtful of you. Cool."

Run and Jay continued recording new songs in the autumn of 1999, and invited Fred Durst to Jay's studio. Durst's rock-rap band Limp Bizkit had scored a major hit on MTV with "Nookie," so Run and Jay knew that fans would welcome Durst as a guest on *Crown Royal*. The song "T'em Girls" featured Durst rapping over Ad Rock's track. "He showed up in the studio and put it down," said Jay. "He came in there with this gang of model-type girls and he was singing about them." D.M.C. was in the studio during Durst's session, and Run tried to include him, but "it was hard," Run claimed. "He didn't have any voice." At the end everyone, including an A & R representative from Arista, received a tape of the session. Clive Davis felt the song would be a big hit, but Durst wanted to change the track. Jay and Run created another one, but Arista preferred Ad Rock's original version.

As a concession to the acoustic sound he wanted, D felt, Run and Jay then invited rapper-turned-singer Everlast onto a cover of Steve Miller's "Take the Money and Run." Arista figured Everlast's presence, along with Santana's, could make this song a hit on rock radio. But when Arista submitted Run-D.M.C.'s completed remake to Steve Miller, his people objected to Run's new lyrics and were reluctant to clear the sample. Miller would take weeks to make up his mind. In the interim, Run-D.M.C. performed a few more shows to earn more money.

Saturday, June 5, 1999, at Top 40 station KISS Boston's Concert 20, Aerosmith joined them for "Walk This Way." After the concert, Run and Aerosmith members discussed collaborating on a song for

Crown Royal, and media outlets throughout America reported that the rock band and Rick Rubin would join Run-D.M.C. on a remake of "It's Tricky."

D.M.C. continued to feel frustration with Run and Jay for excluding him while deciding what *Crown Royal* would sound like. His wife, Zuri, was worried. "If you stop rapping, how we gonna pay the bills?" she once asked. D attended recording sessions with Run and Jay but also continued to record his own songs away from Run-D.M.C. "If we was ever to take a break, I'd probably have to put together a band and just play bars as the D.M.C. Revue or something," he told a reporter. He had self-financed the recording of 150 songs. "So even if I was to stop tomorrow, I would be able to put out a box set of previously unreleased D.M.C. music and ideas."

By mid-August, Run and Jay were recording with Kid Rock in Detroit. "I'm not a big follower of Kid Rock," Jay admitted. "I had his CD in my car; my kids like him because they watch MTV more than me." Rock had started his career as a flat-topped white rapper in the early 1990s, but when rap fans rejected his song "Yodeling in the Valley," he reinvented himself as a guitar-playing, hat-wearing rock-rapper and saw MTV embrace his video for "Bawitdaba." While Run-D.M.C. toured, Rock, a longtime fan, had called them to say, "Please, let's do a record. Let's play together." And when Jay heard a copy of Rock's album, sent by his label, he thought, "Okay, he's on some 'King of Rock'–type shit."

September 9, 1999, a month after the Detroit recording session, which yielded a song called "The School of Old," Run-D.M.C. stepped out of a limo at the MTV Video Music Awards in New York City. "Dag, we couldn't even get tickets last year," Run said at the time. But now, with Kid Rock set to perform a medley of their hits ("Walk This Way," "Rock Box," and "King of Rock") Run-D.M.C. was on the guest list. They wanted to go right in but producers asked them to stand on the red carpet with other guests, models, and VJs for photographers. As they walked toward the entrance, crowds cheered, but D wished he wasn't there. "I got to tell you something," he began, turning to Run. "You don't know what I am thinking." He wanted to say that over the years, the industry had become fake, and that most of these famous celebrities were churning out soulless product; instead, he said, "Nah, this is something I got to keep to myself."

Inside, MTV employees smiled and asked the group if they needed anything. They said not really, and one employee responded, "You guys are so easy to work with. Y'all don't want nothing."

In October, Run invited Stephan Jenkins of the rock group Third Eye Blind onto one of Run-D.M.C.'s new songs. Jenkins arrived at the studio with an idea for a song already in hand, and a drummer named "Brain," part of the "new" Guns N' Roses. Jay thought Jenkins's track was too fast but figured Arista would like it.

When Run saw Ad Rock again at an industry party, Run and Jay had already submitted the new, rock-driven version of *Crown Royal* to Arista. Run had been so busy with guests, tracks, meetings, and D.M.C. that he'd forgotten to call Ad to say they were using the track he'd produced.

Ad naturally asked about the instrumental.

"Oh, man, the song is great and we started working on it and we got Fred Durst to rap on it," he remembered Run saying.

Ad then told the Beasties' manager, "Make this as impersonal as possible but call their manager, and get me off the record. They can have the track. I just don't want to be down with it." He claimed he had nothing against Fred Durst personally but still told his manager, "I just don't want to be down with that."

Their October 1999 release date came and went. Arista couldn't yet release *Crown Royal*, as the label had yet to persuade Kid Rock's and Limp Bizkit's labels to grant permission for use of their vocals on their singles. And singer Steve Miller had yet to grant permission for use of "Take the Money and Run." As a result, Arista executives asked Run and Jay to return to the studio to record music for a single. They wanted to put something out soon, and preferred something with rock or even R & B to draw a wider audience than they imagined a duet with Nas, Fat Joe, or any other rap guest star could attract. But then Jay ran into Fred Durst on an airplane flight. He informed Durst that his manager wouldn't let them include Durst's performance on a single. Durst, a longtime Run-D.M.C. fan, was outraged, and responded, "I'm the vice president of Interscope. I'm doing the song."

CHAPTER 28

Endgame

During winter 2000, in New Jersey, D.M.C. worked on his solo album. With producer Davy D, who had helped produce *Tougher Than Leather,* D recorded his version of Bad Company's 1975 hit "Feel Like Makin' Love" and rapped, "I like Sheryl Crow or Sarah McLachlan. You like them? I listen to them often." He rapped about the Cold Crush Brothers on his demo "Micro Man," set to the Rolling Stones' "Jumpin' Jack Flash" and a quick old-school beat. "Rollin' on the Rhythm" had a woman singing to the tune of Creedence Clearwater Revival's "Proud Mary": "Turntables keep on turning; Crowd gonna keep on yearning; Rollin' on a rhythm." "What's Wrong with the World Today?" described high school students bringing guns to school, while "Come Together" talked about saving the environment and the whales. D was also busy completing a memoir. Run had recently landed a book deal but wanted only to write about religion and life lessons, so he hadn't included D. "I was doing 'words of wisdom,'" Run said of the daily religious e-mail he still sends out to family, friends, and associates.

D felt they should have done a book together, but worked with a cowriter, Bruce Haring, to tell his own story and offer advice about respect and responsibility. D also used a few pages of his book to announce he no longer wanted to record with Run-D.M.C. "I think D didn't want to be part of the group anymore because he felt Joe didn't want him in the group," Tracy Miller said.

For information to include in early chapters about his childhood, D called his parents. He asked his mother, Bannah, about his birth—when and at what time. She told D she'd have to call him back.

When she did, she asked D, "Don't you remember you were adopted?"

He was taken aback.

She said D had been told when he was five years old, but he didn't remember this. D listened to her say his biological mother was sixteen when she'd given him up, and she hailed from the Dominican Republic.

D.M.C. hung up the telephone. "Damn," he thought, "what else is gonna happen in my life?"

He couldn't get it out of his mind.

Confusion turned to rage. He told people he felt like getting a gun and killing a few specific individuals. Run figured he was going through "some type of depression," the same thing he had experienced. "But I love him to death," he added.

At home, D sat in his chair and thought, "I want to kill motherfuckers." But he knew he wouldn't, so he thought, "All right, I don't really want to harm anybody. Let me just take this gun and put it to my own head." And then, "Nah, I don't want to do that. Let me just drink myself to death."

If Jay and Run talked about *Crown Royal* in his presence when they met to perform the occasional show, he'd reiterate how fucked up it was that people ignored his complaints. "But if a motherfucker went and got a gun, then people would listen." It was D's perception that his bandmates kept saying, "Aw, D, you ain't rhyming no more. Your voice is gone. Nobody likes what you're writing about." And he kept thinking about a gun, a gun, a gun: "Maybe he was going nuts," said Run. "This guy probably went through some stuff."

As Run and Jay continued to record a few final songs for *Crown Royal* at Arista's request (for possible use on a single), and as D's depression deepened, D.M.C. told Run, "Yeah, man, see what's gonna happen tomorrow, I'm gonna pull my gun out and kill all y'all."

Run said, "D, don't kill me, man. I got five kids and they love me. I'm not ready to leave."

D said he was joking. "I was very upset; it's human. I had to learn to fucking express my emotions. If I had done shit differently during *Tougher Than Leather* and *Back from Hell*, shit could probably have been different. I was just sitting there going through the motions. And I wasn't about to do it again."

D.M.C. stopped coming to Run-D.M.C. shows, where the group still performed their classics to make the occasional dollar. "When we in Texas this nigga's in New York," said their friend Runny Ray. "He didn't like the album they did without him. Having other niggas rap his part. That's supposed to be D.M.C. but it's 'Run's nephew' or somebody. Bringing all these niggas in: Jay's nephew Boe Skaggz, Randy, all them niggas. D was like, 'Man, fuck that shit; you bringing them in? I ain't coming to no more shows.'"

Learning he was adopted changed the tone of D's material even more. No more lighthearted raps about female celebrities. Instead, new lyrics discussed such things as a child abandoned at birth in a hospital: "Facing doom in a tomb 'cause the kid is alone / but somebody came along and they took the kid home." He evoked the

Cold Crush Brothers by setting this particular new lyric to Harry Chapin's "Cat's in the Cradle," and was so happy with his remake that he wanted to play it for Jay and Run.

Since Arista had rescheduled the release date of *Crown Royal* for March 6, 2001, because of continued delays with guest artists' labels granting permission to use vocals on singles, Run and Jay were still recording songs to replace those Arista couldn't release as singles. D thought they could use some of his new material.

He stopped by the studio with fifty completed songs on demo tapes, and played Run and Jay numbers that used emotional riffs by Neil Young ("Old Man"), Pink Floyd ("Us and Them"), and Crosby, Stills, Nash and Young ("Ohio"). D felt they weren't any different from "Mary Mary" or "Down with the King." But Run begged to differ. "I didn't understand it but that's okay," Run said. "You don't have to understand stuff to like it. He was doing different music. He was listening to John Lennon and stuff. I don't know what he was doing."

Jay didn't know what to make of it either. "At the beginning, it was me, Run, and D, but D's voice is messed up," Jay explained. Run was still competing in his lyrics ("battling motherfuckers, shorties, anyone come into the studio"), and D was initially "cooperative, but the shit we did didn't sound right so D was like, 'Nah, let's put some other shit on there.'" D.M.C. liked what they were doing, Jay claimed, "but he hadn't been listening to hip-hop. He was listening to soft-rock stuff."

Run and Jay had no interest in this soft-rock material D seemed to prefer. "I didn't really care," D.M.C. said. "It wasn't about them. It sounded good to me and to everybody *except them* because they were keeping me in a mold. Like 'If you can't do what the new cats are doing then what you're doing is old.' Instead of just letting me do what I can do."

Run and Jay responded to D's demo with confusion but then agreed to include "Cadillac Cars" on *Crown Royal*. But just as quickly, D claimed they changed their minds, saying, "This isn't gonna work. This is fake."

"It wasn't regular D stuff. Period," Run felt. "It was different." It was also, he told D, inappropriate for Run-D.M.C. "Maybe it *was* a rejection," Run added. "It wasn't acceptable toward what we usually did. I guess when he gave some stuff, and I rejected it, he was hurt, period."

That was that until Arista decided Run-D.M.C.'s song "Rock Show," with Third Eye Blind's Stephan Jenkins, would be *Crown Royal*'s first single. D was at home when Run-D.M.C.'s road manager, Erik Blam, called to say, "D, next week, we're doing a video."

Angry about Run and Jay's refusal to include "Cadillac Cars" on the album, D informed Erik he would take no part. When Erik asked why, D replied, " 'Cause I'm not on the record."

Run didn't call him. D figured he didn't want to have yet another argument. But word reached him that Run had said, "D's fucking up again. He's fucking up again." D.M.C. thought this would be the end of it.

n mid-January 2001, two days before the shoot, Run, Jay, and Erik Blam flew to Los Angeles to meet with Arista and the video's director. When Arista asked about D, Run (D claimed) assured everyone, "D's gonna be here, D's gonna be here."

"And every time Run would tell Arista D's gonna be here," D said, "Run would turn to Erik that evening and say, 'Is D coming?' Erik would say, 'I don't know, Joe.' " As the two days wore on, Arista would also ask Erik if D was coming. "Erik would say, 'Yeah, yeah.' "

On the eve of the shoot, Run decided to call D.M.C. himself. "He tried to get a little mean with me," D claimed.

"But I gave you publishing on records on the album that you ain't even get down on!" Run said.

"But I let y'all put my name on the album," D answered. "Remember the whole issue was that you could have made a 'Run' album."

"Yeah but . . ."

"That was only right. I'm not gonna stand there and be involved in something I had no creative . . . I would have probably did it if you had let me write some fucking music and been involved in the creation."

Run handed their manager the telephone. "Here, Erik, you talk to him."

D then told their manager, "Erik, you know me. You know where I stand."

Erik couldn't justify D's current behavior, though. "Erik was like, 'This motherfucker's buggin' out. He got a fucking old-ass band in there making Beatles records.' " He didn't understand D's new music and couldn't understand why D would hurt the group like this.

Run then grabbed the phone again. "Yo, the shit is tomorrow, we looking stupid," he said. "It was back and forth," D recalled, "and Run started cursing me out. Then Jay got involved, snatching the phone from Run, but before he could say anything to me, I heard Run and Jay arguing in the background. 'Fuck that! D's a sucker!' And Run was like, 'Motherfuck D! Fucking with my shit!' while Jay was like, 'Calm down, calm down.' "

When Jay finally got on the phone, he said calmly, "D, do you have a problem with Run?"

"No, there's no real problem!"

"D, there *is* a problem," he said.

"What problem!"

"D, we're here in L.A. and you're at home."

"That's true."

"D. Just come do the video?"

"Nah, Jay, you know what's going on."

"D, I know that. But I got you, man. Whatever happens, you're gonna come work for my company. I'm making records. You're gonna do my groups and I got my studio, you'll be in there, you'll write, you're gonna be like Dr. Dre's man D.O.C. You're gonna be like that for me. You fucking down for life!"

"I know, Jay, but nah. I just want to go make *my* music, just do what I can do. See, people are looking at what I *can't* do and what they *want* me to do but nobody's taking me for what I *can* do, and that's the most important thing."

"D, I understand all of that. But, D, can you come be in the video? Just do it for me."

This plea touched D. He liked Jay. With a sigh, D said, "All right, Jay. I'll be on a plane in the morning."

"D, will you be on the plane at 9:00 in the morning?" Jay asked.

"I'll be on a plane in the morning," he answered.

D then heard Jay tell Erik: He's coming. Surprised, Erik exclaimed, "What? He's coming?" Then Erik got on the phone: "D, I'm gonna book this ticket now! Don't—"

D told him not to worry. Book the ticket. He'd be there.

In early February 2001, Arista finally released Run-D.M.C.'s first single, "Rock Show," but reviews ranged from respectful to dismissive. Since the rest of *Crown Royal* was composed of similar collaborations, label employees sensed the album would flop. Fans then learned that D's vocals were barely present on the album and objected. Validating D's feelings all throughout the making of *Crown Royal*, influential New York radio DJ Funkmaster Flex cornered D at an industry event to joke, "Motherfucker! Y'all don't need to get with nobody! Just make a fucking album, put it out, and don't care what it do! Y'all fucking Run-D.M.C.! Niggas want to be like y'all!"

Many friends were also saddened to see that D had been excluded. "Them niggas was fucked up," Runny Ray felt. "They doing shit and don't even call him. How can you do that without your man? And I wasn't mad at D when he was mad and not doing shows. You done brought your nephew in, Jay's cousin, Randy on there rapping. That was weak. That's why it didn't fucking sell."

Two weeks after Run-D.M.C. joined Third Eye Blind to shoot a video for "Rock Show," Arista wanted to rush-release Run's new cover of Al Green's "Let's Stay Together" into stores as a single (to squash negative word of mouth about the upcoming album), and asked for a video.

Once again, they called D.M.C. D gave a listen to the song, heard Run say, "Yo, D, you know I love you, let's stay together, man. You know you're my homey," and shook his head. "They thought it would touch my heart," D laughed. "And I'm thinking, 'These motherfuckers are funny! Now they're gonna do a record that's sentimental.' So we went through that whole process again! 'No, I'm not doing that. If it's a record about "where's D at," it's better if no one sees me.' Then I talked to Jay and Erik and they said, 'D, it's good if you show up in the video 'cause it'll at least help your shit.' I said, 'All right. I'll go do the video, all right, cool, fuck it, I'll do it.' "

There was talk of a third video during April 2001, the month *Crown Royal* officially arrived in stores, when Run told a reporter, "D.M.C. is directing our new video. It's called 'Take the Money and Run.' We make our decisions together. That's our secret." But there would be no video for the song. Shortly after Run's comment, Clive Davis was removed from his position at Arista and replaced by L. A. Reid. Plans for the clip were shelved. Critics continued to pan *Crown Royal*, and blamed Run for ruining the album by excluding D.M.C.

The group returned to playing small shows. D kept working on a solo album he now called *Checks, Thugs, and Rock 'n' Roll*. Jay kept doing DJ gigs on the side for money, and on the road during the summer of 2001, Run, D, and Jay began repairing their fractured relationship and planned a new album. Now that he wasn't busy dealing with tons of artists and with Arista, Run sat and really listened to D's solo songs. "When I was doing *Crown Royal* I never took time to listen to what D was saying," he told someone. "I should have put fucking some of D's records on that album."

)n early 2002, with the *Crown Royal* debacle behind him, Run could return to feelings he had nursed early in 2001. Run wondered if he even wanted to record anymore. He was now working with Russell's successful clothing company, Phat Farm. "Me and Russell created this sneaker," Run said, and the final design for the Phat Classic inspired him to joke: "This thing looks like an Adidas, Russ." Russell answered, "Let's just do it," and they quickly sold a million pairs. After that, Run thought, "You know what? I've said enough, I've created enough!" He was ready to say "forget music" and limit his involvement in the industry to working on solo material, producing talented newcomers, or appearing on select remixes. He'd focus mainly on his executive duties at Phat Farm. " 'Cause it's really huge," he said. "This sneaker's making so much money: it's the hugest thing in my life." He also had five kids to support.

However, promoters kept offering gigs, and Run realized he wasn't quite ready to put Run-D.M.C. behind him. They were invited to set their handprints in cement on the Walk of Fame on Hollywood Boulevard outside of Grauman's Chinese Theatre. They made history by becoming the first rap group to do so (alongside other legendary inductees B. B. King, Brian Wilson of the Beach Boys, Carl Perkins, the Godfather of Soul, James Brown, bluesman John Lee Hooker, and country singer Johnny Cash); but Run felt, "I don't want to do it!" Someone close to him, possibly Russell, asked, "What the hell is the matter with you? We want to see you do this!"

So Run reunited with D.M.C. and Jay and went to the theater on Monday, February 25, 2002, to add their handprints to the famous sidewalk. A large crowd that included producer Jermaine Dupri, former Death Row rapper Snoop, and Run's favorite, Jay-Z, cheered for them. "It was one of the biggest days of my life!" Jam Master Jay later said. "From me being the first DJ to put my hands in there, to being the first rap group to be recognized as rock-and-roll stars and putting our hands in RockWalk, it was a really huge thing!"

Run was just as elated. "That was an honor, an unbelievable honor!"

But despite the public show of unity, Jay and D noticed that Run felt estranged from the group. Close to a year after *Crown Royal*'s release and failure, Jay felt comfortable enough to tell D: "Run doesn't fool me. I always know how Run is. Motherfucker was over my house every day during the *Crown Royal* record. Soon as we got the deal with Arista and everything was over with, nigga don't call me anymore. I don't see his ass no more. But while I was making it he was at my house every day!" He added, "D, I understand how you feel 'cause Joe don't fool me."

"And that's all Jay said," D added.

March 14, 2002, Jay went down to the Puck Building on Houston Street in Manhattan, a few blocks away from the old Def Jam office at 298 Elizabeth Street, to attend an induction ceremony for the new Hip-Hop Hall of Fame. Jay saw many old friends. There was Doug E. Fresh, whose beat-boxing Jay imitated during the *Raising Hell* tour, and Slick Rick, whose "The Ruler's Back" single he'd produced in 1988. And Crazy Legs, the talented performer who helped bring break-dancing to the masses by performing in the 1982 film *Flashdance*. And Grandmaster Caz, whom Run and D had started out imitating. And Kangol Kid, who danced during the first Fresh Fest, rapped with the group UTFO, and later inspired "Peter Piper." And Grandmaster Flash: first an idol, now a friend.

There had been ups and downs, moments when all looked lost, but Run-D.M.C. and Jam Master Jay had made it. They'd survived in an industry where rappers released only three albums before losing their audience, and achieved every historic first, opening the doors for everyone that followed. They created 90 percent of the styles used by current rappers and helped move the genre, and Russell Simmons, into corporate boardrooms, clothing stores, movie theaters, rock magazines, and MTV studios. "We had some talent, but God walked through the studio," Run told a reporter. "We're the kings of rap, but he's the king of kings. I know that it's been a lot of luck, a lot of love, and a lot of help from the big man. If magazines keep saying we inspired and created everything, then maybe Run-D.M.C. has five members: Run, D.M.C., Jam Master Jay, Russell, and God."

At the Hip-Hop Hall of Fame ceremony, older, wiser, but reportedly cash-strapped Jay heard Run-D.M.C.'s name called, and peers applaud and cheer wildly. Jay stepped onto the stage to accept the award on behalf of Run and D and looked out over a crowd that included people they'd battled during their earliest days, people whose regime they'd toppled.

After thanking Russell for fine-tuning their look, Flash for inspiring him to DJ, and the Cold Crush for showing Run-D.M.C. the way, Jay said, "Everybody says 'if it wasn't for you cats,' but we know that's bullshit, because we know there was cats before us. We just was the people that were able to take the real beats from the street, which y'all brothers was doing, and put it on TV, let people hear it on wax. It had to be Sugar Hill Gang to bite off my man Grandmaster Caz. It had to be a Puff Daddy to bite off the Sugar Hill Gang. It goes around in circles." He made peace with the empire his group had toppled when they were all so young.

"Run-D.M.C. was the greatest group to do it," said Hurricane. "Their shows were always the best, they put out the hot records, and opened the doors for rap music. Without Run-D.M.C. I don't know how far hip-hop would have gone. So much stuff bounced off of Run-D.M.C.: Russell bounced off of Run-D.M.C., Beastie Boys bounced off Run-D.M.C., Lyor Cohen bounced off of Run-D.M.C., Def Jam bounced off of Run-D.M.C., even though they weren't on Def Jam. So without Run-D.M.C. I don't really know how far hip-hop would have gone."

CHAPTER 29

The Party's Over

When Aerosmith called to invite Run-D.M.C. onto their thirty-eight-date tour in summer of 2002, Run, who had decided not to perform as many shows, returned to the group. Aerosmith was promoting a new two-disc greatest hits package, *Ultimate Aerosmith Hits*, and two new songs, "Lay It Down" and "Girls of Summer," but reporters couldn't stop writing about that night in 1999 when Aerosmith, Run-D.M.C., and Kid Rock performed Run-D.M.C. songs together for MTV. "The MTV medley was well received....People just wanted them," said Tracy Miller. "It was a good show."

The tour started on August 13 in Holmdel, New Jersey, at the PNC Bank Arts Center, and ended on November 14 in Mountain View, California. After years of struggle, Run-D.M.C. was again performing for their mainstream audience. "Back to superstar status," Run said, and he wanted it to stay that way, filling their set with their abiding rock-heavy numbers "It's Tricky," "Rock Box," "Mary Mary," "Walk This Way," and "King of Rock." Because of *Crown Royal*'s lackluster sales, D felt that the tour "was like a blessing. Out of nowhere Aerosmith said they're going on the road and wanted Run-D.M.C. on the tour."

On August 14, 2002, the temperature neared one hundred degrees and the PNC Bank Arts Center was packed. Run-D.M.C. stepped onstage and performed snippets of "Mary, Mary" and "Jam Master Jay." The crowd got even louder when Kid Rock joined them for "King of Rock" and his own hit "Bawitdaba." Then Run-D.M.C. headed backstage, passing four women in flag-patterned bikinis that would join now-shirtless Rock during his own set. "I was so happy to do it," Run said of the tour. "We did good."

They waited backstage until Aerosmith finished their ballad-heavy set with "Dude (Looks Like a Lady)," and everyone grew silent. "Then all of the sudden there's turntables out there on the stage," Jay said. When Jay strolled out on the empty stage, thirty thousand people screamed their heads off. "Jay was definitely the best DJ ever to do it," said Hurricane. He wasn't like modern DJs—who relied on visual gimmicks, spinning around, mixing with their feet in the air—but didn't have to be, Hurricane continued. "It wasn't about that during our era. It was about being able to rock the crowd. If you could DJ and rock the crowd, you did your job. And nobody could do it better than Jay."

From backstage, Aerosmith's lead singer, Steven Tyler, announced, "Yo, Jam Master Jay!" On the turntables, Jay started cutting the opening to "Walk This Way" as Steve Tyler and Run, and Kid Rock (in a T-shirt and holding a can of Pabst beer) and D.M.C. in his "Free Slick Rick" T-shirt emerged from backstage. Onstage, Run, D, and Steven Tyler re-created the little dance they had done in the "Walk This Way" video so long ago. Then Run took his hat off and shoved it onto Tyler's head. They spent a minute or so hugging each other before Run-D.M.C., Jay, and Kid Rock hurried offstage to allow Aerosmith to perform "Love in an Elevator." "We would open the show, went in the middle of the show, and ended the show," Run recalled.

Jay was amazed that so many rock fans still loved them after their last few unsuccessful albums and smaller shows. "There were a few years where the business end of things started to get to me," Jay admitted. "It was frustrating to see the money being made off of the art form during a period of us finding [what sound best suited us]."

Run-D.M.C. was back: Gap commercials, Ted Turner's TNT, the NBA halftime shows, royalties and performance fees for the Nevins remix, Dr Pepper asking the group to film a commercial between tour dates, and a luxury tour bus complete with big-screen TVs and their name on the side, courtesy of Aerosmith.

During the tour, Run-D.M.C. played Burgettstown and Hershey, Pennsylvania; Bristow, Virginia; and Mansfield, Massachusetts, before hitting Wantagh, New York, playing gigantic arenas again, getting flattering write-ups, and performing for the sort of large white crowds some *Raising Hell* concerts had drawn. When a reporter asked D about the tour, he said, "It's going incredible."

In Boston, Run told the media, "We are doing three nights in Boston. Three nights! Twenty thousand people a night! Wow! I don't know what Aerosmith or Kid Rock are used to, what they do in one night," he continued, "but it's amazing to me that this triple headline is doing so much. I told my group, even if *Crown Royal* would have blown up really big I don't know if we'd be at this place anyway," he noted. "We went so far into the R & B area, like really making black records, it's amazing to still have this juice sitting on the other side!"

Jay would follow some concerts with paid gigs as DJ in a local nightclub. After rocking for thirty thousand people, he would catch his second wind and give clubgoers a show as energetic as the one Aerosmith fans had just paid to see. "I'm feeling totally successful, totally blessed, to be thirty-seven years old and still doing it," Jay told the media. "I'm running up and down the court still! The DJ thing really keeps you young."

Run and D meanwhile were becoming tight again. While Run recorded the *Crown Royal* album, they hadn't done as many shows, talked much, socialized, or spoken on the phone about their personal lives. On the road, forced to spend time with each other, they were bonding again. "Me and D are gonna sit down and incorporate his style with mine and make an album with no collaboration," Run said at the time, and D looked forward to recording with him again.

"Joe was more open to D's ideas because *Crown Royal* didn't do what Joe thought it would," said Tracy Miller. "D generally thought they could make a new album, the three of them. That was the goal."

But then Run wondered if it wouldn't be best simply to retire now, while they were riding high. "Sometimes certain bands don't need to make a new record," he thought. With the Phat Farm sneaker doing phenomenally well, he wondered if it wasn't time to enter another phase of his life and career. But then, with Run-D.M.C.'s twentieth anniversary approaching, Def Jam Records offered a recording contract. Russell, who had sold his interest in Def Jam in the late 1990s, was no longer with Def Jam, but the group's former road manager Lyor Cohen was, and while running the label he had sold millions of albums by some of the genre's most intriguing acts.

"It was like, 'Okay, Run-D.M.C. should go out with a bang,'" D remembered thinking. "'We should come home.' We should have been at Def Jam. They should have paid Profile $25 million to get us there on general principle, but it was a battle of business."

Still, Arista had dropped Run-D.M.C. after *Crown Royal*'s poor sales and a new regime arriving to help Clive Davis's successor, L. A. Reid, run the label; meanwhile Def Jam head Lyor Cohen wanted Run-D.M.C. to record a final album that would reflect their original, most heartfelt sound. "You need to use producers," D remembered him saying, "but you ain't gonna go in there with a 'destination.' You're gonna go in there and have fun like you used to. Don't be worried about what you're gonna write. Just go do it." The group couldn't believe it. They were on a huge tour—getting major write-ups every night—and getting along with each other and being offered a new record deal that could potentially earn them millions. And if this was their last album, D felt, so be it. "We would have went to Def Jam and would have probably been home. If you want to end it, let's end it here, though."

Jay happily told reporters about the Def Jam discussions. "It's gonna be a huge event!" he said. "Run-D.M.C.'s gonna sign with Def Jam for the first time. It's our twenty-year anniversary. When they started Def Jam, we were already artists on another label. Everybody came around Russell because of us, and then he got the deal with Def Jam. He needed a way to promote his artists through Run-D.M.C., through our tours."

Jay was also producing an album by a new group called Rusty Waters (an act featuring his business partner, Randy Allen, and Jay's nephew Boe Skaggz) for Virgin Records. Then he would help D.M.C. produce his solo album for Arista (though Run-D.M.C. was dropped, executives still planned to release D's music). "And then Run-D.M.C., the album next year on Def Jam!"

The Def Jam deal could bring them about $25 million, they felt, more than enough for Jay to finally pay the six-figure amount he owed the IRS for back taxes and penalties. They'd be able to take their time creating quality albums, D said. They wouldn't spend three hundred days a year on the road. They might tour once every three years. Said D.M.C.: "That's what we were supposed to be doing as opposed to 'Damn, we got to keep up with Jay-Z, we have to keep up with *Billboard;* we got to worry about SoundScan.'"

A day after Def Jam called with an informal offer, Jay happily told another reporter they were signing to the label. "So it's like 'welcome home.' It's true it's the first time we've ever been signed to Def Jam, but as you may know, we helped to create the label. We were hot, and it helped Russell to start Def Jam. Now, twenty years later, it comes back together."

They wouldn't work with Russell, D said, since Russell openly admitted he was no longer knowledgeable about trends in modern rap music. "Russell will tell you in a minute, 'I don't know no more.' " In addition, Russell was busy running various companies and signing deals. "We would definitely have fucked with Rick Rubin," D continued, "but it would have been us doing what we used to do. Even if we did use a producer's beat, we would have 'just used a beat,' and arranged and produced it ourselves."

Everyone around them was happy for Run-D.M.C. Said Hurricane: "They never wanted to be on Profile once Russell started Def Jam." But Run privately believed a Def Jam album would, unfortunately, have evoked *Crown Royal*. "Without D you were never gonna get a Run-D.M.C. album," he said. "Once D lost his voice a Run-D.M.C. album was dead. It would have been a Run album with Run trying to get something out of D, mainly Run rapping." Either way, the deal hadn't gone through, since Def Jam couldn't get their numbers together. "Run-D.M.C. signing to Def Jam was always the pinnacle of the Def Jam–Columbia deal," Doctor Dre explained. "It just never happened. And as Cory said, 'They will never, ever, ever be on Def Jam' and Cory was right."

Between Aerosmith tour dates in the summer of 2002, Jay stayed busy with side projects. Since JMJ Records' collapse, he'd run his studio and become known as a good talent scout. He discovered rappers, recorded a few tracks, and got them signed to various labels. Sometimes their albums wouldn't come out—like the Ill Hillbillies on smaller label Suave House—but Jay still had friends at majors who remembered the immense success of Onyx's 1993 debut.

Jay hoped to get Millennium Max signed (he included them on *Crown Royal*) and worked with Somebody Ink, a group that included Run's nephew and Run on a few of their songs. Jay was also trying to make inroads in film by producing a movie called *Frank Forever*, which Russell Simmons promised to help shop to studios.

During a break from the Aerosmith tour, in his studio in Queens, Jay received a phone call from his cousin Doc claiming that an associate in Randy Allen's camp pulled a gun on Doc's younger cousin

Fonz and told him, "Yo, get the fuck out the studio. This ain't your studio. This ain't Jay's studio. This is Randy's studio."

Jay was concerned and assured Doc that he'd look into the matter. Satisfied, Doc changed the subject. "I heard you're gonna sign to Def Jam, man," Doc said.

"Yeah, we're gonna sign," Jay answered, then added that life was good: he liked being on the Aerosmith tour, was earning good money, would be doing a few more dates with Aerosmith, and would do a few final DJ gigs before signing to Def Jam.

Doc said that while Jay was on the road, "Randy Allen was running the studio by himself. Lydia High was Jason's personal manager, handling anything pertaining to Run-D.M.C. She was also managing the studio."

But, Doc added, Jay planned to focus on the Run-D.M.C. album and film projects. "I heard he was asked to be director of A & R for Def Jam for $100,000 a year. I think Lyor offered him that but he turned it down 'cause he couldn't see himself in the office every day." He planned finally to close the studio. "He was gonna move on. He was about to drop everything."

Things continued to look up for Run-D.M.C. in early September 2002. Arista released *Run-D.M.C.—Greatest Hits.* An updated version of Bill Adler's 1987 biography *Tougher Than Leather: The Rise of Run-D.M.C.* arrived in stores. And they kept writing songs for a Def Jam album while on the bus. "It's gonna be rock-rap and it's gonna be b-boy," D.M.C. promised a reporter. "We're gonna take it back to the essence of the beat and rhyme like 'Sucker MCs' and 'Beats to the Rhyme.' "

Then, as they were riding toward another concert days before end of the Aerosmith tour, Run decided that he did not want to return to the days of playing smaller, lower-paying club dates, and riding in vans, when he already had a promising, stable job. He went to the back of the bus and told D and Jay, "Yo, tomorrow we're gonna tell them we ain't gonna do the tour. We're going home. Y'all have to figure out what y'all want to do. Because I don't want to perform no more."

Aerosmith was already talking about extending the tour and giving them more dates, so Jay and D both said, *"What?"*

"Let's finish this tour, man!"

"What you talking about!"

"Yo, I don't want to do it anymore," Run said. "I don't want to finish the tour."

"Joe, that's all cool, but let's at least do a couple of shows a month to make sure our soundman, our light man, and our managers can eat," Jay said.

"They're gonna have to figure it out too," witnesses remembered Run saying.

Jay pleaded with Run, then finally said, "Forget you then!"

"Jay probably was hurt over that," said Run. "I was *done.*"

D was just as angry, especially when Run hinted he wouldn't do the new album. "I tried to end it many times," Run explained. "I finally did end it. They wanted me back after a break. I was depressed," Run revealed. "I was starting to feel like I didn't want to do this anymore. And I had a lot of success. And it wasn't as fun."

He was by now president of the entire athletic division at Phat Farm; he had a family; he had church services. "Time to move on," Run said.

But a close friend echoed sentiments shared by many. "Let's just put it this way," this person said. "Run was looking out for Run. Russell's his brother, so he'd be taken care of *without* a Run-D.M.C. show. In the end Run chose to not tour anymore. But if they're your friends and came up with you, look out for them, too. Offer them a job."

It was a shame that it ended like this, many people felt. "And Steven Tyler—I just saw it on VH1—said, 'We were begging them,' " Doctor Dre noted. "He said, 'What is it? Do you need more money? Is it the tour bus? Whatever you guys want, I want you on this tour.' I don't know why they left. That doesn't make sense. It's like, you're on the road, you made money, your ego got involved, and you said, 'I'm not as big as Aerosmith.' But don't worry about being as big as Aerosmith; just go, perform, and have fun!"

CHAPTER 30

Voss and Remembrance

They were off the Aerosmith tour, but Run had agreed to perform with them at the halftime show of a Washington Wizards basketball game, so in his New Jersey home D packed for the trip. He'd have to catch a flight the next morning. It was October 30, 2002. In the background the TV was on, tuned to the news. He heard an announcement for a special report and turned toward the screen. "Rap pioneer Jason Mizell of rap group Run-D.M.C. has been shot," the anchorperson said.

D.M.C. stopped packing. Nah, that ain't true, he thought. Maybe somebody got it twisted, like in late 1986, when someone crashed into Jay's new car, Jay broke his leg, and rumors claimed Jay had been shot and killed. Here we go again, D thought; but still, he began channel surfing. And more newscasts said Jay was not only shot, he was dead. D stared at the screen in abject disbelief. It couldn't be. Seeing footage of Jay's studio, where they had recorded *Crown Royal*, he figured, "Oh, they're saying that because it's Jay's studio. It's not gonna be Jay and it's gonna be all good."

Then his cell phone rang—friends calling to say Jay had been killed in the studio. D still didn't believe it. There might be some mistake. He told his family he was heading out there to see what was up, ran to his truck, and drove to Queens. It was raining and cold, and on Merrick Boulevard, people stood around—police officers, Lyor Cohen, DJ Ed Lover. Fans were placing Adidas sneakers, album covers, Run-D.M.C. posters, candles, and godfather hats at a shrine. Someone had even hung a sign on a fence: "Another Brother Lost to Violence." But D.M.C. didn't believe Jay was dead until he saw Chuck D of Public Enemy in tears.

Chuck had been watching TV at home in nearby Long Island when his friend Kyle Jason downstairs yelled, "Oh, shit, turn on the television!" Chuck heard the name Run-D.M.C. and thought, What the hell happened? Downstairs he watched a news report about Jam Master Jay's murder. "At first I was like sitting there, talking with Kyle and then all of a sudden I just broke out, man. I was like, Yo. That shit hit me on a delay. Like 'Jay got killed.' I looked at it on the TV like it was somebody else and it sat in me like, this was, this was, my friend. And then I kind of like, you know . . . it was a crying type of thing going on. I was like, Yo. That emotion just kind of hit me. And Kyle and me went right on over to Queens. I saw Ed Lover. I saw Big D and um, it was just, it was not good. It was not a good feeling. It was right across the street . . . Jay's studio was right across the street from Encore, the old Encore, which was the place my friend Butch Cassidy first heard Run-D.M.C.'s first 12-inch. That's where Jay's studio was, right at the Jamaica Bus Terminal. And I was like, 'What the fuck.' "

Run was sitting onstage at Zoë Ministries during a service when Erik Blam beeped him. Then the rap duo EPMD's DJ Scratch. Even before returning the pages, Run knew something was wrong.

The next day, Halloween, D.M.C. traveled to Jay's modest

three-story house in Queens. Hurricane was already there. He had flown in from his home down south after someone called and told his wife the news. "I was in my kitchen; I don't remember what I was doing. I remember when she said it to me. It didn't register. I wouldn't believe it." Now D.M.C. and Hurricane were in Jay's home. "I don't remember seeing Run," said Hurricane. "He never came by. It was a sad day basically, a lot of grieving."

Hours after Jay's death, Randy and Randy's bandmate in Rusty Waters, Jay's nephew Boe, were supposedly rehearsing for a promotional tour. The police reportedly wanted to speak with both of them, but a detective told Jay's family that they were hard to reach, and that everyone around the studio seemed to be offering contradictory accounts of what had happened. "They were being uncooperative," someone told reporter Frank Owen of *Playboy* magazine. "Each story Lydia told was different." People in Hollis were also gossiping about Randy Allen, claiming he had relocated Lydia to Las Vegas and was spreading false rumors that Jay had been shot because his wife was involved with a legendary drug lord. Hurricane couldn't believe his ears. "Terri is a straight-up lady, a good mother and an excellent wife," he said of Jay's widow.

To their fans, Run-D.M.C. was a wholesome group that had finished a big tour and was currently writing an album for Def Jam. But industry people who knew them blathered about how Run had disbanded the group on the tour bus. "And a couple of days after that Jay got killed," said a close friend. "Jay wasn't even supposed to be home yet. That's how that went down: Run thinking about no one but himself."

Reporters wanted a statement, so publicist Tracy Miller—now representing only D—got a few quotes from D.M.C. and e-mailed reporters instead of putting D on the phone with them. "As far as Joe, he had been his own person, so I don't know what he was granting or doing." Miller then wrote an obituary for the funeral program. "It was very surreal," she explained. The media kept calling. Cable news channel MSNBC and NBC's high-rated *Today* show wanted her to appear on television. The next morning, one program sent a car to her home, but she didn't go. She granted only one telephone interview. "I thought it was important for people to realize the kind of person Jason was." But she didn't go on TV. "What am I gonna do?" she thought. "What am I gonna say? I'm just gonna sit there and cry." Instead, she kept planning for the funeral, composing a "security list" similar to one for a show, with passes granting certain mourners special access in the funeral home. "But it was, you know, for Jay, and he's dead. It was bizarre."

She took a call from Kid Rock, who offered to provide transportation if any of Jay's relatives needed to fly to New York and couldn't afford to travel. She thought that was cool, since "so many other people just used it as another event to get some publicity."

On the morning of November 4, 2002, Run arrived at the J. Foster Phillips Funeral Home in Jamaica, Queens, with wife, Justine. Three hundred people—many in unlaced Adidas and godfather hats—waited outside in the rain. Radios in passing cars blared "My Adidas" and "Peter Piper." D.M.C., his wife, Zuri, and Tracy Miller arrived from New Jersey in a limousine and walked past hundreds of cameramen, reporters, and fans standing behind metal gates.

Inside, D saw Jay's body in an open coffin. Someone had dressed Jay in his "Rock Box" outfit (the black leather suit, shell-toed Adidas sneakers, hat, and thick gold chain). D saw fans reach Jay's coffin, and burst into tears when they saw him in his outfit.

He also saw people he hadn't seen in ages: Kurtis Blow, Doug E. Fresh, Bill Stephney, even Rod Hui, engineer on their early records. Hurricane, Runny Ray, Big D Jordan, and more of Jay's friends in the Hollis Crew honored him by wearing their own black leather suits, hats, and unlaced Adidas.

D saw a huge floral arrangement from L.L. Cool J that had the word "Student" written on it and red roses, and Ad Rock and MCA of the Beastie Boys standing against a wall with numb facial expressions. "It was very strange," said Ad Rock. "It seemed like everybody was divided. They were different people. Jay was different from [Run and D]. And everybody knew that. Everybody looked to Jay to see what was right. I knew that from the beginning when I met those dudes. If you wanted to know what was what, Jay knew what was what. He was the cool one in the group."

Doc arrived, and heard Run and D speaking with Russell and Lyor Cohen about recording a tribute to JMJ, but Doc felt it was in poor taste. "After a while I'm hearing these clowns, especially D, talk about, 'Oh, we should do a record,' " said Doc. "They were discussing business. Trying to make money," Doc claimed. "They're talking about records and how this can work and I'm looking at these motherfuckers like, 'Y'all have the nerve to talk about how y'all can fucking sell records right now? I can't fuck with you cats.' I mean you at the man's funeral. The body is right in front of you. And all you are talking about is an opportunity to sell records."

At the pulpit, the Reverend Dr. Floyd H. Flake addressed an audience that included producer Jermaine Dupri, Def Jam artist Foxy Brown, A Tribe Called Quest, Whodini, TV personality Big Tigga, Chuck D, journalist Harry Allen, Congressman Gregory Meeks, Russell and his wife, Kimora, Def Jam president Kevin Liles, members of the Fearless Four, Hurricane, music executive Bill Stephney, and Doctor Dre, who said, "I felt empty about everything."

Jay's widow, Terri, sat near their three sons; Jay's mother, Connie; Jay's brother Marvin; Jay's sister Bonita Jones; and a few cousins who are preachers. Randy Allen was also there, but it wasn't visibly obvious to Hurricane that Randy was grieving.

"He didn't live a long life," the reverend told the gathering. "But he lived well by the people whose lives he touched. We are here to celebrate his life." A gospel singer sang two songs, and then the Reverend Stanley Brown said a few words.

D.M.C. got up there with a few pieces of paper. "Jam Master Jay was not a thug," he said, voice breaking. "He was the personification of hip-hop." Fighting back tears, he then led the crowd through his classic verse from "Jam Master Jay": "Jam Master Jay, that is his name / And all wild DJs he will tame / Behind the turntables is where he stands / Then there is the movement of his hands / So when asked who's the best, y'all should say / 'Jason Mizell, Jam Master Jay!' "

Run led the crowd through the Prayer of Comfort. "Jason did what he was supposed to do," Run added. "He helped to create this hip-hop nation. Jason walked in grace, in style, and with class. I didn't know if I should say this, but I believe this is Jason's biggest hit ever: all the support that has come in, all the people that have cried out across the world. I told my brother, I told Lyor and a couple of people. I don't know if anybody understood it. I believe this is the biggest hit ever. This is the most press that he's ever got."

During the funeral, Run and D sat next to each other in numb disbelief. "Joe, Jay's dead for real," D said.

"No he ain't, D. He's really dead? He's not on a plane or playing PlayStation? Jay's dead?"

Many mourners in the church knew about Run leaving the group. "But I understand why they were sitting together," said Ad Rock. "Because it was Run-D.M.C. They had to sit together. And both were like, 'He's where he needs to be.' Saying weird things. 'He's where he needs to be. He did his thing. This is God's plan.' But you know, whatever. We all believe what we want to believe. When our friend gets killed we're all in shock and say things we don't really fully understand in terms of how it appears to people, what it means and all of that."

Reporters who had infiltrated the funeral shoved microphones into Run's and D's faces. D kept his answers brief, but Nelson George, an older black writer who had coauthored Russell's autobiography, *Life and Def*, wrote, "At first their good cheer was disturbing. How could two people who'd been friends with Mizell since childhood be so happy at his [funeral]?"

After the ceremony, Jay's friends in the Hollis Crew carried his coffin down the church steps and toward the white hearse that would convey it to Ferncliff Cemetery in tree-lined Hartsdale, New York. After the burial, D joined his wife and Tracy Miller in a limo and "just went back home again," said Miller.

November 6, a windswept Wednesday morning, D.M.C. arrived at the Rihga Royal Hotel in midtown Manhattan for a press conference. Russell would be announcing a new fund to pay Jay's tax debts, buy Jay's $250,000 home in Hollis, and help his wife and three kids. Many celebrities who attended the funeral—Sean Combs, rapper Busta Rhymes, the Beasties, Foxy Brown, Chuck D, Doug E. Fresh, Russell's friend Andre Harrell, and others—sat in the Majestic East Room, listening to Russell tell the crowd and media that L.L. had donated $50,000, and that Eminem, Jay-Z, Aerosmith, Kid Rock, Lyor, Interscope Records, BET, *The Source, XXL,* Redman, Method Man, Busta, and West Coast Dr. Dre had also made contributions.

In addition to buying Jay's house and establishing college funds for his children, Russell explained, $50,000 of the money would go to anyone providing information leading to the arrest of the person or persons who had murdered Jay. In the audience, many rap artists felt it was weird that Russell, a multimillionaire who had earned an estimated $100 million from selling Def Jam, was asking others to help pay Jay's debts. "Come on!" said producer Hank Shocklee. "A 'fund-raiser' for Jay? It's ludicrous." Even so, people worth $400 million wrote checks for $10,000 and saw reporters describe the contributions in newspaper articles.

Onstage, at the podium, Run told mourners, "The thing that I recognize is that we were just on tour with Aerosmith and Kid Rock and we can't perform anymore. Nobody wants to see Run and

D.M.C. without Jay. Jay was definitely one-third of the group. People might see us on television and be wondering if Jay was a significant part of the group. Yes, he was.

"We split this money three ways," he added.

By his side, D.M.C. nodded his head.

"We're not able to go back out in December with Kid Rock and Aerosmith," Run continued. "We had an endorsement deal with Dr Pepper. We can't make those commercials now. Run-D.M.C. is officially retired."

D was stunned. "I remember D's face looking like, lost," said Hurricane. "He didn't know what the hell was going on."

Run hadn't told him he would be retiring the group, D claimed. "Run needed a way out," D said. "He couldn't get out and Jay's death was the perfect way out. I don't mean to say it like that but that was real. He probably looked at it as God giving him his way out. He doesn't look like the bad guy, because Jay was murdered. That's how I feel. You wanted out but couldn't get out. He was on his *way* out, but this solidified it."

Run kept speaking to the audience. "I can't get out in front of my fans with a new DJ. Some rock bands can replace the drummer. People say that to me: 'Are you the original three members?' I say, 'I don't know any other way but to be the three original members.' That's all I can say—we're retired. Does anybody have a job out there?"

Run stepped aside. "My intention was to retire the group in class," Run explained. "Bad enough we were still running around years later when our career wasn't at its highest point. I mean it was good. We were still good at shows. That's all I can say."

After the announcement, D.M.C. left the stage. Many of D's friends felt it was a lousy thing Run had just done to him. "D didn't know," said Tracy Miller. "We were all shocked and disgusted by that. He [D] was embarrassed, he was angry, but at the same time it was par for the course. It just confirmed everything in D's head that he had wanted to deny about Joe for the past year or two."

Many reporters saw the retirement as a poignant demonstration of unity and brotherhood. Reporters dutifully mentioned the group's many career landmarks and focused on their early works, describing Run and D as two friends with a dream who had somehow managed to unite genres and races during the 1980s. Many in the audience remembered when Run-D.M.C. really was the group described in these articles. "And now years later to see that it is just about the money, buying Rolls-Royces, having Rolex watches, pimping around," said Doctor Dre. "Everything you said you hated about this business you became."

My reaction was that these are all crazy people," said Ad Rock. "But it's also, in a weird way, like a weird family reunion. That's why I didn't get on the mike and say anything. Because 'Big Tigga' and Busta were saying, 'I donate $50,000 to . . .' I don't even know what they were donating money to."

Many attendees assumed this conference would announce a bigger reward for whoever could lead cops to Jay's killer. But Russell and other people controlled the event and said they wanted to raise money for Jay's mortgage and to pay Jay's tax debt of about $230,000. Chuck D finally got onstage. "I was pissed off 'cause they were talking about a fund-raiser," Chuck explained. "And as much as Russell and Lyor had earned from the Def Jam situation, how could you not take care of Jason's arrears? I just thought that was stupid."

At the podium, Chuck discussed how rappers needed to be more conscientious and less greedy. "I don't live in penthouses, suites, $300 hotel rooms. I'm in the communities from here to across the Pacific, and see people that only listen to and watch rappers. It's no reason for us to not be men and women. Yes, we do control the climate. Understand we have the ears of the people. We have to be men and women. I don't want to ruin the atmosphere, but Run, Jay, and D.M.C. made it possible for everybody."

Brushing him aside, Run told the crowd, "Rap is indifferent. It's about whose hands it is in. This shooting, this murder, has nothing to do with rap music. It has to do with an angry, sick mind."

Hurricane was in tears when he and Chuck D left the stage. Chuck was furious. In an out-of-view room, the usually reserved and dignified Chuck punched walls. Sean "P-Diddy" Combs witnessed Chuck's anger and tried to tell Chuck, "It's not about this."

But Chuck replied, "Come on. This is bullshit. How the fuck you gonna have a fund-raiser when motherfuckers are publicly laden in the hundreds of millions of dollars? And you're gonna have a fund-raiser to get Jay's house out of hock? For about $200,000? Get the fuck out of here! That shit is stupid."

Chuck D and many others felt that Russell Simmons and Lyor Cohen should simply have written a check and made a quick and anonymous donation to Jam Master Jay's young widow, Terri Mizell. "The only reason I didn't make a fucking mess out of it was because it was something not to make a mess out of," Chuck said. "It was out of respect to Run, and D. I mean, fuck it. You know?"

(((EPILOGUE)))

Wednesday, December 4, 2002, about five weeks after Jay's murder, Run and D sat in the audience in Los Angeles's Grand Olympic Auditorium. They were at an awards ceremony held by video channel VH1—the "Big in 2002 Awards"—and watching Kid Rock, Chuck D, and Grandmaster Flash perform the Run-D.M.C. classics "Sucker MCs," "My Adidas," "You Be Illin'," "It's Like That," "Beats to the Rhyme," and "Here We Go." Kid Rock performed Run's rhymes, Chuck D shouted D.M.C.'s lyrics, and Flash re-created Jay's cuts on his turntables, while in their seats, Run and D watched with an admixture of pride and sadness. "Me and Run were like, 'Yo, is that what Run-D.M.C. does?'" D.M.C. said that night. "'Cause we never got to see Run-D.M.C. in our lifetime."

After the performance, film star Ice Cube, who had joined Run-D.M.C. on the "Back from Hell" remix eleven years earlier, took the stage to present Run-D.M.C. with a Lifetime Achievement

Award. When a huge video monitor began to air footage of their career and Jay's life, "Me and Run were like, 'We're gonna cry now,' " D explained.

Onstage, while accepting the award, D.M.C.—tall, gaunt, visibly moved—told the audience that Run-D.M.C. had only wanted to make people smile. "So the best way to honor Jam Master Jay is to just keep smiling, man." And Kid Rock and Chuck D would have kept smiling if producers had not told the camera crew to stop filming because the producers wanted the rappers to perform the Run-D.M.C. medley again. The audience sat and waited, watching the closed curtain onstage. Then Rock walked out and told the crowd, "They wanted us to do it with a DAT tape to match the music with the explosions, but fuck that. We did it how Run-D.M.C. did every show and that's live with turntables." The producers decided they could air the television program with the original, heartfelt tribute by Rock, Chuck D, and Grandmaster Flash.

Backstage, reporters asked D about his solo album, *Checks, Thugs, and Rock 'n' Roll*. D said it would include "I'm Missing My Friend," a tribute to Jay. "I ain't talking about him being my DJ," D.M.C. explained. "I'm talking about stuff like how he taught me to swim, he used to sit and do crossword puzzles while we was hanging, a lot of stuff people didn't know about him. That's the legacy I want to leave for him." D.M.C. also said proceeds from the single would benefit Jay's family. "I want to make sure his kids can go to college when they're eighteen 'cause their father was a great musician," he added.

Five days later, D attended (without Run) the 2002 Billboard Music Awards and watched contemporary rap stars Busta Rhymes, Ja Rule, Nelly, Naughty by Nature (members of which produced a song for *Down with the King* and praised Run-D.M.C. in *The Show*), and Queen Latifah perform "Sucker MCs" and "Peter Piper." This time, Aerosmith's Steven Tyler and guitarist Joe Perry walked out and joined the rappers for Run-D.M.C.'s version of "Walk This Way." After the performance, D.M.C. took the stage and tried not to cry. "We just want to thank everybody that ever bought a record, that ever came to a show, because I think Run-D.M.C.'s greatest achievement was longevity. We've been through it all."

Since Jay's murder, a number of rap artists who once held grudges against Def Jam Records for various reasons told reporters that Run-D.M.C.'s former manager Russell Simmons was somehow to blame for Jay's reported indigence, as opposed to Jay's alleged habit of living beyond his means, buying cars and fur coats for friends and associates, and spending thousands on champagne. D.M.C. told *New York* magazine that the group did not earn much money from their first four albums but stressed, "Russell did the best he could." For D.M.C., the terms of certain contracts were to blame, not Russell Simmons. And Simmons himself noted, "Jay's finances were no different from any rapper or rock star [that] hasn't had a hit record in more than nine years. The question you should be asking is, 'Did he make wise investments?'" Russell Simmons did whatever he could—and after a certain point in the late 1980s, whatever the group *allowed* him to do—to help Run-D.M.C. maintain their fame, their status, and their commercial standing in the unpredictable rap music industry.

During his interview for this book, Run claimed that he and D.M.C. were still close. "I laugh with him at least once a week," Run said. "I could beep him right now and ask him something. I beeped him yesterday . . . no, about three days ago and said, 'D, what was that that you said about Cold Crush?' And we were laughing. We laugh all the time."

Run explained that he had spent his entire career pushing for the group "to the day Jay died." He joined D.M.C. and Jay on tour with Aerosmith, and filmed the Gap and Dr Pepper commercials. "We pushed it to the end."

Today, Run continues to join his brother Russell in public to promote Phat Farm sneakers and athletic wear, and describes life as "unbelievably fantastic." He wakes up in his large home in Saddle River, New Jersey; he walks outside to Russell's car (since Russell lives around the corner, they carpool to work); and they costar in commercials. "We make commercials, we design sneakers, and I'm here with my wife and children and a lot of money being made," said Run. Run loves working with his older brother ("He's a great man"), and calls his life a dream come true. "I split my life three ways: 34 percent God, 33 percent family, and 33 percent Russell. Church, family, career." He hangs with his big brother and Bishop Jordan. He donates a lot of his money to Zoë Ministries. He works on solo material from time to time. He raises his children. And he promotes his Reverend Run image even though tour employee Runny Ray claimed, "We were on the fucking Aerosmith tour, and that nigga was still drinking Hennessy and shit like that. Come on, man." At any rate, Run wanted people to know, "I'm a servant of the world, a servant of God, we're all here to serve and that's the deal."

During his interviews for this book, D.M.C. honestly described the group's mistakes, Jay's mistakes with Run-D.M.C., and his own personal blunders. Speaking with a voice that occasionally quavered with emotion, D said he and Run are not as close as they used to be. "He sends me his little 'words of wisdom' e-mail," D.M.C. said. "He sends it to everybody." Run appears on one of D.M.C.'s solo songs, but D last saw Run in person at an annual dinner held by the Biggie Foundation in 2003, and only because Jam Master Jay's mother, Connie, would be present. And that night, D recalled, "Run was like, 'D, what you doing? What's up with you?'"

D.M.C. continues to fly to Hollywood, where film producers have optioned a number of his screenplays. He mentors young rappers and joins them during late-night interviews on New York contemporary rap radio stations. He discusses Run-D.M.C. and Jam

Master Jay's legacy in the media and also puts finishing touches on *Checks, Thugs, and Rock 'n' Roll,* which, at press time, he hoped to release on his own label, reportedly called D.M.C. (Darryl's Music Company) with a video costarring the gifted Sarah McLachlan. "When you hear some of his songs, you'll be shocked at how good they sound," said Hurricane, who said he helped D produce the Jay-tribute "I'm Missing My Friend." "I didn't know what to expect from D with his voice but heard the songs and felt, 'Yo, D can run with this.' Some hip-hop heads will be negative, but if you listen with an open mind you'll say, 'D's shit sounds pretty good.' This is what D always rhymed about but with a twist."

Jam Master Jay's homicide remains unsolved, but since there is no statute of limitations for the crime of murder, Jay's killer may still be brought to justice.

Since Jay's killing, many theories have appeared in the media worldwide. Some articles claimed that Jam Master Jay was killed because he collaborated with Curtis Scoon—never charged with Jay's murder—in a drug deal. According to these unproven published rumors, Jay and Scoon allegedly contributed $15,000 each to purchase cocaine from someone in 1993 and supposedly had the drugs delivered to another person in Baltimore, who instead of selling the drugs and handing Jay and his alleged investor their share of the profits absconded with the drugs.

Curtis Scoon, however, vehemently denied being part of any drug deal with Jam Master Jay and told *Playboy* that Jay did owe him money at one point but for a personal loan. "If Jay was dealing drugs," Scoon told reporter Frank Owen, "it wasn't with me. He paid the debt. I had to get a little heavy with him but he paid. Jay did not owe me a dollar at the time of his death. I hadn't been in contact with Jay for at least four years."

And in October 2003, *New York Newsday* reported that unnamed "detectives have no evidence Mizell was involved in any illicit activities before his slaying, nor have they been able to confirm any of the allegations that have surfaced since his death."

Jay's friend Eric "Shake" Williams meanwhile told *Playboy*, and Web site AllHiphop.com, that while sitting with Randy Allen in a car on November 4, 2002, Shake questioned Randy's version of events. Randy had reportedly claimed that after Jay was shot, Randy grabbed a pistol they kept in the studio and ran out the back door, ostensibly to chase the killer. Shake claimed that in the car he asked Randy, "Why didn't you shoot?" Allen allegedly replied, "Dude was gone." Shake then claimed that he asked Randy why he dropped the gun outside in the alley, and that Randy said he did not want the police to find it in the studio. Shake then claimed to have told Randy, "Randy, it's just me and you. Who did that to Jay?" Shake claimed that Randy told him, "Shake, the nigga that killed your best friend and mine is Curtis Scoon," and that Randy knew this because studio bookkeeper Lydia High allegedly recognized the visitor when she opened the door. However, Randy Allen told *Playboy*'s Frank Owen, "No such meeting took place."

Since there is no reliable, concrete evidence linking Jam Master Jay to the distribution of illegal narcotics, this book does not focus on claims made about Jay after his death. "Jason is at peace, regardless of what they say about him," his sixty-nine-year-old mother told a reporter.

Another prevalent theory described by individuals interviewed for this work involves Randy Allen. For a time, headlines pointed every which way—to Jay's alleged fellow investor in a decade-old drug deal, to Jay's former road manager and the road manager's son, to a currently imprisoned New York City drug lord and the record label that federal law enforcement officials suspect the drug dealer financed—but many sources allege that a few of these theories emanated from Randy Allen.

No one has ever said Randy actually killed Jam Master Jay, and the police have certainly never accused Randy Allen of any crime or of involvement in the murder of Jason Mizell. Some of Jay's friends and family members simply note that some of Allen's alleged actions confused them.

The police's reported standpoint on the matter is that no one knows why Jay was murdered. There are too many theories, reluctant witnesses, witnesses recanting their versions of events, suspected masterminds, and possible lookouts pointing fingers and offering too many contradictory versions of events. In fact, for all anyone knows, all of the facts reported to the police and the public—through the media—about Jam Master Jay's murder may be false. "Everyone in this case is lying," one law enforcement source told *New York Newsday* in late October 2003. Whether anyone really walked up a flight of stairs to kill Jay, or whether Jay hugged his murderer—stories provided to police by individuals at one time suspected of involvement—remains unknown. Jay might simply have been playing video games when someone already present in the studio decided it was time to get this done.

All that is known is that someone killed Jay with a gun; police found Jay's body in a recording studio; and some people present that night might have seen who committed this murder.

(((INDEX)))

INDEX